FROM CONTENTION TO DEMOCRACY

FROM CONTENTION TO DEMOCRACY

Edited by
Marco G. Giugni
Doug McAdam
and
Charles Tilly

ROWMAN & LITTLEFIELD PUBLISHERS, INC.
Lanham • Boulder • New York • Oxford

ROWMAN & LITTLEFIELD PUBLISHERS, INC.

Published in the United States of America
by Rowman & Littlefield Publishers, Inc.
4720 Boston Way, Lanham, Maryland 20706

12 Hid's Copse Road
Cumnor Hill, Oxford OX2 9JJ, England

Chapter 2, "Social Protest and Policy Reform," originally appeared in
Comparative Political Studies 25, no. 4 (January 1993), 579–607. Reprinted by
permission of Sage Publications, Inc.

British Library Cataloguing in Publication Information Available

Library of Congress Cataloging-in-Publication Data

From contention to democracy / edited by Marco Giugni, Doug McAdam,
and Charles Tilly.
    p. cm.
    Includes bibliographical references and index.
    ISBN 0-8476-9105-5 (alk. paper).—ISBN 0-8476-9106-3 (pbk. :
alk. paper)
    1. Social movements. 2. Social change. I. Giugni, Marco G.
II. McAdam, Doug. III. Tilly, Charles.
    HM101.F7736 1998
    303.48′4—dc21   98-7079
                                                 CIP

Printed in the United States of America

∞ ™ The paper used in this publication meets the minimum requirements of
American National Standard for Information Sciences—Permanence of Paper for
Printed Library Materials, ANSI Z39.48—1984.

Contents

Abbreviations

AC	Civic Assembly
AD	Democratic Alliance
APD	Association de la Paix par le Droit
CFDT	Confédération Française Démocratique du Travail
CND	Campaign for Nuclear Disarmament
CTC	Copper Workers' Confédération
DDC	Directorate of Development and Cooperation
EU	European Union
FAC	Aid and Cooperation Fund
FEN	Fédération de l'Education Nationale
FoR	Fellowship of Reconciliation
FPMR	Manuel Rodriquez Patriotic Fund
ILP	Independent Labour Party
LICP	Ligue Internationale des Combattants de la Paix
LNU	League of Nations Union
MDB	Movimento Democràtico Brasileiro
MDP	Popular Democratic Movement
MIR	Movement of the Revolutionary Left
NAFTA	North American Free Trade Alliance
NGO	nongovernmental organization
NMWM	No More War Movement
NUWSS	National Union of Women's Suffrage Societies
NUWW	National Union for Women Workers
OECD	Organization for Economic Cooperation and Development
PCCh	Communist Party (Chile)
PPU	Peace Pledge Union
PSCh	Socialist Party (Chile)
SDC	Swiss Agency for Development and Cooperation
SDP	Social Democratic Party
SFSF	Svenska Freds-och Skiljedomsföreningen

SMO	social movement organization
SNES	Syndicat National de l'Education Secondaire
SNESup	Syndicat National de l'Education Supérieure
SNI	Syndicat National des Instituteurs
SPE	Swiss Society for the Protection of the Environment
TSMO	transnational social movement organization
TUC	Trades Union Congress
UER	Unité d'Enseignement et de Recherche
UCS	Union of Concerned Scientists
UNEF	Union Nationale des Etudiants de France
WCG	Women's Cooperative Guild
WLL	Women's Labour League
WSPU	Women's Social and Political Union
WTUL	Women's Trade Union League
WWF	World Wide Fund for Nature

Preface

Social movements sometimes fizzle, sometimes make marginal differences to politics as usual, but sometimes produce substantial social change. When, how, and why? Students of social movements have concentrated so heavily on where social movements come from, who takes part, and how participation affects their individual lives that we have little systematic understanding of social movements' impacts on the world at large. Considering that social movement activists spend much of their effort trying to change the world, our ignorance is a surprise and a shame.

From Contention to Democracy begins the work of reducing collective ignorance on social movement outcomes, especially outcomes that affect the degree and character of democracy in a polity. Rather than detailed studies of particular movements and their outcomes, it concentrates on theoretical problems and research opportunities. We asked a dozen social movement theorists to reflect explicitly on the relationship between movements and social change processes. We asked them to focus on how movements influence those processes instead of how social change influences or generates social movements, which more often preoccupies specialists in the subject. Our authors have taken their responsibilities seriously. They have challenged students of social movements to rethink their subject.

This volume has a twin sister. In fact, our original idea was to pull together a series of essays—both theoretical and empirical—on the consequences of social movements. The colleagues and friends whom we invited to write took up the challenge so enthusiastically that we ended up with too many good chapters for a single volume. Hence we decided to produce two books instead of one. The present one is mostly concerned with broader issues such as the incorporation of movements in the polity, existing institutions, or the cultural definition of society, including the ways in which such movements can lead to a transformation of social and political structures and contribute to the democratization of society.

Thus, theoretical issues are at the core of this volume. The other book (soon to be published by the University of Minnesota Press) is more specifically focused on the various types of consequences of social movements and brings more empirical material to the discussion. Together, the two books provide a good picture of the current state of affairs with regard to the study of the consequences of social movements, a field which is still characterized by a lack of systematic research.

Before going fully into the discussion of the role of social movements for change, we wish to make several acknowledgments, starting with all the authors who have accepted our invitation to write a chapter and who have skillfully provided the material for the book. Then we would like to thank those who have made the publication of this volume possible at Rowman & Littlefield: Dean Birkenkamp, Vice President and Executive Editor, who has believed in our project since the first time he saw a sketchy outline; Rebecca Hoogs, Editorial Assistant, who has been constantly in touch during the earlier stages and provided warm encouragement and helpful advice; Dorothy Bradley, Production Editor, who has managed to get the manuscript as quickly as possible through the production process; and Carol Bloom, who put her copyediting skills to the book's benefit. We also acknowledge *Comparative Political Studies* for granting permission to reprint chapter 2 by Sidney Tarrow. Finally, Marco Giugni is particularly grateful to the Swiss National Science Foundation for a research fellowship that allowed him to conduct research abroad and to work on this project.

Introduction

Social Movements and Change
Incorporation, Transformation, and Democratization

Marco G. Giugni

There is no clear-cut definition of social change. Generally speaking, it is:

> relatively wide and non-temporary, though not irreversible, variation or difference or alteration in the properties, in the state, or in the structure of the social organization of a given society, that is, in the relations between the major social systems that form it—be they related to the economic, political, state, religious, or family spheres or within one of such systems or in one or more institutions among those linked to it, observable at a certain moment with respect to a previous one, considering the identity of the unity to which one refers and the variables taken into account to single out the variation. (Gallino 1993, 437)[1]

Given this broad definition, the importance of inquiring into the impact of social movements on change lies, not only in the lack of systematic studies in the present state of affairs, but above all in the variety of social aspects that movements can potentially modify, thus contributing to the development of contemporary societies. Theoretical work on the impact of social movements, and more generally of contention, on social, political, and cultural systems would unveil the mechanisms that can lead to such impact. However, the assumption that social movements affect the society in such a significant fashion to transform it must be not only theoretically addressed, but also empirically confirmed, unless it is to become a self-fulfilling prophecy.

As several authors have pointed out, the study of the consequences of social movements is a tricky task (Berkowitz 1974; Gurr 1980a; Rucht 1992). The same holds true for their impact on social change. Most important, the dimensions of change are many and variegated. Furthermore, it is not easy to determine the causal mechanisms involved. The only manageable way is to delimit the task by focusing on a particular aspect of change and by suggesting a number of possible processes of change. The first of the three broad processes that we will discuss in some detail is the *incorporation* of social movements, or part of them, in the existing institutional arrangements of society. In its most common variant, it is the well-known process of institutionalization, which some observers have mistakenly seen as the end point of all movements. Actually, it is only one among several possible trajectories. Second, movements can bring about a *transformation* of social as well as political institutions. This type of impact is apparently more profound than the first one, but still, transformation may concern only some minor aspects. Finally, *democratization* is a further potential outcome of social movements. As we will argue, this is a surprisingly poorly studied outcome in the light of the assertion—often made among scholars and the general public alike—that movements are powerful sources of democracy. A separate part of the book is devoted to these broad processes of change. We do not claim that these processes are mutually exclusive. For example, democratization is obviously also a transformation, though not necessarily incorporation. Yet, they arguably cover much of the terrain open for movement influence. In any event, we stress that their function is purely analytical: to distinguish between the general modalities of change due to the presence and action of social movements. Before we outline in broad strokes the processes of incorporation, transformation, and democratization, we must address distinguishing, defining features of social movements. For we cannot assess an outcome until we first have a clear picture of a movement's principal features.

Past and Present of Social Movements

Not everyone in the field agrees on the nature and characteristics of social movements.[2] In our view, most of the definitions commit two mistakes that make the task of studying the role of social movements in social and political change more difficult. These mistakes are reification and confusion. *Reification:* When we think of a social movement, we tend to identify it with the actors that belong to it. In this view, the labor movement, for example, would consist of the workers and organizations that mobilize to defend their interests vis-à-vis the owner of the means of production. Similarly, all people and organizations that act to protect the environment against pollution caused by the intervention of man on nature would form the ecology movement. In this view, social movements are groups. In the worst of cases, a single organization becomes the movement itself, as is often heard and read in mass media reports. As a corollary of this first mistake, there is the assumption that social movements have a continuous and logical history from generation to decline, independent of changes in their surrounding environment. *Confusion:* social movements are publicly visible through their overt activities, most notably when they engage in street demonstrations. In trying to detect a movement through its activities, however, we face the risk of mistaking these actions for social movements. Social movements do not stage all protests. Other forms of struggles—feuds, civil wars, electoral competition and campaigns, insurrections, riots, and so forth—manifest themselves through protest actions.

In order to avoid these two mistakes, we must devise a definition that both departs from a substantialist view of movements and sets them apart from other types of contentious politics. That provided by Charles Tilly (1994, 7) is a good starting point:

> A social movement consists of *a sustained challenge to powerholders in the name of a population living under the jurisdiction of those powerholders by means of repeated public displays of that population's numbers, commitment, unity, and worthiness.*[3]

In this relational definition, a social movement is a particular kind of social interaction, a cluster of political practices whereby a group of challengers (who are indeed part of the definition, but by no means exhaust it) engage in mutual claim making with powerholders with the aim of influencing their decisions and behaviors. This distinguishes them from other types of contentious politics, defined as "collective activity on the part of claimants—or those who claim to represent them—relying at least in part on noninstitutionalized forms of interaction with elites, opponents, or the state" (Tarrow 1996, 874).

Social movements are not only conceptually distinct from other contemporary forms of collective contention, but also historically contingent. According to Tilly (1986, 1995a), they came into being less than two centuries ago. He is even more precise, stating that they were invented in Britain between the 1760s and the 1820s (Tilly 1982). Why Britain? Of course, this is in part a metaphor. However, in Great Britain the processes of state formation that are intimately linked to the birth of the social movement took place earlier than elsewhere in Europe. The formation and consolidation of the national state, the centralization and parliamentarization of politics, the emergence of mass electoral politics—all these mutually related processes have had an impact on the ways people publicly and jointly express their desires that other parties act in certain ways affecting their interests. Collective claim making became increasingly autonomous, proactive, and national in scope (Tilly, Tilly, and Tilly 1975).

In front of centralized and effective authorities who could respond to publicly articulated demands and grievances, people began to call for public attention and support by displaying their numbers, commitment, unity, and worthiness. The older repertoire of contention began to be replaced by a new repertoire made of mass meetings, mass-membership organizations, intergroup coalitions, protest marches, street demonstrations, strikes, petition drives, public statements, and the like. Thus, the modern social movement took shape.

Since then, the forms of social movements have remained more or less unchanged, inventing new forms of actions from time to time; the movements have modified the content of their claims. In this respect, Raschke (1985) has made a distinction between three broad types of movements that have characterized the modern society according to the central paradigm underlying their mobilization: the "older" movements for fundamental citizenship rights (i.e., the French Revolution), contending the (political) authority paradigm; the "traditional" labor movement, mobilizing around the (economic) distribution paradigm; and the new social movements, whose claims rest on the (cultural) lifestyle paradigm. While this classification is somewhat too rigid, it points to changes in the dominant social movement of a given historical period. However, it is important to note that in today's world all three types of claims are present at the same time: nationalist movements can be seen as the modern form of authority-paradigm claims, while labor movements and new social movements have followed a process of institutionalization—self-evident in the case of the former, less obvious for the latter—but remain nevertheless active through noninstitutionalized forms of action. The question, then, is how the various types of co-existing movements are affected by large-scale processes of change and, conversely, how movements provoke social change. The former question has received a great deal of attention from scholars (e.g., McAdam 1982; Melucci 1996a; Piven and Cloward 1979; Smelser 1963; Tarrow 1994a; Tilly 1986, 1995a; Tilly et al. 1975). The latter question is the focus of this volume.

Incorporation

There are a number of typologies of social movement effects in the "tool kit" of sociologists and political scientists. Among the most notorious are certainly Gamson's (1990) distinction between acceptance and new advantages (as two clusters of movement success), Kitschelt's (1986) procedural, substantive, and structural impacts, and Gurr's (1980a) trilogy of effects on the group fate, policy changes, and societal or systemic effects. Other useful classifications have been proposed, among others, by Schumaker (1975), Rochon and Mazmanian (1993), and Kriesi (1995). They agree that social movements can bring about changes on three distinct levels: (1) to alter power relations between challengers, authorities, and third parties, (2) to force policy change, and (3) to produce broad systemic changes, both at the structural (institutional) and cultural level.

These three levels of change correspond to social and political reality, but of course, they do not tell us how movements provoke such changes. In addition, despite its heuristic advantages, this typology suggests an inductive reasoning—it starts with the empirically demonstrated effects of social movements. Instead, one should perhaps start with possible processes and mechanisms that movements may influence. Within our conception of change—incorporation, transformation, and democratization—movements potentially intervene in two main trajectories of social change. Most typically, movements gradually become incorporated in existing structures and procedures, yet without transforming the basic rules of the game. This path may lead to institutionalization, but also simply to the integration of the movements' demands into public agendas and policies. Sometimes, however, they provoke a transformation of some aspects of the existing social and political system. This transformation can occur "from without" (endogenous), that is, as challengers that have no access to the system, or "from within" (exogenous). Ideally, what distinguishes incorporation from transformation is whether, in the process, there is a *transfer of power* that fundamentally alters the distribution of power within society. Finally, the process of democratization develops when a transfer of power couples with a modification of the mutual *rights and obligations* between the state and its citizens. Democracy may be affected in the absence of a transfer of power, leading to what we may call democratic adjustment. In this volume, however, we only focus on the impact on democracy that social movements make through transfers of power. Figure A illustrates these distinctions.

The relation between social movements, incorporation, transformation, and democratization is illustrated in figure B. Social movements as well as the three processes of social change are visually represented as "bricks" to signify that they are broad categories that include a variety of aspects. Movements may spur both incorporation and transformation. In addition, as Rochon and Mazmanian (1993) have suggested, incorporation (which, in terms of existing typologies, corresponds roughly to procedural effects) can, under certain conditions, facilitate transformation (grossly, substantive or structural effects); hence, the downward causal arrow. In turn, incorporation and transformation can lead to a process of democratization, but only under certain conditions that pertain to the mutual rights and obligations between the state and its citizens, forming the basis of modern democracy (see below). The "screen" formed by

FIGURE A
Three Processes of Social Change

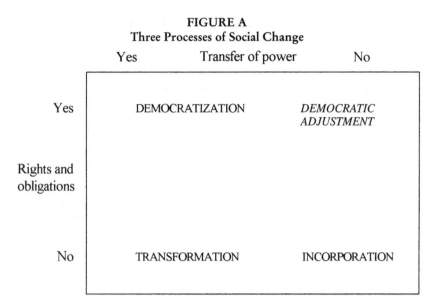

democratic rights and obligations is meant to denote the obstacle that movements have to pull down if they are to bring about the democratization of society.

Let us reiterate that incorporation, transformation, and democratization do not exhaust all processes of change. We do claim, however, that they cover a wide range of movement outcomes and that they point to crucial ways by which movements can produce social change. Also, of course, they must be intended as ideal-types rather than actual processes of change. However, it is important to analytically distinguish incorporation from transformation and from democratization. This distinction re-

FIGURE B
Relation between Social Movements and the Three Processes of Social Change

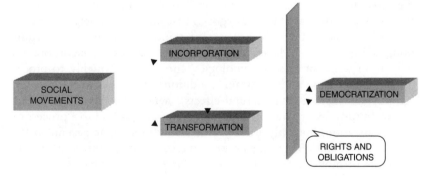

flects an approach to the study of the consequences of social movements that proceeds by (1) formulating theories of the causal processes by which social movements can provoke change, (2) identifying instances of the effects, then determining whether the causal chain was operating, and (3) identifying instances of the causal process, then determining whether and how the effects occurred (Tilly forthcoming).

Power Relations Change

Incorporation is probably the most common among our three processes of social change. The institutionalization of labor movements in the polities of all western countries is a typical example. Labor movements, intended broadly as "the overlapping networks of trade unions, *ad hoc* class-based organizations, and working-class political parties that had emerged almost everywhere in Europe by 1914" (Hanagan, in this volume), have been incorporated in the political system in at least three ways. First, labor organizations—unions, that is—have become part of interest-mediation arrangements that occur in the conventional political arenas, thus taking advantage of the opening of institutional channels for claim making. Second, the action repertoire of labor movements has institutionalized. In most countries, the strike is nowadays accepted as a legitimate means of action by the working class. Its form and content is often negotiated with the powerholders. Unlike in the past, it has become a conventional way of doing contentious politics. Finally, labor movements have followed a process of incorporation into political parties that, as Hanagan maintains in his essay, has often resulted in the persistence of movement activities within party structures and eventually allowed them to exert enduring influence on social policies.

Policy Change

Labor movements are not alone in their increasing integration into institutional channels and procedures. As Hanagan's essay makes clear, other movements have shared a similar fate. He gives us the example of peace and women's movements, which have followed a historical path of consolidation and incorporation into political parties, especially between 1920 and 1960. But the example of new social movements suggests that incorporation can take forms other than integration within state and political institutions. Even where the institutions are less permeable to outside challengers, movements can influence social change through the process of incorporation in at least two ways, both related to their claims. On the one hand, analysts of social movements have often stressed their effects on policy, particularly on existing legislation, as an indicator of their degree of success (e.g., Amenta, Carruthers, and Zylan 1992; Banaszak 1996; Burstein 1979, 1985; Burstein and Freudenburg 1978; Costain and Majstorovic 1994; Gelb and Lief Palley 1987, 1996; Huberts 1989). In terms of our focus on process, policy outcomes correspond to the incorporation of movement claims in governmental agenda, legislation, or public policies in general. Two crucial questions, then, are: How can challengers succeed in putting a theme in the governmental agenda? How can they force changes in legislation and policy? The former question has received a great deal of attention by agenda-setting and agenda-building theories (Cobb and Elder 1983); the latter, as we said, has been the main focus of research into the consequences of social movements. The chapter by Sidney Tarrow in the present volume deals with this aspect through the example of the French student movement.

Systemic Change

Finally, on a more general level, incorporation refers to the process by which movement claims are taken up by sectors of the society or public opinion. Through this process, challengers contribute to social change by influencing individual as well as public opinions, attitudes, and values. As William Gamson argues in his essay, contemporary movements have a crucial forum to attempt to advance their goals through public discourse: the mass media. Thereby, they may be able to bring about cultural change, but also to have a vicarious impact on public policy.

Transformation

If incorporation is a quite usual path followed by social movements today, transformation is a process by which they can aspire to producing more fundamental changes. In fact, it could be argued that the incorporation of some aspects of movements is unavoidable once claim making is performed. As a result, the question is about the extent of incorporation rather than whether it occurs or not. On the other hand, to take place, transformation implies the presence of a number of conditions. The task of analysts, then, is to define and ascertain the conditions for transformational social change as it is (co-)produced by social movements.

Revolutions are the most profound, yet the least frequent, transformational outcomes of contention. Here we use the general term of *contention* rather than the more specific label of *social movements.* Revolutionary outcomes are forced transfers of power in situations of multiple sovereignty, transfers of power that can be the result of social movements, but usually involve a wide coalition of (institutional and noninstitutional) actors. In fact, as Jack Goldstone maintains in his essay, social movements and revolutions are two possible outcomes of contentious collective action that originate in similar circumstances, but evolve and diverge in consequence of the interplay of protest movements, state response (i.e., the severity and character of repression), the broader environment of social support, and cultural evaluations of state and protest actions. Here we have an important insight into the conditions for transformation, conceived as revolutionary change: the form and outcome of collective action is not determined by movement emergence. Instead, contention evolves in a transformational process, above all, as a consequence of state action.

This volume, however, is most concerned with social movements as a particular form of contentious politics. In this regard, transformation often means institutional change, which we may define, following Elisabeth Clemens (in this volume), as "noncatastrophic transformation of the basic rules of the game or principles of order that characterize a particular society at a particular point in time." Her suggestion to take inspiration from the new institutionalism in sociology, political science, and history (Powell and DiMaggio 1991; Scott 1995; Steinmo, Thelen, and Longstreth 1992) in order to single out the conditions and mechanisms of institutional change is particularly illuminating in this respect. It points to the importance of the existence of alternatives for movements to produce institutional change and to the need of looking, not only at the characteristics of movements but also at institutions, if we are to fully grasp the process of transformation. Here we get a second important insight— transformational change is largely shaped by the character of whatever social movements are changing. As a result, movements will encounter either more or less resistance on the part of those affected by the prospective change, whether powerholders or third parties. It is much easier, at least in theory, to alter relatively new and peripheral rules than to modify long-standing practices that are deeply anchored in the social structure. But here we go back to a process of incorporation rather than transformation. Nevertheless, even as regards fundamental modifications of the basic rules and procedures, not all changes are equally salient for social actors, thereby being either more or less difficult to produce.

The discussion so far concerns social institutions, that is to say those durable or regular aspects of social life emerging from day-to-day interactions. However, when we deal with contention, political institutions become particularly relevant for a discussion of the movement-institution nexus. The question here is: Under what conditions and how do social movements affect political institutions? Specifically, under what conditions and how do social movements *transform* the existing institutions? To be sure, neither this introduction nor the three chapters devoted to transformation will provide a definite answer to this question. Our aim is much more modest; namely, to offer a reflection on the relationship between social movements, on the one hand, and social and political institutions, on the other hand.

Democratization

Sidney Tarrow (1994b, 1) pointed out that "[a]t its dawn in Western Europe and North America, modern democracy was unquestionably a social movement." Given the joint emergence of democracy and social movements, he concluded that it is quite surprising that the relationship between movements and democratic development has received only scant attention. We agree that much more must be done in this domain. The wave of democratization that has swept several South European and Latin American countries has spurred a number of studies on the development of democracy, yet mostly elite-centered models. Nor has the more recent wave of democracy movements in eastern Europe pushed scholars toward the analysis of how social movements may be part of the democratization process. Here we present three essays that look at democracy under the prism of social movement theory in order to redress the elite-centered bias. Two essays deal with southern Europe and Latin America.

In our conceptualization of social change processes, shown in figure B, democratization presupposes incorporation, transformation, or both. In addition, to contribute to democratization, social movements must affect at least one of four elements that define democracy (Tilly 1994): (1) broad citizenship; (2) relatively equal citizenship; (3) binding consultation of citizens to state policies and personnel; and (4) protection of citizens, especially members of minorities, from arbitrary state action.

According to this definition, which lies between purely institutional criteria (such as elections, courts, etc.) and purely substantive criteria (such as justice, equal opportunity, etc.), ideally a state is democratic to the extent that it asserts citizens' rights and obligations, which cover a large share of people under its jurisdiction, which distribute with relative equality among citizens, which include binding consultation of citizens to policies and personnel of the state, and which offer citizens, especially minorities, protection against arbitrary action by state agents. Hence, social movements ideally have a democratizing impact when they succeed in affecting all four elements of democracy. The crucial questions here are obviously (1) whether movements do have an impact on democracy and, if so, (2) under what conditions. Unlike proponents of elite-centered models, many of whom point to the authoritarian threat posed by popular mobilizations (e.g., O'Donnell and Schmitter 1986), most students of social movements would not hesitate to give an affirmative answer to question 1 (e.g., Cohen and Arato 1992; Kitschelt 1993), but they also tend to skip question 2 in favor of a general positive assessment of the democratic contribution of movements. Yet, as Alberto Melucci and Timo Lyyra argue in this volume, there is no automatic correlation between the rise of social movements and their supposedly "positive" or "progressive" (i.e., democratizing) effects. Clearly, social movements' contribution depends on a series of circumstances.

To begin with, if we assume that a polity is democratic to the extent that it establishes clear rights and obligations with regard to the four elements mentioned above (but see Melucci and Lyyra's broader definition of democracy in complex societies), the democratizing impact of movements increases with the proliferation of movements that explicitly aim at affecting those rights and obligations. However, as one of our authors has pointed out elsewhere, any assessment of the effects of social movements on democracy should take into account not only the pressure exerted by protest actions, but also historically specific opportunity structures as well as the dispositions and strategies of elites (Tarrow 1994b). Thus, if we acknowledge the contingency of both opportunity structures and social movements, democracy appears as a contingent outcome of political conflicts. This ascertainment encourages Tilly (1994, 22) to conclude that "the proliferation of social movements only promotes democracy under limited conditions: it only occurs when movements organize around a wide variety of claims including explicit demands for democracy and the state gains capacity to realize such claims at least as fast as the claims increase."

Second, democracy bears different meanings in different contexts, and the hypothetical impact of popular movements on democracy varies according to the polity's previous configuration, though it is difficult to say in which direction. On the one hand, it could be argued that a polity in which basic democratic rights are more or less warranted provides a better ground for movement impact, as compared to profoundly nondemocratic polities, because elites are more sensitive to and the general public more supportive of demands for more democracy. On the other hand, the opposite might well be true: the absence of democratic rights—especially in an increasingly globalizing world—might spur pressures from below, which, if they received support from political elites and parties, might push democratization farther and faster. Perhaps, the relationship between social movements and democracy is curvilinear rather than linear, combining the two kinds of reasoning. Furthermore, as the chapters written by Patricia Hipsher and Salvador Sandoval suggest, the impact of social movements on democracy also varies according to the phase of the democratization process. As opportunities, constraints, costs, and risks of mobilization are not the same in the later stages of transition from authoritarian rule and in the early phases of civilian rule, the impact of movements on democratization should vary accordingly.

Finally, it should also be noted that not all movements contribute in equal terms to the process of democratization. Although it might be argued that social movements in general, at least under certain conditions, promote democracy by contributing to the creation of a public space and the transfer of power over states, historically different types of movements have had an additional and specific impact on democracy (Cattacin, Giugni, and Passy 1997). Thus, labor movements could be said to have occasioned what we may call *distributive democratization,* insofar as they have acted upon the principles that govern the policies of redistribution of wealth in the society. Similarly, the student movements of the sixties and seventies have perhaps promoted *ideological democratization,* for they challenged the dominant (i.e., bourgeois) values by offering alternative worldviews and value systems. Finally, the so-called new social movements have certainly contributed to *participatory democratization,* thanks to the expansion of the rights of citizens to protest and to the enlargement of political participation. However, while this may hold in western societies—that is, in social settings in which some kind of basic democratic rights are granted—it is doubtful whether it can be applied to nondemocratic contexts.

The Essays in This Volume

The present volume has three parts, each one devoted to one of the three processes of social change outlined in this introduction. Part I deals with the incorporation of movements into partisan politics, state policies, and public discourse, respectively. Part II focuses on transformation due to contentious politics. Here are discussed the possibilities for movements to alter the basic patterns of relationship between them and the state, to produce institutional change, and to bring about a fundamental (i.e., revolutionary) transformation of the entire society. Finally, Part III addresses the capabilities of movements to promote democratization, both in already democratic countries and during transitions to democracy.

Chapter 1, written by Michael Hanagan, discusses the relations between social movements and political parties in historical perspective. Rejecting the dichotomy implicit in much of the literature that social movements are either fully independent and active or else quiescent, Hanagan argues that the incorporation of left-wing social movements into political parties has often resulted in the persistence of movement activities within party structures and that incorporated social movements have exerted enduring influences on social policy. The incorporation of social movements into parties and their disengagement have followed a historical pattern that provides a framework for analyzing the secular path of social movement evolution and the development of movement identities. Through the examples of labor, peace, and women's movements in various countries, the author shows that the conditions of movement integration into political parties in the past have shaped the development and outcomes of social movements in succeeding periods.

In chapter 2, Sidney Tarrow applies his well-known theory of protest cycles on the protest wave that occurred in France in 1968, with a particular focus on the effects on policymaking. In so doing, he gives us an example of how social movements can force the incorporation of their claims into policy. In particular, he draws three implications from the case under study: first, protest waves not only take advantage of political opportunity structure, but become a component of it and, hence, provide a window for reform; second, protest waves are not sufficient to produce significant reforms, but need the presence and entrepreneurship of well-placed reformists; third, waves of mobilization can produce temporary coalitions for reform, but are often too brief, divided, and multivoiced to give sustained support to reformists when the fear of disorder disappears.

Chapter 3 is also related to the question of incorporation, this time into the world of public discourse. William Gamson extends his well-known work on the impact of challenging groups to the realm of culture and looks at the factors for movement success in the forum formed by the mass media. He does so by adapting his typology of movement success based on the distinction between obtaining acceptance and gaining new advantages. Acknowledging that students of social movements have largely failed in demonstrating the effects of cultural challenges, Gamson proposes to assess movement impact on cultural change through public discourse. Following this approach, success reflects the movements' skill in relating to journalists and depends on offering attractive frames that integrate public discourse with the other two main resources movements use in this context: experiential knowledge and popular wisdom. Thus, his contribution is also an attempt to link strategic and symbolic aspects of social movements.

With chapter 4, written by Marco Giugni and Florence Passy, the discussion shifts to the relationship between social movements and institutional change. In a way, their essay bridges the processes of incorporation and transformation. Here the path that allows movements to transform the rules of political interaction via their incorporation in existing procedures is at center stage. The authors offer an alternative look at social movements, not only as part of a conflict system, but also as engaging in cooperation with state agents and structures. They argue that this aspect of movements is becoming increasingly important in the context of complex societies. Their comparison of two movements in France and Switzerland suggests that the degree of cooperation is more prominent in

Switzerland and stronger in the solidarity movement than in the ecology movement. In particular, in the Swiss system the operational level is more important, whereas in the French system the consultative logic still seems to prevail, in spite of an increasingly deep integration of movements in state institutions. In some cases, cooperation is so strong that, at least in the domain of aid to development, it is often difficult to distinguish between movement organizations and state institutions. In the end, the authors ask quite provocatively whether the social movement as a specific cluster of political performances is not being replaced by a new cluster, characterized by a new type of interaction with powerholders, whereby contention gives place to cooperation.

In chapter 5, Elisabeth Clemens goes to the core of the problem of transformation by providing us with a broad theoretical reflection on the possibilities of institutional change for collective action. She argues that, if social movements matter in part because they produce social change, then a theory of movement outcomes must be a theory of the relationship between protest or insurgency and durable aspects of social organization. Starting from a broad definition of institutional change (see above), she asks how it is possible to transform a part of the social order without disrupting the whole, producing the cascade of indeterminacy that figures prominently in classic accounts of revolutions, given that so much is at stake in existing institutional rules. After posing this dilemma, her essay draws on recent developments in institutional theory to characterize sources of more bounded indeterminacy, moments and social locations in which not everything is possible, but more than one thing is. To do so, the author draws from various new institutionalisms, which provide a vocabulary for identifying different dimensions of social durability and for locating organizational alternatives in situations unmarked by widespread institutional breakdown.

Jack Goldstone's essay, which forms chapter 6, extends the discussion to other types of contentious politics, in addition to social movements, and makes a strong case for a dynamic analysis of what he calls contentious collective action, which includes a variety of protest phenomena, from movements to revolutions. Specifically, he suggests that we look at the political context of protest, which determines whether protest takes the form of social movements, rebellions, or revolutions. He argues that the character of a regime, rather than the aims or intentions of challengers, are the key determinants of the forms and outcomes of collective action. In his view, successful revolutions, social movements leading to reform, cycles of protest, and guerrilla or terrorist activities are best thought of as a family of related phenomena, originating in a similar set of circumstances, but evolving and diverging in consequence of distinct patterns in the interplay between protest movements, state response, the broader social environment, and cultural evaluations of state and protest actions. The form and outcome of contentious collective action is not determined by the conditions of movement emergence. These characteristics are themselves emergent and contingent on the responses of various social actors to the initial protest actions.

Chapter 7, by Patricia Hipsher, opens Part III, devoted to democratization. Starting from the remark that social movement theorists have paid scant attention to the effects of social movements during transitional periods, she analyzes the variable impact of social movements during the transitions to democracy in Latin America and southern Europe, with reference to a particular case study, the shantytown dwellers' movement in Chile and, to a lesser degree, various other social movements in Spain, Chile, Brazil, and Portugal. Her essay indicates that transitions from authoritarian rule not only provide opportunities for social movements to mobilize and democratize the political process, but also may place certain constraints on movements' abilities to remain insurgent. As she maintains, generally in the early stages of democratic transitions the impact of social movements is strongly felt, as movements push transitions beyond mere liberalization. Movements push transitions farther and faster and contribute to the reconstitution of the civil society by functioning as schools of democracy and agents for restoring the public sphere.

In chapter 8, Salvador Sandoval addresses similar issues by looking at the role that protest movements have played in the processes of democratization of Spain, Portugal, and several Latin American countries. He argues that social movements have been key actors in establishing stable democratic regimes in situations where opposition elites included these collective actors in the pro-democratization coalition. In situations where social movement actors were not included in the opposition coalition, but rather subordinated to the internal conflicts of the opposition elites, the end result was a transition from authoritarian rule to relatively unstable democratic regimes, characterized by the continued presence of military intervention in civilian rule.

Finally, chapter 9, written by Alberto Melucci and Timo Lyyra, addresses the relationship between social movements and democracy in complex societies. The authors show that contemporary complex societies pose new threats as well as provide new opportunities for movements to influence the democratic process. In this context, the democratic outcomes of social movements depend, more than before, on the autonomy of the social space for collective action. This, they maintain, is only partly a result of the interaction between movements and the state, and it involves the various social areas in which the autonomy of movement action constitutes itself, not only at the political but also at the personal level. In addition, the authors argue, nothing assures us that movements always make society more democratic, and this is true also for the so-called left-libertarian movements that have dominated the unconventional political arena during the last few decades. They suggest that it would be wrong to proceed from a normative point of view which assumes that the contributions of social movements are positive in all circumstances. Such a view would mean mistaking reality for our desires and taking for granted something that must be demonstrated empirically.

In the conclusion, Doug McAdam's essay offers us his speculation about the future of social movements as we have known them for the last two centuries. He envisions four broad trends as we enter the new millennium: the growing institutionalization of social movements and the rise of a so-called movement society, the global spread of the social movement form, the rise of transnational advocacy networks and the exportation of the movement form, and finally a future of movements as multilevel games within a world made of composite states.

Notes

1. Translated from Italian.
2. A more elaborate discussion of the nature and characteristics of social movements as opposed to other forms of contentious politics, which has inspired the present discussion, can be found in Tilly (1994).
3. Emphasis in original.

Part I

Incorporation

1

Social Movements

Incorporation, Disengagement, and Opportunities—A Long View

Michael Hanagan

In evaluating the outcomes of social protest, a fuller array of relations among social movements and political parties must be considered than is generally offered in the literature on collective action.[1] This essay rejects the dichotomy implicit in much of the literature that social movements are either fully independent and active or else quiescent (Taylor 1989). It shows that the incorporation of left-wing social movements into political parties has often resulted in the persistence of movement activities *within* party structures and that incorporated social movements have exerted enduring influences on social policy. For much of western and central Europe over the last century and a quarter, it maintains that the incorporation of social movements into parties and their disengagement have followed a historical pattern that provides a framework for analyzing the secular path of social movement evolution and the development of movement identities. Finally, it asserts that conditions of movement integration into political parties in the past have shaped the development and outcomes of social movements in succeeding periods.

Three phases in the relationship between political parties and left social movements can be identified, and they follow a distinctive rhythm: *disengagement/social movement independence (1870–1914), consolidation/social movement integration (1919–1960),* and *disengagement/social movement independence (1960-present).* First, in the years between 1870 and 1914, western, central and northern Europe proved particularly fertile in generating left social movement organizations (SMOs). Organizations of working men and women, birth-control advocates, students, educational reformers, trade unionists, peace activists, child labor reformers, tenant farmers, suffragists, opponents of sweated labor, unemployed

3

workers, and many more engaged in boycotts, petitions, rallies, demonstrations, marches, general strikes, and many other forms of collective action. The second phase, between 1919 and 1960, offered countercurrents. Freeing themselves from the influence of existing parties, labor movements transformed into political parties. The development of labor movement parties had direct repercussions on related social movements, which were drawn into the periphery and became satellites; while labor movements became more independent, allied social movements became less. During the third phase, beginning in the 1960s and continuing to the present, social movements broke from the labor orbit and reasserted their independence.

Drawing on the rich history of European social movements over the last 125 years and employing historical and comparative methods, this essay emphasizes the importance of what Sidney Tarrow (1992, 24) defined as "social movement sectors"—dense and interactive spheres of activity in which movements compete and cooperate. Emphasizing the continuity of collective action, this study finds that the forms of social movement and their relationship to one another within left social movement sectors have changed depending on whether they sought to influence states directly through independent action or to influence them indirectly through political parties.

Social Movements and Political Parties

Five basic relationships between movements and parties can be identified: articulation, permeation, alliance, independence, and competition. The first two of these positions seriously limit movement autonomy; the last two are the least restrictive.

Articulation

SMOs are organized around the party program and articulate the policy positions of parties to constituencies where parties hope to mobilize support and to recruit members. In France, in the post–World War II period, the communist-influenced Unions des Femmes Françaises and the Combattants de la Paix are extreme examples of this type, but the Labour party-controlled Hydrogen Bomb Campaign Committee and the women's sections of the Labour Party in Britain might serve as more typical examples. Even while such organizations are directly controlled by political parties, they often exert an independent influence on the party. Their success in mobilizing the masses strengthens the party's commitment to a particular cause. In return for routine access to the center of party power and institutional support for their cause, movement activists are expected to follow party guidelines and instructions.

Permeation

SMOs have operated within parties to recruit them to their cause; the Campaign for Nuclear Disarmament (CND) in the United Kingdom, the group around Clara Zetkin and the paper *Gleichheit* in pre-1914 Germany, and the women's sections within the contemporary Swedish Social Democratic Party (SDP) are examples. To have prospect for success, such strategies presume considerable preexisting support within the political party. Although permeation implies that the party is not as fully committed to a particular goal as movement activists should wish, it also necessarily involves SMOs' acknowledgement that they share a broad range of goals with the political party of which they are members. Loyal to the party, movement activists expect to receive a fair-minded hearing for their cause and, employing routine channels for exerting influence, to have a reasonable chance of winning the party to their point of view.

Alliance

SMOs may negotiate *ad hoc* alliances with parties or factions of parties that involve close collaboration on specific issues but in which both party and SMO retain their own separate organization and overall freedom of action. Examples here include the coalition between the Labour Party and the National Union of Women's Suffrage Societies (NUWSS) in Britain between 1912 and 1914 and the fleeting link between the French trade union, the Confederation Française Démocratique du Travail (CFDT), and segments of the peace movement in more recent times in the early eighties. Coalitions imply that each side expects to obtain specific and concrete benefits; coalitions dissolve if these expectations are disappointed. Next let us consider the two more autonomous strategies.

Independence

SMOs act independently of political parties, pressuring them to make concessions at the risk of losing voters who support the movement. In 1907, following its break with the Independent Labour Party (ILP), the Women's Social and Political Union (WSPU) became an independent movement; founded in 1960, the British Committee of 100 was formed for this purpose from the very beginning. Frequently the choice of such a strategy implies sufficient support for the SMO within a political party that a failure to make concessions will lead to defections within parties— and serious electoral consequences. A willingness to inflict serious electoral losses on those it wants to influence puts an SMO in a strong bargaining position, but, if it actually does so, it risks diminishing its own prospects for achieving any measure of reform while at the same time losing support within the party.

Competition

SMOs turn themselves into political parties. The labor movement in many European countries provides the key example here, although at various times and places, peace parties and women's parties have enjoyed a brief existence. Typically, SMO parties began as "parties of protest," intended to articulate the grievances of ongoing social movements. Over time, if these parties grow, they are presented the possibility of becoming "parties of power," influencing state policy through their own electoral power or through governmental participation rather than as simple mouthpieces for social movements. Serious debates within SMOs and SMO parties have generally occurred over the feasibility of combining electoral politics with those of social movements; social movements feel most comfortable within "parties of protest" but obtain the most benefits within "parties of power."

SMOs never have the full range of choices, as outlined above, available to them. Choices are limited by the prevailing political context, which itself is a product of past political struggles. Almost no political issues arise absolutely *de novo* and, in almost every circumstance, some strategies for obtaining political goals are backed by force of tradition, institutional support, and ongoing organization while others are untried or discredited. Without strong and compelling reasons, few SMOs will break with successful past practices and institutional commitments. The big and relatively rapid changes in the strategies of social movements described here were produced by a *combination* of changes both in the mobilization of political groups and in the political opportunity structure. When we refer to "political opportunity structure," we refer to the political context for social movements (Eisinger 1973; McAdam 1982). For present purposes, this essay concentrates on changes in the situation of those political parties through which social movements seek to exert influence. Depending on circumstances, either major party successes or failures can produce realignments. Major party successes can force SMOs into closer relationships with political parties as the only vehicles capable of winning benefits for them. Alternatively, they can sunder existing bonds if a victorious party fails to make what an SMO considers "adequate" concessions. Party defeat can break ties by decreasing the possibility of gaining benefits or it can tighten bonds if SMOs find no other source of support. In addition, the realignment of the movements we examine were greatly accelerated by changes in the ability of SMOs to mobilize their constituencies. The expansion of suffrage strongly affected all European SMOs in this period. The increase in the size of social groups that were the constituencies of SMOs—working men and women, white-collar professionals, and students—was also important. Finally, the decline of religious parties, by freeing up the loyalties and allegiances, enlarged the constituencies to which SMOs could appeal.

In discussing how SMOs evaluate their choices, it is important to consider that changing strategies entails forging new identities and, in this way, affects the very interest criteria adopted for making strategic decisions. An SMO's decision to employ a strategy of working within a political party involves its members increased identification with the party's other goals; in time, members become more willing to sacrifice SMO priorities for that of their party. In contrast, SMO independence focuses members' attention in a more concentrated fashion on specific movement demands emphasizing their centrality and importance. Justifications for movement independence are powerfully enhanced if large portions of the political world can be shown to revolve around just those points that the movement establishes as central. The self-absorption and tunnel vision of some independent social movements should not be seen as the cause of movement independence but its result. Shifts in movement strategy involve not only pursuing existing interests in new ways but in reconfiguring collective interests themselves.

Before fleshing out this argument in the European context, let us first explain our focus and define some terms. In this essay, we concentrate on western, central, and northern Europe, areas in which movements spread most densely in the late nineteenth and twentieth centuries. The reasons for this spread are not mysterious, for these were the countries in which elections played the most important role and those in which rights to organization were most securely recognized. Nonetheless throughout most of the early period under study, the majority of adults in all these countries, sometimes the large majority, were excluded from the vote and, during most of the period under consideration, limitations on the right to organize varied greatly and were sometimes exceedingly restrictive.

The three most important and enduring social movements belonging to left social movement sectors in modern European history are the center of our investigation: the labor movement, the peace movement, and the women's movement. "Peace movements" indicate groups of activists identified in scholarly jargon as "pacifist" and "pacifistic," including both those who think "war is always wrong and should never be resorted to," as well as those who think that "war, though *sometimes necessary,* is always an irrational and inhumane way to settle disputes, and that its prevention should be an over-riding political priority" (Taylor 1958: 51).

Between 1870 and 1990, peace movements included groups in favor of compulsory arbitration in international affairs, supporters of unilateral disarmament, organized draft resisters, and those groups opposed to the U.S. deployment of an antiballistic missile system. "Women's movements" signal gender-conscious groups that include feminists who fight to advance women's rights and interests as well as other politically oriented groups in which "women are acting consciously *as* women" (Bogan and Yellin 1994, 2). Both the explicitly feminist Women's Social and Political Union (WSPU) and the not explicitly feminist Women's Cooperative Guild (WCG) fit into this category. Not all "women's movements" belong to the left social movement sector examined here. For example, in France, women's movements would include the Catholic and anti-republican Le Féminisme Chrétien and Action Sociale pour la Femme. Both supported votes for women, but had almost no relations with suffragists in the left-wing movement sector.

"Labor movement" indicates the overlapping networks of trade unions, *ad hoc* class-based organizations, and working-class political parties that emerged almost everywhere in Europe by 1914. Socialist and labor (and, later, Communist) parties were all part of this group. The great strength of the labor movement was rooted in the growth of trade unions and in the spread of the strike as a form of protest to every European nation. Even in countries like France where the national trade union movement remained aloof from socialist parties, local trade unions provided support and bitter strikes supplied the occasion for the spread of socialist propaganda. Its base in an established trade union constituency with a national organization and widespread regional connections helps explain why labor was uniquely able to form and sustain political parties.

1870–1914
Disengagement
Social Movement Independence

In the late 1860s and early 1970s, great majorities in labor movements, peace movements, and women's movements identified themselves with a politics that styled itself as "liberal," "republican," or "radical." Ties that had been strained or broken in the wrenching conflicts between 1848 and 1851 had been almost entirely reknit—although not, as events were to show, entirely forgotten. Strategies of articulation and permeation dominated almost everywhere. In the late 1840s in France and Great Britain, leading liberal spokesmen, such as Frédéric Bastiat, John Bright, and Richard Cobden, initiated the peace movement. At its foundation, the Trades Union Congress (TUC [1867]) was little more than a pressure group of the Liberal Party, and many British feminists began their careers in such organizations affiliated with the Liberal Party as the National Liberal Federation (1877) and the National Reform Union. In Germany, August Bebel, later one of the chief pioneers of German Marxism, was an activist in the Verband des Deutschen Arbeiter (Bildungs) Vereine whose main concern was working with liberals for reform and democratic national reunification (Breuilly 1992). K. Hjalmar Branting, the first Social Democrat elected to the Swedish *riksdag*, ran on a liberal political slate.

Nevertheless, between 1870 and 1914, networks of activists distanced themselves from liberal or republican parties. In western and central Europe, the combination of industrialization and suffrage expansion shook the established political order. In France and Great Britain, successful liberals refused to make the concessions their trade-union supporters required. In these countries, liberal parties were becoming "parties of power" inured to governing and to the compromises that it entailed. As liberal parties edged toward a policy of conciliation with militarists and social conservatives, they became incapable of fulfilling the hopes of workers and social reformers, hopes they themselves had first stimulated and encouraged. Liberal landslides, such as those of 1906 in France and Great Britain, resulted in legislative achievements that seemed to exhaust the liberal program, leaving them a spent force. In central Europe, in the Austrian and German empires, liberalism increasingly became too weak and divided to contain rapidly growing labor movements.

The Peace Movement

In 1889, France commemorated the centenary of the French Revolution with an international exposition that provided the setting for an outburst of international organizing. The Second (Socialist) International was founded in Paris in that year as was the Universal Peace Conference. Because it failed so ignominiously, little attention has been paid to a European peace movement tracing its roots to the International Peace Congresses of 1848 to 1851 and the International League of Peace and Liberty of 1867 (van der Linden 1987). Before 1914, hundreds of peace societies were founded throughout Europe, each promoting the idea of compulsory arbitration in international disputes and rigorous respect for neutrality; national peace councils with paid directors were created in France, Italy, Germany, Belgium, Denmark, Sweden, Norway, and the United Kingdom (Cooper 1991, 60) Liberal politicians were the main targets of the peace movements, and, of the three movements under consideration in the pre-1914 period, the peace movement retained the strongest ties to liberalism in almost every European nation. Still, the spread of pro-imperialist and nationalist sentiments within liberalism made it an uncertain home, and increasingly peace activists began to organize separately. In 1898, the unexpected call from the Russian czar for a peace conference at the Hague strengthened activists' convictions that peace initiatives could come from unlikely quarters.

Favorite peace movement tactics were the organization of international congresses that issued appeals to national governments to submit their grievances to arbitration; the sponsorship of discussions among peace activists from rival nations or cultural exchanges—Franco-German events were particular favorites. Peace movement activists organized mass petition campaigns to build international support for the Hague Peace Conferences of 1899 and 1907; they celebrated International Peace Day, originally designated as February 22 (George Washington's birthday) but later changed to May 18 (the opening of the first Hague Conference). The leaders of the peace movement were often middle-class intellectuals, and it appealed disproportionately to the middle classes, but these were not the movement's only audience. In France, for example, labor organizations such as the Bourses du travail, cooperatives, and working-class universités populaires were affiliated to the peace movement (Cooper 1991).

The geographic strength of the peace movement is difficult to ascertain, but the broad outline is sufficiently clear. England was easily the strongest center of the European movement, followed by France. In the United Kingdom, peace organizations headed by Quakers, nonconformists, feminists, and socialists participated in the British National Peace Council, and leading Liberal politicians, such as David Lloyd George and Sir Henry Campbell-Bannerman, hailed its actions. In France the peace movement received support from the Radical, Radical Socialist, and Socialist Parties, and a 1909 meeting of the Association de la Paix par le Droit (APD) was endorsed by historians Ernest Lavisse and Gabriel Monod, the sociologist Emile Durkheim, numerous senators and deputies, and such key political leaders as Léon Bourgeois, Emile Loubet, and Stephen Pichon, minister of foreign affairs (Cooper 1991). In the middle ranks of the peace movement were Belgium, Italy, the Netherlands, Switzerland, and the Scandinavian countries; in the smaller European nations the rights of neutrals were often the major focus of peace activists. Although the peace movement was not negligible in Germany and Austria, it was relatively weak there (Chickering 1975).

The Women's Movement

Increasingly, the peace movement found itself supported by the growing women's movements that played an important role in the world of European protest. Organized women marched, petitioned, paraded, chained themselves to lampposts, protested at polling booths, and ran as candidates for political office. In western Europe, women's organizations also began to distance themselves from liberal parties. In the United Kingdom, after the failure of Liberal leaders to support the expansion of the suffrage to women in the Reform Bill of 1884, women's organizations began to take a more distant attitude toward the party. The refusal of leading Liberal Party politicians, such as Herbert Asquith, to support women's suffrage, even when presented with an overwhelming political majority in the House of Commons, encouraged a decisive turn toward independence within the women's movement. The violent acts militant feminists of the WSPU carried out against Asquith's government were based on the assumption that, since many liberals supported women's suffrage, militant tactics would increase the pressure on Asquith within the party. Although fewer in numbers, French feminists were moved toward organizational independence by the same forces. The main obstacles to women's suffrage there were the opposition of Radical Socialists in the Senate; while using the pretext that women would vote as their confessors instructed them, Hause and Kenney (1984) showed that many were also social conservatives, fearful of a threat to the family.

The geography of women's movements is also reasonably clear, and it differs from that of the peace movement and, as we shall see, from that of the labor movement. In a continental context, Great Britain had been the originator of the movement and remained its leader, although Scandinavian movements soon threatened to catch up. While success is not a certain measure of relative strength, it is not coincidental that Finland and Norway were the only European countries to grant women's suffrage before 1914. After the United Kingdom and Scandinavia, Germany had the strongest women's movement; the Latin nations followed well behind.

The sudden growth of Scandinavian women's movements was largely due to regional political and economic circumstances. There, liberalism was both newer and more progressive than in much of Europe. In most of Scandinavia, industrial development came late, mostly occurring after 1900, and it proceeded with great rapidity, transforming agriculture as much as industry; in Finland and Norway, pre–World War I development was mainly confined to agriculture and lumbering (Gourevitch 1986). Scandinavian nations were too small to be involved in great power conflicts, except as innocent bystanders, and had little opportunity to involve themselves in colonial adventures. The central problem of Scandinavian liberalism was that its explosive economic growth created mass support for liberalism at a time when socialist parties were already beginning to compete for support among the masses and to join liberals in demonstrations in favor of expanding suffrage. Without traditional links to a mass working-class constituency, Scandinavian liberals were forced to prove their credentials and became more reliable and thoroughgoing champions of women's suffrage than liberals in the rest of Europe. Scandinavian countries developed quite strong women's suffrage associations, which received support from both socialist and liberal political parties but generally remained more closely associated with liberal parties.

The Labor Movement

Of all the social movements in the pre–World War I European world, labor was undoubtedly the largest and the best organized. In the 1870s, the labor movement was still largely a social movement committed to mobilizing masses of workers in the streets and workplaces to put pressure on the established order. Between 1870 and 1914, labor distanced itself from liberal parties. Starting in 1890, every May Day, trade unionists and socialists showed off their strength in public marches, and, after 1895, mass strikes were occasionally employed as a method of protest. By 1914, in those areas of Europe where the working class had even partial access to the suffrage, labor had made serious steps toward transforming itself into a political party.

Although the specific reasons for the break with liberalism varied greatly, the working-class abandonment of liberal political parties is clear enough (Stone 1983). German liberals had been committed to the cause of a democratic nationalism, but these liberals with whom working-class democrats, such as August Bebel, had first been associated were stunned by Bismarck's military triumph in uniting Germany by "blood and iron." German liberals had earlier believed that German unity could only be won by a democratic revolution modeled on 1848. In the wake of the Austro-Prussian War of 1866 and the Franco-Prussian War of 1870–1871, the division of liberals between those who rallied to Bismarck and those who opposed him, led young workers like August Bebel to decide that they must strike out on their own and turn to Karl Marx. French workers became disgruntled in the early days of the Third Republic when the leaders of the republican left, led by Léon Gambetta, compromised and created a conservative republic with little to offer workers. English workers' ties to liberals lasted longest, but the Liberal preoccupation with Ireland led to worker dissatisfaction, and the split between Unionists and Liberals and the later battle over protectionism created conditions favorable for the growth of an independent labor party (Cohen and Hanagan 1995).

To one extent or another, all the SMOs we have studied broke or strained their ties with liberals in the years before World War I, but only labor movements turned themselves into political parties. Besides the support of trade unions, what allowed the labor movements to successfully undertake this move was the vast expansion of manhood suffrage occurring in Europe between 1870 and 1914, as well as the great increase in the number of industrial workers. Almost everywhere, large sections of the working class were getting the vote, and, when labor movements broke with liberalism, they were able to put their case before whole sections of the electorate that had never been recruited to other parties.

Scandinavian countries arrived at the same break but exhibited a pattern different from England and France. British liberals and French republicans had built up a strongly entrenched position within their labor movements. In Britain and France, particularly, the break was piecemeal and occurred in a series of traumatic ruptures over decades. In Scandinavia it was not so much a growing tension between liberals and socialists as it was that liberalism less successfully dominated the space for working-class politics. The Scandinavian cases are interesting because they show us that programmatic responsiveness is not the sole determinant of parties' relationships to social movements; political parties must have entrenched sources of strength within the politically active population in order to make it worthwhile for an SMO to enter their ranks. Scandinavian liberals' relations with labor were weaker, and socialist parties were in existence in these countries before the advent of large-scale extensions of the suffrage so, once suffrage was expanded, socialists went ahead and appealed directly to the ranks of the uncommitted.

All of the parties that developed from European labor movements were parties of a "new type." They were designed to be mass membership parties with constitutions that spelled out how candidates were to be nominated, how party policy was to be determined, and how elected party representatives were to be disciplined if they failed to carry out party policy. The sense of party membership and involvement generated by working-class parties was unprecedented in European experience. Real socialists were "card-carrying socialists." Party discipline was also unprecedented. Over the course of the following decades, all of these parties, including the British Labour Party and the Swedish Social Democratic Party, expelled elected representatives who failed to carry out party-mandated policy on key issues. The strength of party discipline enhanced the value of strategies of articulation and permeation by giving authority to party pronouncements and, thus, real power to the social movements who could win party support. The heartland of socialist parties could be found in the Scandinavian and Germanic world. Table 1.1 shows the percentage of socialist votes in western, central, and northern European nations in the last election before World War I.

As the labor movement broke free from the liberals, it developed a new identity. A party led by a network of trade unionist or working-class supporters of liberalism proclaimed itself the "party of the proletariat." This new identity was not manufactured out of wholecloth but hand-crafted from available facts and selective cases; nonetheless, like the claim of women's movements to represent "women," the claim of labor movement parties to represent the "proletariat" was more a goal than a reality. In the pre–World War I period, for example, active socialists were typically urban, male skilled workers from a secular or Protestant religious background. Arrayed in the armor of "the proletariat," socialist leaders might mock the condescension of the middle-class women who often led organized protests against sweated domestic labor. Condescension there sometimes was, but many a woman social reformer possessed more knowledge of conditions in sweated labor than did socialist leaders—and sometimes a great deal more sympathy.

Early in their development, socialist parties oriented their programs and their approaches outside work-based issues. In the last years before World War I, individual parties and the Socialist International turned their attention to issues of peace and gender. In 1907, the Socialist International set up a Socialist Women's International, which in 1910 called for the celebration of International Proletarian Women's Day. The Socialist International made clear that it expected socialists to organize their own peace and women's movements with a socialist orientation and as part of the socialist movement; in regard to other social movements, socialists sought to build SMOs that would articulate party programs and distrusted independent social movements. The first congress of the Socialist Women's International at Stuttgart in 1907 resolved that "socialist women must not ally themselves with the feminists of the bourgeoisie, but lead the battle [for the vote] side by side with the socialist parties" (Evans 1987, 58). Socialist women were encouraged to organize women's sections within socialist parties that would appeal to women as housewives and/ or as workers. In much of Europe, socialist youth groups devoted much of their effort to antiwar issues.

The proclamations of the Socialist International are only indicative. But in this case, the Socialist International reflected a sentiment widely prevalent among pre-1914 socialist leaders: as socialists, they were suspicious of organizations dominated by middle-class liberals; as political leaders, they were distrustful of organizations seeking to influence party policy outside established channels; as heads of household and chief breadwinners, they were wary of independent organizations of women. The Socialist International's resolutions were based on preexisting divisions; serious fractures within women's movements between socialist and nonsocialist women already existed in Austria, Finland, France, Germany, and Sweden (Evans 1987).

The policy followed by socialist parties in the peace movement closely resembled their policy in the women's movement. International socialism defined itself as "the party of peace" and, at the founding congress of the Socialist International, French socialist Edouard Vaillant had proclaimed:

"peace is an indispensable condition for the emancipation of the proletariat" (Haupt 1972, 11). But only in the last few years before World War I did socialist movements become very concerned about the threat of war. Their efforts to organize antiwar demonstrations during the Morocco Crisis of 1911 and the Balkan War of 1912 marked their dramatic entry into the antiwar movement, but they did so on their own terms with no regard to the existing peace movements in the field. Mutual suspicion prevailed between socialists and the peace movement. Peace movement activists were frightened that the socialists would use their numbers to take over their organizations and felt that class war was only another kind of war. Socialists insisted upon the necessity of recognizing the capitalist roots of militarism and expressed their belief that socialism was the necessary prerequisite for international mediation and arbitration. In Austria, a leading member of the small Austrian Peace Society emphasized "the serious work of scientific and moderate pacifism as against socialist endeavors," while in 1907 a leading socialist woman activist confided in her diary that "The [Hague] peace conferences move much too slowly—the Revolution will overtake them" (Wank 1988, 46).

1919–1963
Consolidation
Social Movement Integration

After World War I, as socialist parties grew, their efforts to build SMOs to articulate party policies became much more significant (see table 1.1). Between 1918 and 1960, almost everywhere, labor movement parties replaced liberal parties as the largest party of the left; under socialist party pressure, social movements abandoned strategies of independence and turned toward articulation and permeation. Within party structures, SMOs continued to organize rallies, demonstrations, and petitions, but now they often did so as much to influence their own party as the state. SMOs were also subject to repression for violating the rules of party constitutions that sometimes imposed more constraints than did state repression. Where labor movement parties were less politically dominant, social movements were usually more successful in preserving their independence.

The Labor and Women's Movements

The integration of SMOs into labor movement parties was not accomplished easily. The process by which this occurred in the women's movement can be seen clearly in the British Labour Party, the party that had the best relationship with independent feminist and women's groups. In

TABLE 1.1
Votes for Labor Movement Parties*

	Last National Election up to 1914	First National Election after 1918	First National Election after 1945
	(1914 included)	(1918 included)	(1945 included)
Austria	25.4% (1)	40.8%	44.6%
Belgium	30.3%	36.6%	44.3%
Denmark	29.6%	28.7%	45.3%
Finland	43.1%	38.0%	48.6% (2)
France	16.8%	21.2%	49.9%
Germany	34.8%	45.5% (3)	29.2% (4)
Italy	17.6%	32.3%	39.6%
Netherlands	18.5%	24.3%	38.9%
Norway	26.3%	31.6%	52.9%
Sweden	30.1%	29.7%	46.1%
Switzerland	10.1%	23.5%	31.3%
United Kingdom	6.4%	21.4%	48.0%

*% of voting population that cast ballots for communist, socialist, and labor parties (1) Austrian kingdom of Austro-Hungarian empire (2) includes *Suomen Kansan demokraattinen liitto* (3) includes *Unabhängige Sozialdemocratische Partei Deutschlands* (4) West German election, 1949

Sources: Peter Flora *et al. State, Economy, and Society in Western Europe 1815–1975*. Vol. 1. Chicago: St. James Press, 1983; Chris Cook and John Paxton. *European Political Facts: 1918–73*. New York: Facts on File, 1975; Chris Cook and John Paxton. *European Political Facts: 1848–1918*. New York: Facts on File, 1978.

1914, while it was still evolving from a social movement to a political party, British Labour Party leaders had a variety of ties to various women's movements. Between 1912 and 1914, the party had reversed its earlier stand supporting only universal suffrage and worked in close coalition with the NUWSS for the extension of the existing suffrage to women. Affiliated to the party was the Women's Labour League (WLL), a group dedicated to supporting Labour candidates but which had also independently carried out its own campaigns for inclusion of women in the National Insurance Act of 1911 and anti-sweating and public health legislation (Collette 1989). The WCG, another important women's group, had passed a resolution agreeing to a "closer alliance between Cooperation and the other Labour forces." The TUC also allowed considerable leeway for women's organization. Organizations that focused on organizing women and representing the interests of working women, such as the Women's Trade Union League (WTUL) and the National Union for Women Workers (NUWW), were loosely affiliated to the TUC.

In the next few years, the labor movement's strength grew dramatically, and, as it did, its relationship to the women's movement also changed; everywhere relations characterized by independence or alliance moved toward articulation or permeation. Labour, a very junior partner in the progressive coalition in 1906, became the senior partner in the governing coalition in 1924. A new constitution, adopted in 1918, laid the basis for the party's future organizational development. The WLL became the women's sections of the Labour Party; in the process it lost most of its autonomy, but, by 1924, the WLL had acquired 150,000 members and became one of the party's major constituency organizations. During the same few years, the party's relationship with the WCG grew more intimate. Although retaining its organizational independence, the WCG allowed its local groups to affiliate directly with the Labour Party and more than 100 branches took this course (Webb 1927). At the same time, the coalition with the NUWW no longer functioned. The Representation of the People Act, adopted in 1918, gave women over thirty the right to vote and abolished virtually all property qualifications for voting. While full women's suffrage was not yet attained, the great hurdle was overcome and electoral equality was clearly a matter of time (it came in 1928). After 1918, the Labour Party and the NUWSS went their separate ways. A parallel policy was also implemented in the trade union movement when, in 1919, the NUWW was dissolved into the National Union of General Workers, and the WTUL became the women's section of the TUC (Rowan 1982).

But the reconfiguration of power in favor of the labor movement was actually much greater than the mere reorientation of organizations in the women's movement suggests. In the years between 1918 and 1960, membership in the Labour Party and the women's sections of the Labour Party tended to become much more central to the preoccupations of women activists. An excellent example of this evolution is that of Selina Cooper and her network of family and acquaintances, politically active in the Nelson area of Lancashire between 1899 and 1947 (Liddington 1984). By the 1900s Cooper had been involved in the Burnley Weavers Association, the Social Democratic Federation, the ILP, the WCG, the Labour Party, the WLL and, through her membership in the NUWSS, had become paid organizer and a national figure in the women's suffrage campaign. Throughout her entire political life, she considered herself a socialist, a trade union activist, and a suffragist. In 1907, disappointed by the Labour Party's refusal to support the expansion of women's suffrage in its own right, she devoted her own very considerable energies to the cause of women's suffrage.

In 1918, with the success of suffrage expansion, in common with many women's activists, Selina Cooper found herself adrift. At first, she supported the efforts of the NUWSS to transform itself into the National

Union of Societies for Equal Citizenship, an independent feminist organization to deal with the economic and social conditions of women. Yet her own local branch of the organization, the Women's Citizens' Association, was unable to survive in working-class Nelson. The reason for this lack of popular interest is not hard to find, for the years immediately following the war witnessed a dramatic resurgence of class militancy. In 1918, working-class political activists' eyes were focused on the Russian Revolution and on the wave of industrial militancy sweeping all of Europe, including Britain. Cooper became involved in the Labour Party's campaign to withdraw British troops from Russia and was deeply stirred by the joint declaration of the Labour Party and the TUC in support of a general strike if Britain intervened further in the Russian civil war.

Cooper's activities in support of the Russian Revolution drew her inevitably more deeply into the Labour Party. Initially, she had opposed the existence of separate sections in the Labour Party for women, but in 1918, finding herself the only woman out of twenty-two members elected to the Executive of the Nelson and Colne Constituency Labor Party, she turned her attention to the Women's Sections. For the next twenty years, Selina Cooper devoted most of her time to the party, fighting for many of the same issues that had concerned her during her years in independent suffragist organizations. Cooper organized petitions and marches for the public dissemination of birth control information and, during the Depression, to prevent the passage of laws prohibiting the employment of married women. She also joined a women's antiwar organization, Women against War and Fascism, that worked to win the Labour Party to the cause of a United Front to fight fascism. Her increasing willingness to work with Communists eventually led Cooper into fundamental conflict with Labour Party leaders, and in 1940 at the age of seventy-six, she was expelled from the party.

The campaign for a United Front between 1933 and 1939 provides an exceptionally clear picture of the new reconfiguration of social movement organizations. Stimulated by the British Communist Party, the drive was an organized movement *within* the British Labour Party, using the tactics of social movements, to change party policy. The movement for the United Front reached its peak in 1939 when an important supporter, Sir Stafford Cripps, submitted a memorandum in its favor to the Labour Party National Executive Committee. Cripps knew that his memorandum would be rejected but that its rejection would make his position public, and his memorandum was really, in Pimlott's words, a "manifesto" intended for "the rank and file" (Pimlott 1977, 171). Supporters of the United Front, drawn from the Communist Party and left-wing groups like the Left Book Club and Women against War and Fascism, circulated the document throughout the party. Cripps addressed rallies calling for the formation of a United Front. A National Petition Campaign was organized, calling for the Labour Party, the Liberal Party, and elements within the Conservative Party to work together to defend democracy.

The incorporation of women's movements such as the WLL and women activists like Selina Cooper into the women's sections of socialist parties was hardly unique to Great Britain; in fact, the Labour Party was late in following a policy already dominant in Germanic and Scandinavian Europe. In 1908, the repeal of German laws forbidding women's participation in political activities gave the party the chance to integrate the new women's sections into its own party structures. As in the United Kingdom, German socialist women gained representation on the party executive committee, but women's organizations were also subordinated to the decisions of the party congresses. Women's organizations soon became an important component of the SDP. By 1931, 22.8 percent of the party's membership, numbering around 230,000 women (Pore 1981, 56; Quataert 1979, 5). Austria followed the German model, and, by 1911, over 28,000 women were enrolled in the women's section of the party. In Scandinavia socialist parties played the leading role in establishing women's sections, and everywhere they were an important component of the party's strength (Haavio-Mannila 1981).

While socialist parties significantly limited the autonomy of socialist women's groups, it also gave them institutional representation in the highest councils of socialist parties. What did the women's movement gain from institutional incorporation? Here the case of German Social Democracy is probably typical. Although committed to an ideal of the "mother housewife," German Social Democracy, prompted by the demands of organized women, worked to educate working-class women on methods of birth control and defended access to birth control. It promoted reform in the areas of marriage, divorce, illegitimacy, prostitution, and the protection of mothers. It also opposed laws that discriminated against women in their biological capacity (Pore 1981). Sometimes, socialist women were able to employ this maternalist rhetoric to promote programs that empowered women in the broader economic and social arena. In the 1930s Swedish socialist women championed the idea of the Swedish state as a "People's Home," which should provide help for everyone and in whose construction everyone should participate (Hobson and Lindholm forthcoming). Further, on occasion, women's representatives on the SDP's leadership councils could play a role in mobilizing support on issues, such as peace, which has been a historical concern of socialist feminists. In 1955, for instance, the Swedish government was debating the acquisitions of atomic arms and a strong defense program; the cabinet was deeply divided. The peace party, according to Alva Myrdal (1982, 86), was strengthened by "strong mass support . . . organized by an indefatigable campaign of the Social-Democratic Women's union."

The Peace and Labor Movements

Although by 1950 the peace movement was to be incorporated into European labor movements, in the interwar period, European peace movements' relationships with socialist parties proved to be stormier than with women's movements. Certainly World War I and its aftermath made peace a far more central issue that it had been in the prewar era. Millions of men and women in Britain, France, and Germany had actual experience with the horror of warfare or had lost husbands, sons, and brothers in the trenches. They were willing to consider any alternative to the prospect of another war. What made peace so central a concern, however, was that the unstable diplomatic equilibrium after the Versailles settlement, added to the rise to power of dictators—first in Italy, then in Germany—and the exclusion of the Soviet Union from world diplomacy, increased the likelihood of war.

Yet, to explain the peace movement's growing political independence in the thirties, it is necessary to take into account the dramatic change in the political bases of support for peace movements. In the twenties, in the largest European nations, socialist support for pacifism seemed to pave the way for the incorporation of peace movements into labor movement parties.

As in the pre–World War I period, the heart of the European peace movement was in Great Britain and France, with strong support from Scandinavia. But the two regions took different approaches toward peace. During World War I, a number of Scandinavian states, Denmark, Norway, and Sweden, as well as Holland and Switzerland, had remained neutral. In those countries, the old pre-1914 support for neutralism remained dominant and, in some countries, became part of the national consensus, shared by all parties, including the socialists. In the years up to 1917, the Swedish SDP had been shaken by left-wing opposition, similar to that in the rest of the European continent in the prewar years, which opposed socialist support for the national defense budget. In 1917, the left was decisively defeated, and Swedish Social Democrats abandoned the socialist emphasis on the capitalist roots of war to adopt a policy of neutrality, support for national defense, and the democratization of the army (Koblik 1988; Tingsten 1973). Where most European parties were skeptical of a capitalist-dominated League of Nations, the Swedish Social Democrats were ardent champions of international organizations and supported the League until it lost its credibility in the thirties. Following the Swedes, the Swiss SDP formally embraced neutralism in 1935 (Masnata 1963).

In contrast, in the belligerent nations, particularly in France and Great Britain, the transformation of the peace movement in the interwar period was dramatic. Labor movements, which generally maintained their commitment to joining together both socialism and the peace issue, increased their influence over the peace movement. In the twenties in Britain and France, labor-dominated peace movements aggressively competed for membership with liberal movements.

The strong emergence of pacifism, initially with the support from most of the labor-movement left, was the chief new feature of interwar peace movements in Britain and France. Starting in 1921, the ILP-inspired No More War Movement (NMWM) gained rapid ground. The NMWM broke with the mainstream of the prewar socialist tradition in that it was a secular pacifist organization. It required its members to "declare it to be my intention never to take part in war, offensive or defensive, international or civil, whether by bearing arms, making or handling munitions, voluntarily subscribing to war loans, or using my labour for the purpose of setting others free for war service." Its declaration ended by adding the obligation "to strive for the removal of all causes of war and to work for the establishment of a new social order based on cooperation for the common good" (Ceadal 1980, 73–74). Blanket opposition to war proved more rhetorically powerful than opposition to particular wars, perhaps one reason why the communist-inspired Amsterdam Congress against Imperialist War in 1932 met with limited response. In Scandinavian countries, where socialist parties endorsed neutralism instead of pacifism, pacifist-oriented peace movements remained in the liberal domain; in Sweden the Svenska Freds-och Skiljedomsföreningen (SFSF) found its membership growing under the influence of radical pacifist Christians, led by the "white general," Albert Wickman (Lindkvist 1990). In 1922 Norway was the first country to extend legal recognition to "conscientious objectors."

As the rush toward war accelerated in the thirties, in Britain and France, peace movements lessened their ties to parties, either labor movement or liberal, and struck out on their own. This new independence was made possible by the radical political realignments occurring in national politics. In the twenties, as in the pre–World War I period, support for peace movements had largely coincided with the left-right division in politics. Labor movement parties and significant sections of liberal and republican parties shared a commitment to peace. In the mid-thirties, a momentous political reconfiguration occurred. Faced with military aggression by fascist and authoritarian forces in Germany, Italy, and Japan, many activists within liberal and labor movement parties began to reconsider their position on rearmament and collective defense. After 1933, the Communist parties marched in favor of a defensive military alliance with the Soviet Union, and liberal and socialist parties in Britain and France were divided between pacifist and pacifistic camps and advocates of rearmament. Conversely, conservative parties, hitherto resolutely militaristic and chauvinistic, began to divide on the wisdom of confronting Adolf Hitler and Benito Mussolini; Sir Samuel Hoare, Sir John Simon, and Lord Halifax appeared to join the antiwar camp. The division of all major parties (except the Communists where public division was not permitted and internal division discouraged) on the issue of peace versus rearmament created the opportunity for an independent peace movement.

As labor movement socialist parties began to reconsider their total opposition to war, secular integral pacifism broke free of their hold and became an independent social movement. In Great Britain, the liberal League of Nations Union (LNU), a pre–World War I period organization, dedicated to arbitration and multilateral disarmament, continued in the forefront. In 1934, the LNU organized a "peace ballot," and its membership peaked at a little over 400,000. But small religiously inspired pacifist movements like the Fellowship of Reconciliation (FoR), whose origins dated to the pre–World War I period, tripled their membership during the interwar years. Far more significant were the appearance of new secular "integral pacifist" organizations that maintained an uncompromising pacifism. By 1930, in France, the old prewar APD had waned, and a new, integral pacifist Ligue Internationale des Combattants de la Paix (LICP) had formed and in the next few years became France's major peace organization (Ingram 1991). In 1936 in the United Kingdom, the integral secular pacifist Peace Pledge Union (PPU) opened its offices and rapidly began to challenge the LNU for leadership of the peace movement; by April 1940, 136,000 people had sent postcards to the PPU main office that read "I renounce war and never again will I support or sanction another" (Ceadal 1980, 223).

As it became independent, the peace movement began to fashion its own image of itself. The formation of a peace activist identity had begun in the religious pacifist organizations. In 1924 a member of the FoR Council had remarked that "The genius of the Fellowship was that it was not merely a propaganda body but something like a religious order. We were called to commit ourselves to a certain way of life" (Ceadal 1980, 65). Secular pacifist organizations developed in the same direction. "At the first Peace Pledge Union camp at Swansea" an early member recollected, "there was a large table for vegetarians and as the days went by the number of people at the vegetarian table grew steadily . . . until the crowd was almost equally divided" (Ceadal 1980, 228). If pacifists increasingly adopted a way of life that allowed them to identify themselves, it also gave their enemies a convenient stereotype to caricaturize them. Martin Ceadal (1980, 83) has suggested that George Orwell's malicious characterization of ILP socialists in the twenties was better applied to the pacifists of the thirties:

> typically a prim little man with a white-collar job, usually a secret teetotaller and often with vegetarian leanings, and a history of Nonconformity behind him, and, above all, with a social position he had no intention of forfeiting.

Yet the opportunity for the independent peace movement in the thirties to develop a full-fledged identity was brief. Events in Munich in 1938, the invasion of the Czechoslovak rump-state in 1939, and, then, the outbreak of World War II severely weakened it. Already by 1935, the clear majority of the British Labour Party had rallied to support programs of rearmament and national defense; in that year, George Lansbury, the Labour Party's leader, was replaced because of his pacifism. Between 1933 and 1939, French socialists were more divided and fought interminably and inconclusively over the issue of armaments and pacifism (Bilis 1979). The decline of the peace movement left a much reduced number of pacifists in the field when war broke out in 1939; they were joined in their isolation briefly by the Communist parties, reeling from the Hitler-Stalin pact, but the communists returned to the pro-war fold in June 1941 with the attack on the Soviet Union.

In the few years after 1945, in much of Europe, whatever was left of antiwar sentiment found shelter in the labor movement camp, a labor movement that had made giant political gains (see table 1.1). In 1955 Labour Party members had formed the National Council for the Abolition of Nuclear Warfare. The Swedish Social Democrats played a leading role in the Aktionsgruppen mots Svensks Atoombom. In 1958, the German Social Democrats helped launch the Kampf dem Atomtot but did not long support it (Carter 1992). In France socialists expressed little interest in forming a peace movement. French socialists were too divided by the bitter memories of the interwar antagonisms, and they had little chance of taking away this issue from the Communist Party. In France, according to Jolyon Holworth, the party's activities "gradually led to the identification, in French political culture, of 'peace' with 'communists' " (Holworth 1984, 27).

The formation of the British CND around the issue of nuclear disarmament in 1958 was less directly tied to a labor movement party than earlier groups, but in the words of CND official Peggy Duff: "a great many people saw the Labour Party as the only road to ban the British bomb. First, you had to change Labour Party policy. Then you had to get labour elected. It sounded quite simple" (Duff 1971, 118). CND leaders were deeply involved in organizing mass marches and in the internal politics of the party and the trade union movement. After some initial successes, their policy was decisively rejected in November 1960 when the Labour Party followed the TUC in rejecting the CND program. As Duff (1971, 193) noted "The defeat was a major catastrophe for the leaders of CND. Victory through the Labour Party had been their one basic strategy. What could they do now?"

In fact, CND did not develop an alternative but continued its tactics until eventually many of its former activists abandoned it, joining the anti-Vietnam campaigns of the New Left and its program of mass protests. Duff's reflections on why the CND did not evolve are telling and offer insight into why the New Left grew:

> Any really independent presence required a much more radical analysis of politics and a very considerable broadening out of the concerns of the movement. Issue-orientated campaigns carry within them the seeds of their own extinction, unless they can be rapidly attained. And our particular issue could not be quickly achieved through the Labour Party because it required a major revolution in foreign and defence policy. The Labour Party was not that revolutionary. To have maintained its momentum, the campaign would have had to extend itself at least to the whole field of foreign politics. (Duff 1971, 200)

The dilemma Duff described is quite general. A change in the movement's strategic reorientation, from articulation or permeation to independence, implied changes in the movement's identity. Independence requires that an issue be perceived not only as important but supremely important, sufficient to be worth publicly attacking and confronting Labour Party officials and risking condemnation from one time comrades. In the process of this reorientation, networks of activists must reassess their priorities. Since social movements within or without political parties have always been built on heterogenous coalitions, the wrenching decisions for independence always entail losses—a break with whole networks of allies who will not follow. What is lost in shedding political ties will hopefully be recompensed by changing the movement's identity so it attracts new members, either inside the party ranks or from outside. Shaken by frustration, social movements may leave political parties over single issues, but as they reconstitute themselves as independent social movements, it becomes necessary to extend the issue as far as it can go in providing a serious political alternative to the party they have abandoned.

1960 to the Present
Disengagement
Social Movement Independence

The failure of the CND takes us to the watershed of 1960. In that year, under the leadership of Bertrand Russell, the Committee of 100 was formed, an organization dedicated to building an autonomous peace movement. Its use of massive civil disobedience was designed to pressure the Labour Party but, like the feminists of the WSPU, from outside the party rather than from inside. The Committee of 100 really began the current era of more independent social protest.

Roots and Patterns

To fully understand the movements of the last three decades, it is necessary to analyze their roots in the late forties and fifties; the relations between parties and SMOs existing during that decade and a half have continued to influence the opportunities for the expansion of independent SMOs. During this period, many labor movement parties entered governing coalitions; their participation in power was no longer viewed as extraordinary but as a routine fact of political life. Once in power, parties were faced with the problem of allocating scarce resources and clearly defining priorities. In the fifties and sixties, the highest party priority was the demands of the trade unions, which had provided the rock on which the labor movement parties had built, and the sentiments of the majority of voters who elected labor movement candidates. Farther down the list came attention to the concerns of peace activists and organized women's groups.

Unfortunately, there were important areas of difference between trade unionists and popular sentiment and those of both the peace and women's movements. Following the trade unionists' lead, tacitly or not, European labor movement parties had supported a highly gendered conception of work in which women were expected to bear the major burdens of child rearing and men were expected to be the major breadwinners. The social security systems, which were the pride of the most successful Social Democratic countries, reflected these assumptions as did the contracts negotiated by communist and socialist trade unions (Schirmer 1982). Such policies might have reflected the status quo in most European countries in 1950, but, in the sixties and seventies, in many European countries, women's labor participation rates began to rise, at a time when an increasingly large number of children did not live in traditional families.

Those concerned with questions of peace also felt themselves abandoned. During the early days of the Cold War in 1947 and 1948, most European socialists were concerned about the Russian threat. Several Scandinavian nations and the Low Countries—though hesitantly—rejoined their European comrades. During World War II, neutrality had not worked for Denmark, Norway, Belgium, or Holland, and they joined NATO, but the doctrine of neutrality survived; it had worked for Sweden and Switzerland, and they were joined by the diplomatically mandated neutrals, Austria and Finland. As the Cold War lengthened, however, and U.S. foreign policy came under the influence of a saber-rattling John Foster Dulles, many European socialists had second thoughts. Still, party leaders were convinced that support of anticommunism and the U.S. alliance were necessary to appeal to moderate voters and prevented party-dominated antiwar groups from too overt criticism.

During the sixties, women's groups and peace activists resented their relegation to an inferior position, and, influenced by the U.S. civil rights and student movements, they opened a new period in the relationship between political parties and social movements; other social movements would follow in their wake. In this period, like that between 1870 and 1914, social movements disengaged themselves from political parties. But the departure of social movements from labor movement parties in the sixties and seventies was not so sharp or so complete as that from liberal parties between 1900 and 1920. Where labor movement parties had provided an alternative to liberal parties in the earlier period, no serious political alternative was available to the social movements of the sixties and seventies.

The failure to develop a coherent political alternative was not due to intellectual disarray; independent social movements on the left that emerged during the years between 1960 and 1990 shared many common principles. Unlike in the United States, most social movement activists in Europe were socialists of one stripe or the other. The feminist movement may have begun as a response to male insensitivity within the New Left, such as in the peace movement, but within a decade there was widespread support and recognition of feminism within almost all European peace movements (Meyer and Whittier 1994). Indeed, the ideological interpenetration of various movements on the left, as well as the middle-class character of movement activists, helped create the misperception that these movements were really reflections of a socially homogenous popular base, sharing a set of values, often labeled "postmaterialist" or "participatory democratic." Such a view ignored the real dynamics of independent social movements that depended on the existence of networks of mainly middle-class activists who exalted movement independence and led lives built around movement principles. At the same time, their political strength depended on their appeal to rank-and-file members of mainstream parties who remained attached to these parties in most respects but who were frightened by the introduction of cruise missiles or appalled by legislation prohibiting abortion. Also, while movement principles were often shared across independent social movements, movements remained absolutely separate organizationally—if anything, organizational separateness increased over time. Individual movements made political judgments on the basis of their particular movement concerns—not from the perspective of the whole social movements family of which they were a part. SMOs were not inclined to make major compromises; they resisted absorption, and they refused to work together on the basis of their shared ideas.

Although the viability of individual movements varied, some patterns can be found to the appearance of strong independent social movements. Independent social movements never arise *de novo*. Indeed, in a sense there are no "new" lefts or "new" social movements, for all grow out of old lefts and old social movements and inherit the dilemmas, strategic locations, and ideological debates of their predecessors. The network of activists of the sixties and seventies and their strategic and tactical decisions were powerfully shaped by the networks of social activists existing within political parties in the forties and fifties. Movements that successfully adapted to changing political opportunities appeared newer than they were.

All the networks of social movement activists that emerged in the sixties and seventies were conditioned by the movement networks that surrounded them. Not all labor movement parties of protest changed into parties of power. In France and Italy, Communist Parties, while powers at the regional level or within the trade unions, remained on the peripheries of national power and continued to support protest movements. The threat of independent movements combined with the continuing crisis of communism generally forced Communist parties to give more leeway to the movements that they dominated, but their ability to retain considerable influence in social movement sectors seriously limited the ability of SMOs to develop (Beckwith 1985). In such countries Communists also continued to inspire imitators who sought to build their own parties of protest along the same lines but with more radical principles and closer relationship to social movements; Lotta Continua in Italy or the Ligue Communiste or the Gauche Prolétarienne in France are examples of these organizations (Tarrow 1989a). In England, Sweden, and West Germany, independent social movements grew up, but important sections of the social movement sector continued to work within labor movement parties to change their orientation; in Britain, feminists lamented the split between "political" feminists who worked within the Labour Party and "cultural" feminists who developed their own autonomous women's subculture outside it (Lovenduski and Randall 1993). In countries like Holland and Switzerland, labor movement parties had never fully succeeded in incorporating important peace movements, and these continued to look to support from religious and liberal parties, as well as to the socialists. This produced a thriving climate for social movement organizations.[2] In much of Europe, social movement parties grew up that attempted to

compete with labor movement parties, but these generally proved temporary and unsubstantial.

Implications

Our long view of the changing relations of social movements and political parties has several implications for the study of social movements and
their outcomes. Scholars have emphasized that movements' effects should
include their influence on long-term political structures as well as on contemporary events—on the foreign policy process as well as on the war
in the street (Gamson 1990; Kitschelt 1986). A neglected yet significant
structural outcome of protest movements is incorporation into political
parties. Over the last century, parties have proved more enduring and
resourceful than independent SMOs. Although risky and sometimes
threatening essential identities, more than anything else, control over parties has empowered social movements. While less rewarding, at least the
subordinate incorporation of movements into parties has provided routine political access denied to independent movements.

The failure to consider the influence of incorporated social movements
on working-class parties is not simply aberrant; the drift of modern social
movements has been away from parties, and nothing is more foreign to
contemporary political activists than hierarchical subordination within
parties. For many, subservience is still a painful memory. In the case of
women's movements, for example, incorporation typically involved a
thoroughgoing subjection to male-dominated trade unions and a predominantly male electorate. Nonetheless, as the constituency of European socialist and labor parties changes to include a larger proportion of
professionals and females, and as independent social movements wither,
unable to sustain themselves in a more conservative European environment, new opportunities for the reintegration of movements within parties may be emerging. Roger Karapin's study of social movements in West
Germany in the eighties shows that independent social movements were
most successful when working in tandem with organized factions of the
SPD (Karapin 1993). In the nineties, as left-wing social movements have
declined in Europe, some former activists have sought haven in labor
movements and social parties. More attention must be paid to the conditions of sanctuary. Considering the outcomes of social movements on
political parties, then, we must look not only at its programmatic elements—the extent to which parties embrace social movements' demands
and translate them into a public policy—but at its structural aspects—the
degree and manner in which social movements incorporated into parties
are situated as they exert an ongoing influence on policy formation.

This survey of social movements over a relatively long historical period also confirms Marco Giugni's view that outcomes must be seen as a dynamic process; in his view, too much attention has been given to the success or failure of individual social movements, too little to interrelationships among social movements and their social context (Giugni 1994). An examination of European social movements over the long haul shows that one way in which changing configurations within families of social movements affect outcomes is by reorienting the goals of social protestors. The bargaining position of independent social movements is stronger to the extent that they can recruit members willing to put movement loyalties above party ties. Social movements preach the transcendent importance of movement goals. Sidney Tarrow has analyzed in detail the cycle of social protest, characteristic of the recent past, in which initial successes achieved by independent social movements provoke imitators who accelerate a cycle of protest that climaxes as the number of independent social movements cascade and their successes decline precipitously (Tarrow 1994a).

But the movements of the sixties, seventies, and eighties are not the only model of social protest in the European experience. Powerful protest movements swept Europe between 1917 and 1950 based on political parties and the ability of incorporated social movements to mobilize their constituents for protest. The configuration of movements dominating in that period favored a broader political identity. Social movements working within political parties inevitably shared some of the party's larger goals; in such circumstances, success was viewed in relation to both movement purposes and party goals. While the rigid subordination of constituent social movements to the priorities of labor must not be repeated, still the ability of parties to forge a common identity out of a variety of disparate movements is well worth studying; it represents both an important outcome of past struggles and an alternative form of mobilization for future conflicts.

In conclusion, this essay has argued for the continuity of social movements and maintained that this continuity is often neglected because students of collective action fail to note the existence of social movements embedded in political parties. The thrust of this argument is to integrate the study of social movements more closely with that of routine politics, to locate social movement within parties, and to emphasize the ongoing dialogue between movement and political parties. Social movements are not politics by different means, but politics *tout court.*

Notes

I would like to thank the following colleagues for their many helpful suggestions and criticisms: Miriam Cohen, Jeff Goodwin, Helmut Gruber, Roger Karapin, Jason Kaufman, Doug McAdam, David S. Meyer, and Elisabeth Wood.

Michael Hanagan

1. Recent work by Sidney Tarrow and Roger Karapin has helped to clarify my thinking on this topic (Tarrow 1994a, Karapin 1993).

2. For some of the most important and interesting work on the relationship between politics and contemporary social movements, see Kriesi, Koopmans, Duyvendak, and Giugni 1995, Koelble 1991, and Rochon 1990.

2

Social Protest and Policy Reform
May 1968 and the *Loi d'Orientation* in France

Sidney Tarrow

The politics of reform has most often been viewed as incremental process—which indeed it is, under most circumstances. The model for this mode of analysis is found in Aaron Wildavsky's (1974) work on the budgetary process. The best predictor of the size of a public budget in year *n*, Wildavsky observed, is the size of its predecessor in year *n* − 1. Given the number of constraints and inhibitions that prevent policy innovation under most circumstances, writes John Keeler (1993, this issue) "those rare governments that have surmounted such obstacles . . . have thus commonly been discussed simply as interesting exceptions to the patterns of what might be termed ordinary policy-making."

But from time to time, major waves of policy innovation emerge above the gentle plain of ordinary politics. For understanding these breakthroughs, incremental models of policymaking are not nearly as helpful as models based on changes in political opportunity structure. Major electoral realignments; political crises, the ends of wars or military threats, leadership succession; and the emergence of new social coalitions—such nonincremental changes frequently trigger periods of reform. What Valerie Bunce (1981, 225) wrote of succession can be extended to a number of different types of political change: "Major changes, if they occurred at all, tended to be introduced in conjunction with the rise of new chief executives." But what of the effect on policy innovation of the threats to routine politics coming from challengers to the polity? Although Bunce's (1981) *Do New Leaders Make a Difference?* examined the impact of leadership succession, Rose (1980) has analyzed the impact of party differences on policy, and Keeler (1993) analyzed the importance of political crisis and electoral landslides, we still know little about the impact of social protest on policy change. As Marx and Wood (1975, 403) wrote:

Given the variety of places that one can look, the extreme difficulty in most cases in determining causal relations, and the long time periods that may be involved, most statements about the consequences of social movements are primarily descriptive or taxonomic. The systematic study of social movement consequences is much less developed than that of the prior conditions that give rise to movements.

Most scholars of movements have assumed with Turner and Killian (1972, 256) that one of the necessary aspects of a social movement is "a program for the reform of society." But how often do movements bring about anything as global as "the reform of society"? Even in less grandiose terms, we have very little idea of the impact of movements on reform for few scholars have looked systematically at the effects of movements on reform.[1]

One of the reasons for this gap is that reform has often been conceived of as a top-down extension of citizenship (Marshall 1964), either through incorporation (Rokkan, Campbell, Torsvik, and Valen 1970) or by elite policy diffusion (Heclo 1974). A second reason is that social movements often coincide with political changes of a more conventional type, making it difficult to sort out their degree of responsibility for a particular policy change (Burstein and Freudenberg 1978). A third is that scholars most often focus on movement *emergence,* giving less attention to the slower, less dramatic processes of policy elaboration, negotiation, and implementation. Rare is the movement that is sufficiently focused and powerful to stimulate a direct and visible policy response—except where that response is repression.[2]

May 1968: A Window for Reform

But we do have a near-laboratory case for studying the political impact of a major wave of protest on policy innovation—May 1968 in France. As two of that period's most acute historians observed:

> despite the retreat of the movement and its rejection in the ballot box, the events were the carriers of potentialities that, by one means or another, durably mortgaged the French political scene in a way that had to be immediately faced. (Capdevielle and Mouriaux 1988, 219 [my translation])

This is a puzzle; for how could the May crisis "durably mortgage the French political scene" when it produced few coherent policy proposals, left a disorganized and almost-collapsed movement in its wake, and led to an enlarged conservative majority and a dispirited and divided opposition? The answer we give to this question depends on how we think social movements influence reform—either directly, through the power of the people, or indirectly, through changes in the political opportunity structure that they trigger. If we proceed from a pure "protest leads to reform" model, we will have difficulty explaining why *any* reform effort should have followed the May movement, for that movement was soundly defeated. But if we understand policy innovation to be mediated by changes in the political opportunity structure—for elites as well as for the mass public—it is less surprising that a wave of protest was followed by a major reform.

In the months following the June 1968 national elections, in which the Gaullist party achieved a major electoral triumph, the government—not without internal dissent—boiled down the jumble of demands for educational change that had erupted during May into a major law for educational reform—the *loi d'orientation* of Minister Edgar Faure. The movement of May arose suddenly and unexpectedly and collapsed just as quickly, but the policy response was rapid and directly addressed the universities, where the events had begun.

The law that resulted was intended to restructure the university system around three broad goals: autonomy, pluridisciplinarity, and participation (Chalendar 1970, parts 2, 3; Fomerand 1974, chap. 5). It replaced the old faculties with departments (Unités d'Enseignement et de Recherche [UER]), it broke up the massive University of Paris into twelve different "campuses," and it provided the machinery for all the French universities to elect governing councils and create their own internal statutes.[3] It would be difficult to imagine so major a change being introduced into the sclerotic structure of French education without the impulse of a major political earthquake.

What is the implication of this story for the theory of policy innovation? In what follows, I will show that, as Keeler suggested, an exceptional electoral mandate and a threatening political crisis open a window for policy innovation. But the brevity of the French crisis and the disorganization of the movement of May left the initiative for reform to elites, leaving it to become ensnared in the mechanisms of parliamentary politics. As the political struggle receded from the streets to the halls of Parliament and the cabinets of ministers, the game of ordinary politics decided its future. As I shall argue in the conclusions, this has implications for reform that go beyond the case at hand.

Political Opportunities and Reform Cycles

Before reviewing these events and my interpretation of them, it will be important to make clear what I mean by the term "the structure of political opportunity" and how it can be used to link the *enragés* of May—few of whom were at all interested in reform—to the reformers of October. The social movement literature on political opportunities has usually employed the concept to understand when movements emerge and the strategies they choose when they do so.[4] It has less often been extended to understanding the political opportunities opened up by a wave of protest for a movement's allies and opponents and for political elites.

Scholars of movement emergence and strategy have mainly emphasized four elements of political opportunity structure: electoral realignments (Piven and Cloward 1977), the opening of institutional access (Eisinger 1973), the presence of influential allies (Gamson 1990; Jenkins and Perrow 1977), and divisions within the political elite (Tarrow 1989a, chap. 2) and how these provide incentives for movement formation and collective action.[5] A fifth element—the availability and extension of new frames of meaning—has received far less attention but can also be critical in triggering a new movement (Snow and Benford 1988, 1992).

But new movements themselves sometimes produce changes in political opportunity: for participants in the original movement who can see what succeeds and what fails; for allies and opponents who adopt their models of collective action and use their collective action frames for new purposes; and for members of the political elite who use the movement to gain political advantage. Major waves of movements create opportunities for others by demonstrating new or innovative forms of collective action, placing new frames of interpretation on the agenda, and making clear either the threat of an opponent or the promise of a new constituency.

For example, the protest cycle initiated by the U.S. civil rights movement demonstrated how nonviolent resistance tactics, employed in the spotlight of national television, could gain majority support for a minority movement. Second, it provided a dramatic and fungible "rights frame" that other minority groups were quick to take up—what Snow and Benford (1988) call a "master frame." Third, it demonstrated the existence of a large African-American constituency for reform, a signal that the Kennedy and Johnson administrations were quick to exploit (Piven and Cloward 1977, chap. 4).

But the American movements of the 1960s also show how a protest cycle's endogenous development helps to produce its demise. As the nonviolent movement in the South gave way to more aggressive collective action in the North and to a more violent rhetoric from younger militants, a split was induced between moderate older organizations and their newer competitors and—in part because of the rhetoric of exclusiveness of the latter—between the movement as a whole and its White "conscience constituents." Militant tactics and violent rhetoric, although in a distinct minority in the movement, helped to turn public opinion against it and to justify a shift from the facilitative policies of the reformist Johnson administration to the punitive ones of the Nixon years (Button 1978).

This parabolic model of a protest-reform cycle can also be applied to France after May. Spurred by fear of renewed agitations in the streets and encouraged by a constituency for reform, the French reformers of July 1968 quickly drew up a scheme for the reform of higher education. But as in the United States—although far more rapidly—the cycle had an internal dynamic from protest to reform to consolidation and retreat. As the threat of contestation evaporated, the reformists were forced to scale down their ambitions to meet the objections of their conservative opponents (Fomerand 1974, chap. 8). And by the spring of 1969, with the defeat of de Gaulle's referendum and his sudden retirement, the reform lost much of its sting, resulting in a greater gain for the conservative professorate than for the dissatisfied students. This is a story that French specialists know well; what can we learn from it about the politics of policy breakthrough?

The Opportunity for Reform

Three major factors facilitated the reformers' task in the summer and fall of 1968: first, an informed debate about higher education that predated May by several years; second, the very suddenness and brevity of the May–June crisis; and, third, the strength of the Gaullist electoral mandate. Taken together, these factors provided Education Minister Faure with fertile political ground and gave the reform an unusually smooth beginning.

The Reformist Background

In thinking back to the conflagration of May 1968, it is easy to forget that the 1960s were a decade of discussions, debates, and attempts at educational reform—in France as elsewhere.[6] From the reform projects of the Resistance, which culminated in the never-implemented Langevin-Wallon report of 1947, to the two important *colloques* of Caen in 1956 and 1966, through the passage of the Fouchet reform of 1965, "the 'modernisation' of the universities became a major issue in certain sectors of education, in certain industrial circles and among certain groups in the world of politics and the higher administration" (Bourricaud 1982, 37).

Groups of reformers, including some of the most distinguished names in French academia, called at one time or another for most of the reforms that would later appear—admittedly in different from—in the *loi d'orientation*. Summarizing these proposals from Bourricaud's (1982, 38–44) extensive treatment, they included, notably: increased support for research, the opening of the university to society, the modernization of teaching, the replacement of the faculties with something approaching the American department, the removal of barriers between universities, a degree of autonomy in the financing of research units outside the state's annual budgets, the elimination of certain chairs, and even—in one version, the limited participation of students in university governance.

Nor were the reformers either isolated or disorganized. They had an interest group—the Association for the Development of Scientific Research—and maintained close ties with important officials in the ministry, even succeeding "in enlisting the support of a number of politicians" (Bourricaud 1982, 37). Although the shift from the Fourth to the Fifth Republic denied them the help of some of their closest allies—for example, Mendès-France—they retained a position of trust with the ministry and especially with two successive directors-general for higher education, Gaston Berger and Pierre Agrain (Bourricaud 1982). This coalition for reform was partly responsible for placing—and for keeping—educational reform on the policy agenda during the 1960s.

But the reforms did not attack all the defects of the system with equal vigor. Grignon and Passeron's (1970) summary of the major reforms that were implemented between 1954 and 1967 in four of the five main faculties showed that the significant reforms were mainly concerned with the organization of degrees. They left out the problem of the structure of the faculties or universities, methods of teaching, and the relation between teaching and research. Although the faculties of law and medicine implemented significant reforms under government prodding, where the arts and sciences were concerned, the "new system . . . [did] not necessarily imply a break with the old teaching organization and still less with the system of traditional attitudes" (Grignon and Passeron 1970, 32).

What was important about this for the period of *l'après-mai* was that, by 1968, a cadre of educational reformers could be identified by Faure for his cabinet and as an elite support base. These had ties throughout the educational establishment and could draw on ideas that had been circulating since the colloques of Caen. May brought new and unruly actors on to the stage, but it exploded onto the political scene in the context of an ongoing debate about the future of higher education.[7] Faure had only to pick up the existing threads of proposals and use the fear of a renewed May to produce a political response. He could do this, first, because of the extraordinary nature of the crisis.

A Short and Abrupt Crisis

The May crisis was quite short, which strengthened the reformers' hand, against both those whose instinctive response was for greater law and order and against their sworn enemies. Even adopting the kind of broad definition used by Schnapp and Vidal-Naquet (1988), the French May was over very quickly compared, for example, to its German and Italian counterparts. In fact, the sudden beginning, the lightning diffusion, and the rapid collapse of the May–June events were its most visible characteristics.

The actual beginning of the cycle is in some dispute. Some see the agitation against the Fouchet educational reform in 1964 to 1966 as the most important gestation stage (Passeron 1986), a view that is reinforced by Converse and Pierce's (1989) findings about the widespread dissatisfaction with the educational system before May.[8] Others find the beginning in the anti-Vietnam war protests of 1966, while still others see it in the early signs of working-class insurgency in 1967 (Capdevielle and Mouriaux 1988). What is certainly true is that the rise in collective action associated with the actual *themes* of May began in the fall of 1967 and continued sporadically through the winter and early spring of 1968.[9]

The same suddenness marked the end of the events. But while most would regard the sudden drop in collective action after the elections of June as the sign of the collapse of the movement of May, some see the end of the cycle coming much later—in the conflicts over reform that succeeded the passage of the loi d'orientation and ended with the last major university strike in 1976 (Passeron 1986).

It is certainly true that the movement was effectively neutralized when the Sorbonne and other faculties were cleared out at the end of May and that the movement as a whole suffered a major collapse with the Gaullist electoral victory of June. By the *rentrée*, solidarity had so broken down among student groups and between the students and their supporters among the faculty that they posed no real threat to the authorities. It was this lassitude, against the general fear of the renewal of contestation, that gave the reformers the pause they needed to shift the center of gravity from the streets to the political arena.

But the demobilization of the students over the summer of 1968 was only a part of the picture—and perhaps not the most important part. The major reason why the French crisis can be said to have ended by June 1968 was the return to work of the working class with the signature of the Accords of Grenele.[10] To the extent that factory militancy continued, it was linked to the issue of union rights in the workplace in December 1968 and to the favoring of collective bargaining by the Chaban-Delmas government in September 1969 (see Bridgford 1989, 103, 111 for these changes).

The May events largely exhausted the capacity for collective action of the other major sectors of French society too. Although groups as different as cadres (Groux 1988), white-collar workers, public employees, farmers, Catholics (Hervieu-Léger 1988), parents' associations (Vernus

1988), and even football players (Wahl 1988) were swept into the move-ment of May, their attitudes to the crisis were sharply divided. By June the Parisian middle class—which had been outraged by police brutality in the Latin Quarter in May—voted in overwhelming proportions for the Right.

The Crisis and the Mandate

The movement of May was surely one of the shortest springs in the history of French protest cycles. But as it ended, no one could predict what the students would do at the rentrée and how their actions would affect the workers and others who had joined them in May. We know that uncertainty is one of the major resources of protest movements (Eisinger 1973; Tarrow 1989a). This uncertainty, and the desire of the shaken Gaull-ist party to provide palliatives for the masses of students who had turned out in May, provided a major opportunity for reform.

With the virtues of hindsight, we can see that there was little prospect for a renewed May at the rentrée of the fall of 1968. But in July, when Faure was appointed, no one really knew whether the movement of May was dead. The rapid paralysis of the university system and of virtually every part of French society in May had shocked the political elite out of its *suffisance* and convinced reformists that something had to be done to prevent a recrudescence of revolt. The fact that the summer vacation brought a deadly quiet to the educational establishment might have meant that the movement was over or it could have meant that its leaders were regrouping for the next round of contestation.[11] Faure's appointment was a response to this fear, and he was quick to take advantage of it, as the major studies of his tenure as minister show (Chalendar 1970; Fomerand 1974, 1975).

The most direct source of the opportunity for reform lay in the enor-mous triumph of the Gaullists in the elections of June. Their success was even more remarkable when we consider that, as late as May 24th, General de Gaulle had attempted to deal with the crisis through a referendum on participation—one that he might well have lost. How great their success was can be judged from table 2.1, which compares the swing in votes to the Gaullists and their allies in June to previous electoral swings in the Fifth Republic.

It was not only the Gaullist victory that explains the strength of Faure's mandate but the humiliation de Gaulle suffered in May, when he found his political space constricted by the enormity of the conservative victory and the refusal of his supporters to organize the referendum he wanted (Charlot 1989). By putting a reformer like Faure in charge of the educa-tion ministry and giving him a sweeping mandate for reform, General de Gaulle hoped to strengthen his own position vis-à-vis the Gaullist party.

TABLE 2.1
Electoral Change in France, 1958–68

Year of legislative election	First ballot		Total swing from Left to Government[a]
	Left parties	Government	
1958			
Percentage	41.9	17.6	—[b]
Seats	90	212	—
1962			
Percentage	42.1	36.4	18.6
Seats	107	269	8.8
1967			
Percentage	41.5	37.7	1.9
Seats	194	242	−71.3
1968			
Percentage	36.5	43.6	11.9
Seats	83	354	103.5

Source: Ehrmann (1983, 220).

a. Index for votes: Percentage of change in Goverment vote from last election minus percentage of change in Left vote from last election. Index for seats: Percentage of change in Goverment seats from last election minus percentage of change in Left seats from last election.

b. Excludes changes from Fourth to Fifth Republic.

This can best be understood in the coalitional terms used by Peter Gourevitch (1978) to understand de Gaulle's later resignation after the referendum of 1969. The Gaullist coalition had never been limited to loyalists and conservatives; it had from the beginning appealed to "modernizers" who wanted to make France into an advanced industrial nation. As in the stillborn referendum that spelled his defeat the following spring, de Gaulle may have seen educational reform of 1968 as a way to regain the support of the modernists, short-circuit the power of the conservatives, and reestablish his personal links with the electorate.

For such a coalitional juggling act, Edgar Faure fit the bill very well.[12] A former radical who had never been central to the Gaullist coalition, he was suspect to many in the Gaullist party because of his identification with many of the Fourth Republic's excesses. But he was far more palatable to the General, whose previous efforts at educational reform had been undermined by Pompidou and Peyrefitte.[13] More than anything, Faure's leadership was characterized by a deft political touch and a degree of light-footedness that some saw as opportunism. He was once quoted as saying that "France is not ungovernable. It can be ruled by skill and dissimulation" (quoted in Wright 1987, 527).

Politicization and Factionalization

Given the conflicts surrounding higher education in May, it might be sup-
posed that a reform like the one Faure proposed in October 1968 would
stimulate tremendous controversy from the activists of May. But movements arise quickly and seldom focus on the details of reform. In addition, *this* movement had rapidly left educational issues behind to focus on
national politics and had internal divisions that were so severe as to reduce
its capacity to return to the issue of university reform. Both of these features of the movement of May gave Faure a relatively free hand to enunci-
ate a major reform project.

A Focus on National Politics

If the May movement began in the universities, once it had evolved
from the terrain of student demands to that of political power, there was
no turning back. As Passeron (1986, 382 [my translation]) observed:

> If the raging conflict in the universities acquired a privileged position for the
> tensions that triggered the escalation of the revolt, the student movement
> soon ceased to have—if it had ever had them—goals that were strictly speak-
> ing related to the university.

Encouraged by the overreaction of the minister of education in clearing
out the courtyard of the Sorbonne in May and by the police brutality
that met the ensuing demonstrations, the students quickly focused their
energies on the political arena. Their main slogans were at first largely
tactical: the reopening of the faculties, amnesty for the arrested students,
an end to police presence. But once these goals were achieved—and they
were effectively achieved soon after Pompidou's return in mid-May—the
movement could not rest on its laurels if it was to survive. As Passeron
(1986, 382 [my translation]) wrote: "The united front against the traditional university exploded as soon as the disdained institution was no
longer available to bring together its attackers and paper over their opposing criticisms."

Scanning the documents that have been assembled by Schnapp and
Vidal-Naquet (1988, parts 2, 3), one cannot help but be struck by the
rapidity with which a great number of student groups focused their attention on politics. The major exceptions were the *instances de fait* that had
sprung up in faculties around the country, which devoted themselves over
the summer to questions internal to the university. But these were divided
and dispersed and were easily co-opted into the reform projects of the
minister and his cabinet. The result was that the greatest student mass
movement in the country's history lacked an educational counterprogram

at precisely the time when a strengthened Gaullist majority put forward a major program of university reform.

Whether the movement's rapid concentration on national politics was the result of the inherent centralization of the French system (Schnapp and Vidal-Naquet 1988, 50), of the instinctive Jacobinism of the Left, or simply of the pace and direction of events, it is difficult to say. What was unusual about the French May was the rapid diffusion to movement organizations around the country of slogans that invested the national political system and the rapid disappearance of a radical discourse about the need for educational change. This was in part responsible for the gravity of the May crisis, but when it was over, it left open a window of reform for the elite.

Factionalization

Nor was there any such thing as a unified movement for university reform in French society. Had Edgar Faure and his collaborators wished to reflect movement opinion in the law they proposed to Parliament in October, they could not have found a coherent representative of these views among the student organizations, the teachers' unions, or the universities in general. This was as true of students and teachers as it was of the relations between various student groups and of various levels of the educational establishment.

Students and Teachers

The most obvious cleavage was between students and teachers. The mythology of May 1968 has left the impression that the students enjoyed considerable faculty support. This is in part the result of a few, highly publicized translations of books by university professors and in part due to a confusion between the "heroic," national phase of the movement—when the stakes were the installation of a new kind of regime—and the more prosaic concerns of students and teachers. In terms of the latter issue, there was a deep cleavage between the radical student groups that emerged from May and the bulk of university professors—even those on the historic Left.

This cleavage had already emerged in the debates of the large, unorganized assemblies that developed in many faculties in May. A number of younger faculty and even some professors joined these student groups to design ambitious schemes for university reform (Salmon 1982). In June, even full professors were encouraged to participate by the ministry. But these instances de fait, rather than soldering a reform coalition around the goals of May, demonstrated the great gap in perspective between the students and most of the teaching staff and produced humiliation and resentment among the latter. As Salmon (1982, 68) wrote: "Even to those who had favoured reform, many of the ideas developed in the assemblies and seconded occasionally by colleagues seemed both childish and certain to cause a complete collapse of all forms of higher education."

The shock administered to conservative professors by these reform schemes[14] was reinforced by the reform strategy of Minister Faure, who appeared ready to embrace the students' demands for *co-gestion*. The differences went well beyond the assemblies of May and June, as professors, maîtres, maîtres-assistants, assistants, and technical and administrative personnel carved out different positions on the prospect of changes in the university.[15]

Students and Students

If there were sharp cleavages between teachers and students, the ideological differences among the student groups were even sharper. Before May, some of these groups had been reformist; others had reformist tendencies within them; whereas others rejected the university as a relevant arena from the beginning.[16] Although these differences were obscured by the unifying target of the state in May, by June they began to emerge more clearly, both in the debates in the unofficial assemblies being held in various faculties and in the tactical attitudes of various groups toward participating in the elections. Differences in strategy that preceded May, together with those that resulted from clashing interpretations of the events, combined to produce divergent attitudes toward the reform.

The Union Nationale des Etudiants de France (UNEF) provides a well-documented example. The organization was deeply split when the movement of May exploded, between a "universitist" tendency that "gave primacy to the allocation of studies," and a "structuralist" one that "insisted on the need to present 'counter-plans' to the government's projects" (Monchablon 1988, 17). Competition for the support of newly radicalized students led UNEF to adopt a more radical stance as the movement of May ended. Its leaders were "conscious that 'in many places the struggles [of May] had taken place outside' of l'UNEF" (11). To gain their support, it needed to maintain a radical *élan* that went beyond reforming the university. Faced at its national assizes in July by the presence of many delegates outside its control, the UNEF leadership proposed a new charter that would make it "a mass political movement" and liquidate the vestiges of unionism (11).

Teachers and Teachers

The bulk of the French professoriat had never been enthusiastic about a movement that some of its members saw as juvenile, whereas others feared it for what they saw as its subversive dangers. Influential conservative groups like the Société des Agrégés and professional associations like the Syndicat Autonome of university professors weighed in heavily against *any* student participation in university policymaking. Distinguished academics like Georges Vedel and Charles Debbasch argued forcefully against the dangers of encroachment on professors' freedom of choice.[17]

Divisions among the teachers' organizations that had participated in the May movement were almost as broad as those within the student movement. The best example was the Fédération de l'Education Nationale (FEN), which was constitutionally only a federation of teachers' unions, but that had considerably increased its importance during May. Even at the height of the movement, FEN's internal constituencies were divided. Although the Syndicat National de l'Education Supérieure (SNESup), under gauchiste control, joined the students in their movement in the university, the secondary school union, SNES, which was controlled by the Communists, opposed *contestation* and tried to brake the movement in the *lycées*.[18] Although some of the FEN's leaders were present at Charléty, others took a more moderate line, hoping to increase the organization's influence with the government after the crisis ended.[19]

These divisions may well have been partly responsible for the Federation's incapacity to put forward a viable alternative to the Faure reform when, in October 1968, it held its "Etats Généraux de l'Université Nouvelle" (FEN 1969). The constituent unions divided at the conference on mainly sectoral lines.[20] Remarkably, this national conference failed to discuss the forthcoming university reform altogether (FEN 1969). It was only through a focus on "common demands for the allocation of greater financial credits" that the cleavages among FEN's main constituent unions were covered up (FEN 1969, 207–8).

It should be obvious from this brief survey that, in the highly politicized crucible of tendencies and organizations that emerged from the movement of May, there was no unified movement for university reform. Had Faure and his collaborators wished to reflect the movement's views in the law they proposed to Parliament in October, they could not have found a coherent representative of these views among the student organizations, in the teachers' unions, or in the universities in general.[21] The absence of such a coherent movement made it easy for Faure to maneuver, but, as we shall see, the collapse of the movement and its internal divisions after the rentrée removed the threat that was the major incentive for reform.

Reform and the Political Process

Faure's strategy was to build a coalition for reform out of some elements of the former movement, some educational modernizers, and Gaullist loyalists. He wasted no time in making contact with modernists who wanted to build a university in tune with the modern world, and with radicals who wanted to see the Napoleonic system dismantled. Distrusted by the conservatives, he nevertheless made contact with representatives of the Catholic educational hierarchy and met surreptitiously with student leaders in the evening.

Faure's first formal move was to set up a number of study commissions and to make contact with many of the instances de fait that had organized spontaneously in the effervescence of the spring, and began a series of meetings with interested groups—some of them sub rosa.[22] He drew the FEN into his plans and met privately with Confédération Général du Travail leader Georges Seguy, convincing him—and through him his Parti Communiste Français comrades—not to oppose the reform.[23] In the months following his appointment, Faure diverted attention from the much-feared renewal of mobilization in the streets by creating a *"bouillonnement au sommet"* around himself and his cabinet.[24]

Faure sounded very like a progressive in the fall of 1968, but his true strategy was to take advantage of the political opportunity structure of a disorganized, but still potentially dangerous, movement and a strengthened Gaullist majority. He built a political and ideological coalition based on the desire of the conservatives to preserve social peace, of the modernists to create universities that would be adequate for a modern society, of liberals who wanted university autonomy from the state, and of progressives who hoped for real student participation in university decision making. In legislative terms, the coalition-building exercise was a success; by November 7, only four months after he took office, the reform passed both houses of Parliament with overwhelming majorities (Fomerand 1974, chap. 4).

But Faure's coalition was temporary, depending as it did on fear of a renewed May among the government's supporters, the disorganization of the opposition, and General de Gaulle's personal support. It also failed to take account of the institutional power of the professorate to turn reforms to its own advantage—a capacity that the reform actually increased. As fall gave way to winter and winter to the following spring, with the reform's implementation and de Gaulle's sudden resignation, the cracks in the reformist coalition became fissures.

The Weaknesses of the Reform

Seldom had so many sweeping changes been proposed in such haste or had to be implemented in so short a time.[25] In fact, at the end of the legislative process, even the idea for a provisional year to put the system into gear was scrapped. By December 31, 1968—within two months of the law's passage—some six hundred provisional UERs had been created. By April, elections for new councils had been held for students and faculty all over the country. The new universities almost immediately elected their presidents and submitted draft statutes to a commission of the Conseil d'Etat. By the 1970 rentrée even the thorny problem of dividing the University of Paris into thirteen new universities had been largely completed.[26]

The UER Problem: Creating Resources for Your Opponents

But a number of unfortunate results followed from this haste.[27] The greatest problem had to do with the creation of the new departments—or UERs—and their integration into the newly created universities. For rather than following the educationally rational course of first creating the new universities and then allowing them to define their own internal structures, Faure's cabinet created a "provisional" list of UERs very rapidly—by December 1968—and only then moved to the broader step of aggregating them into universities.

The problem that this created was that the provisional UERs—some of them no more than new names for old faculties and institutes—quickly gained an institutional base from which they could defend their interests and constrain the shape of the new universities. Although the fear in governing circles was that radical students would take over the provisional UERs, the real danger in this procedure was that the professorate could use them to consolidate its position and prevent real educational innovation from being carried out. Although, here and there, creative new interdisciplinary units were created as a result of the procedure, one disappointed reformer wrote that "a certain number of associations were created only to gain greater autonomy and control over more resources, while many were created from the desire of teachers from the same political or philosophical tendency to stay together" (Chalendar 1970, 177).

The problem was reinforced by the reluctance of the prime minister's cabinet to see the law implemented in the frenzied atmosphere of l'après-mai. Not everyone in the administration shared Faure's enthusiasm for reform.[28] Under French constitutional procedure, only the prime minister or the president had the right to pass the decrees that would be necessary to create the universities.[29] If the prime minister—or members of his staff—were unconvinced of the necessity of the law, serious delays could result.

Although Faure and his staff proceeded almost immediately to the designation of the new universities—naming seventeen of them by March 1969 and thirty-seven more by June (Chalendar 1970)—the prime minister's office was not happy over the plans to apply the law to the *grandes écoles* (189). "Under different pretexts," his staff found reasons for delay and "the signature of the Matignon was held back until Faure's departure as Minister" (193).[30] There was an even longer delay in the case of Paris, but this related more to the need to find a solution to feuds and political differences within the old Sorbonne than to high politics. But while the government delayed, academic mandarins who had no enthusiasm for reform had time to regroup.

The Revenge of the Mandarins

Faure and his cabinet expected the newly created UERs to be provisional for two reasons: "The Minister could himself complete or modify [the plan], and the councils of the new universities, once elected, could equally question them in creating their statutes" (Chalendar 1970, 175). But they calculated without taking account of two factors: First, it would require a continued commitment for the spirit of the reform to survive; and second, they took insufficient account of the power of the academic establishment to delay or reshape the reform.[31]

The power and factional divisions of the academic community were particularly important in the big cities, where more than one university was created. In smaller towns like Caen, Clermont, Dijon, Nice, and Poitiers, where only one university was created, true "pluridisciplinary" institutions resulted (Salmon 1982, 78). But in the bigger cities, like Aix-Marseilles, Lyon, Lille, Bordeaux, Strasbourg, and Toulouse, the law set numerical limits on the number of students and more than one university had to be created.

In principle, there was no reason why this could not have been done on an educationally rational basis. But most often, professors would collect on personal, political, or disciplinary bases.[32] Some who favored reform found their way to such experimental universities as Vincennes or to Paris VII; others created solutions of convenience like Paris I; and those who dreaded change could remain in the old faculties of law and medicine in Paris, which were virtually unchanged, or join conservative "new" universities like Lyon I. The reformers' urgency in beginning the reform with the UERs, while the government delayed in creating authoritative university institutions, left it hostage to the revenge of the mandarins.

Business as Usual

No doubt, had an actively reformist education ministry remained in place, led by a minister with the political will to defend his reform, provisional arrangements that were based on hasty decision or on poor educational policy could have been revised. But the season for reforms, like the season of protest, was very short. After less than one year in power, and as the result of de Gaulle's ill-considered referendum and resignation, Faure was removed from power by the new Pompidou government and his reformist cabinet dispersed. An educational conservative whose brother-in-law was president of the Société des Agrégés, Pompidou replaced Faure with Olivier Guichard, a Gaullist loyalist who administered the law without personal conviction or political imagination. And Guichard's tenure coincided with a series of administrative and management shakeups of the ministry that left little time or energy for reform. He was followed by Joseph Fontanet and, after Pompidou's death, by Jean-Pierre Soisson, Valery Giscard d'Estaing's first education minister.

This merry-go-round of ministers and their cabinets did little good for the newly formed universities. Each new government attacked the problem of educational reform anew, unintentionally contributing to the turmoil in the universities by reinventing the wheel many times over (Passeron 1986). In the absence of a reformist hand at the helm, the orientation law was "diverted according to local power relations, here to the profit of the continuity of the powers in place; there as a camouflage for demagogic practices" (Passeron 1986, 386). These constant changes gave the ministry the chance to reaffirm its tutelage over many aspects of educational life and left room for an educational conservative like Alice Saunier-Seité to attack the spirit of the law when she became minister for the universities in 1978.

The Narrowing Window of Reform

But if the reform failed in its boldest aspirations, it was not primarily because of the power of the educational establishment or because Faure had lost his position. The reform passed so swiftly because Faure and his collaborators had built a coalition on the fear that—barring reform—there was danger of mobilization in the streets. Their coalitional base was wide but temporary. Some favored reform for its own sake, but many others supported it only because of their fear that the rentrée would bring renewed student strife and a return of insurgency to French society. When that fear abated, so did the impulse for reform.

Even before de Gaulle's resignation and Faure's replacement at the ministry, Faure lost the marginal power he had enjoyed over the summer and during the fall. This was not only because of the normal wearing away of reformist initiatives by the give-and-take of the political process or of administrative resistance, but more fundamentally because the industrial and educational rentrée provided evidence that—except for small groups of isolated agitators—the movement of the previous spring was dead.

It was the challenge from outside the polity that had given the reformers their political opportunity and it was the decline of that threat that reduced their leverage vis-à-vis a cautious government, a conservative Parliament, and an aroused academic establishment. This can be seen in the sharp decline in collective action in general—and of confrontational protest in particular—at the rentrée. As the reported time line of student demonstrations, public marches, and violence from July 1968 through June 1969 in figure 2.1 shows, it was mainly *after* the reform was passed, and during the period of the election of student councils, that contestation was renewed.

In fact, the reform helped to bring student protest back to where it had started. In contrast to West Germany and Italy, where the same period saw a move out of the universities into the streets on the part of student radicals, the election campaign for the student councils envisioned by the reform law brought the student movement back to the campus, where both violent and nonviolent collective action accompanied the election campaign. Although the press featured the most violent encounters when radical groups attempted to stop students from voting, in fact, most of the collective action surrounding these elections was peaceful and the 60 percent quorum of participation was not always reached (Fomerand 1974, 240).[33]

It was in Parliament that the first signs of the declining threat of mobilization appeared. Each step of the legislative process led to whittling down of the liberality of the initial reform plan. Many of the amendments were

FIGURE 2.1
Total Codable Student Events in France, July 1968–June 1969

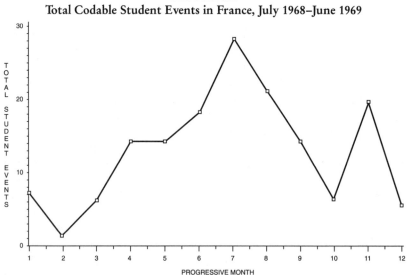

inspired by the academic establishment, either working through the prime minister's office or through individual members of Parliament. As a result, in the final text and in the implementation of the law, each of the bill's original principles was compromised.[34]

Second, in the electoral colleges, the weight of the maîtres-assistants and assistants was reduced from Faure's generous proposal of August (Chalendar 1970), and that of the students made dependent on their level of electoral participation—a limitation that was never suggested for the other categories of voters. As for the cherished goal of opening up the university to the outside, little was said about it in the final text of the law, but external groups held a statutory proportion of seats on the university councils.

Third, the regional councils foreseen by Faure to coordinate educational policy were never created, for after de Gaulle's ill-fated referendum on the regions, there was little enthusiasm in the government that succeeded him for decentralization. Instead, the group of university presidents who had begun meeting informally as an association was turned into an official council by ministerial decree and eventually came to exercise real power.[35] The replacement of Faure's cabinet of reformers by Guichard's, which was made up largely of current or future members of the Conseil d'Etat and had come mainly from the conservative law faculties, set the seal on reform for a generation.[36]

The defects of the loi d'orientation will be familiar from a number of countries that attempted systematic education reform; whereas other defects appear to be results of the traditional French system and cannot be blamed on the law or on its implementation; and others have to do with characteristics of later periods of French politics. But in assessing the outcome of this case of extraordinary policymaking, it should not be forgotten how far the French system had come from its Napoleonic roots.[37] If the universities that emerged from the Faure reform were less autonomous, less pluridisciplinary, and less participatory than the reformers had hoped, they were an advance on the situation they replaced, where there had been no structure even resembling the university system common to other advanced countries. Faure may have failed in his more ambitious undertakings; but given the parallelogram of forces resisting reform, his achievement was no mean feat (Passeron 1986).

Conclusions

The major implications of the loi d'orientation for the comparative theory of extraordinary policymaking are three.

First, like critical elections and major crises, protest waves like that of

May 1968 do not simply take advantage of an existing political opportunity structure but become an important component of that structure and, through it, provide a window for reform.

Second, although they may help unleash a reform process, protest waves are not sufficient to produce significant reforms—they also require the presence and entrepreneurship of well-placed reformists who can turn the impetus for change into concrete proposals and pilot them through the political process.

Third, waves of mobilization can produce a temporary coalition for reform, but they are often too brief, too divided, and too multivoiced to supply reformers with sustained support when the fear of disorder evaporates.

These conclusions can be highlighted and illustrated by comparison of the French educational reform of 1968 with other recent mobilization waves. First, with respect to the co-occurrence of protest and reform, although there is no evidence that reform *must* result from protest, sustained collective action frequently impels elites to move in the direction of reform. In the United States, argued Piven and Cloward (1971, xiii), "relief arrangements are initiated or expanded during the occasional outbreaks of civil disorder produced by mass unemployment." Similarly, Shorter and Tilly (1974, 145–46) concluded from their analysis of the history of French strikes that "the great wave-year mobilizations . . . were invariably rewarded with some kind of legislative success, the ultimate touchstone of the value of political action."

Periods like the Popular Front in France, the New Deal and Great Society in the United States, and the 1968 to 1972 period in Italy all saw a co-occurrence between protest and reform. As the Tillys concluded from their study of a century of conflict in Europe:

> No major political rights came into being without readiness of some portions of those (protesting) groups to overcome the resistance of the government and other groups, consequently without considerable involvement of those groups in collective violence. (Tilly, Tilly, and Tilly 1975, 184)

This occurs not through a direct translation of protest into reform, but because protest movements become part of the political opportunity structure and provide reform-minded elites with openings they otherwise would lack.

Second, it was not the movement of May itself that produced the educational reform in France, but a realignment in the governing coalition triggered by that movement and exploited by skillful political entrepreneurs. In analytical terms, much of the variance in the outcomes was explained not by the independent but by intervening variables.

The same was true in the reform period of the 1960s in the United States. "Protest," to paraphrase the work of Browning, Marshall, and Tabb (1984), was "not enough" to produce reformist outcomes for minority groups without the intervening influence of elections, political realignments, and leaders able to take advantage of a widening political opportunity structure. This suggests that the study of social movements will remain fatally incomplete unless scholars become more sensitive to the relations between protest and politics.

Third, the implementation of the French Orientation Act shows that, although protest is necessary for a reform process to begin, it is not sufficient to sustain it. A reform that takes shape during a period of crisis quickly loses its steam when the threat of crisis has passed. It took the May crisis to give French reformists the political opportunity to put in motion reform plans that predated May; they seized it by constructing a broad coalition for reform stretching from some elements of the student movement to educational modernizers and Gaullist loyalists. But the window of opportunity opened by May was not wide enough, nor did it stay open sufficiently long to allow the reform to be implemented in its original spirit.

In the same way, the distributive policies of the Johnson administration in response to the riots gave way to the "law and order" expenditures of the Nixon administration (Button 1978). In Italy, the repressive policies of the authorities followed rapidly on their initial confusion and permissiveness faced by the protest wave of the late 1960s (della Porta 1992). Like the French May and its reformist aftermath, these examples suggest that, although protest can put reform on the agenda, it is insufficient to guarantee its success. Whether this is equally true of other sources of extraordinary policymaking will only be known as the result of systematic comparative analyses.

One final note: The outcomes of a cycle of protest and reform cannot be measured only by its immediate results. Like the troughs of major movements in other countries—for example, in the United States (Rupp and Taylor 1987) and Italy (Lange, Tarrow, and Irvin 1990), the doldrums following a period of mass mobilization like that of May 1968 can disguise a slow and capillary process of cultural transformation that leaves a heritage of values and practices for the next cycle of protest.

Notes

This article is dedicated to the memory of Annick Percheron, who both experienced the events described here and immeasurably facilitated the author's research. This is a much revised version of an earlier report on social protest and reform in Western democracies, funded by a National Endowment for the Humanities Interpretive Research Grant. I am grateful to Denis Barbet, Beldon Fields, David Goldey, Peter Hall, John Keeler, René Mouriaux, René Rémond, and Ezra Suleiman for their help and advice on the earlier report, as well as to the people cited herein who agreed to be interviewed. I would also like to thank Mark D. Bayer, Anita Lee, and Sarah Soule for their invaluable assistance in preparing the tables and graphs. Of course, only I am responsible for the accuracy of any claims made.

1. For some exceptions, see Astin, Astin, Bayer, and Bisconti (1975), Burstein and Freudenburg (1978), Button (1978), Gamson (1991), Gurr (1980), Piven and Cloward (1977), and Tarrow (1989a, 1989b).

2. But see the study of the U.S. ghetto riots by Button (1978), who demonstrated a fairly clear cross-sectional relationship between the intensity of violence and increases in federal spending in cities.

3. Jacques F. Fomerand's (1974) thesis, "Policy-Formulation and Change in Gaullist France: The 1968 Orientation Act of Higher Education" is the best existing analysis of the policy process surrounding the Orientation Act and its policy outcomes. Fomerand also included a basic chronology of the policy process (pp. 6–7) and the full text of the law (pp. 342–55). Also see Fomerand (1975) for a summary of his most important findings.

4. For the development of the concept of political opportunity structure in relation to social movements, see the survey in Tarrow (1988). The most important signposts are Eisinger (1973), McAdam (1982), Kitschelt (1986), Katzenstein and Mueller (1987), Tarrow (1989a, 1989b), Kriesi (1991), and Rucht (1990).

5. The most systematic study based on a political process model is that of Doug McAdam (1982), who argued in the case of the U.S. civil rights movement that a model based on the political process provides a far better explanation of when the movement emerged than other available models.

6. See Bourricaud (1982), Fomerand (1975, chap. 2), Grignon and Passeron (1970), Passeron (1986). As Grignon and Passeron (1970, 27–28) wrote:

> The immobilism of the university and the inflexibility of its organization and curricula have been constantly denounced over the past 15 years, until finally denunciation became unanimous and the effects of the rise in enrollments succeeded in rousing even the most conservative academics.

7. In fact, an examination of the reform proposals of Education Minister Alain Peyrefitte was scheduled for an Assembly debate on May 14th (Aubert, Bergouni-oux, Martin, and Mouriaux 1985, 204).

8. Converse and Pierce (1989) conclude, from their analysis of the relationship between public opinion in 1967 and demonstration participation in May 1968 that

> Attitudes towards education opportunities and the role of government in promoting education, *expressed more than a year before the events,* had more independent impact on the May demonstrations than either the classic leftist issues of unionism and income distribution or even lack of trust in the governing authorities generally. (pp. 232–36, emphasis added; see also table 2)

9. The first event that Schnapp and Vidal-Naquet (1988, 106ff.) related to the May crisis took place on November 25, 1967. No other major conflicts appear in

their careful itinerary of university protest until the celebrated events of March 22 at Nanterre.

10. Statistics provided by the French Ministry of Labor show that the number of days lost to strikes in the years following the May outbreak was actually lower in 1969 and 1970 than it had been in 1966 and 1967 (Capdevielle and Mouriaux 1988, 107). Although there were signs of continued worker militancy after May— for example, in a greater willingness to occupy plants during strikes (p. 108)—the accords of Grenelle of June 1968 effectively closed the crisis as far as industrial relations were concerned.

11. In a personal interview, Michel Alliot recalls that, when visitors would complain to General de Gaulle of the damage that the Faure reform might do to higher education, he would remind them of the collapse of the system in May (2 April 1990).

12. Failure had ambitions for the post well before May 1968. Alliot recalls discussing it with him as early as 1964. Although Faure was not named to the post until July, it was in June that the two had their first conversation about Faure's plans for the ministry (interview, 2 April 1990).

13. I am grateful to David Godey for reminding me of this, as well as for identifying the Faure quote that follows.

14. The most serious were produced by the "Conférence InterFacultés," meeting in Toulouse in July (Chalendar 1970, 13).

15. As Schnapp and Vidal-Naquet (1988, 47) concluded:

Pour nombre d'assistants ou de maîtres-assistants, la revendication de la suppression des hiérarchies à l'intérieur des universités passait par leur propre élévation au rang de professeurs. Des professeurs de province estimaient que l'occasion était unique de se faire nommer à Paris, d'autres qui avaient moins de 40 ans déclaraient avec candeur que la direction de l'Université devait être confiée aux professeurs de moins de 40 ans.

16. Before May, for example, the Union des Etudiants Communistes were "divided among 'orthodoxes,' 'italiens,' and several varieties of extremists" (Schnapp and Vidal-Naquet 1988, 16). The various Maoist groups, both before and after May, never had much interest in the university—except as a site for the recruitment of militants for the factories (151). The one surviving Maoist document on the university, which is reproduced by Schnapp and Vidal-Naquet, 359–60), called for the subordination of the movement to the cause of "serving the people." Even the movement of the 22nd of March rejected what its leaders called "a corporatist spirit" (149), and viewed the movement for transforming the university with a critical eye, affirming that "ni pratiquement ni théoriquement on ne peut créer un îlot socialiste à l'intérieur d'une société capitaliste" (152).

17. Divisions could by no means be reduced to a Left–Right axis. Although many conservative Catholic supporters of the *école libre* were in favor of educational reform (the same was true for the majority of Jewish professors), the lay Left was divided. For to the extent that the reform was thought to attack the unity of French education (and Edgar Faure tried to project exactly this impression), it could be understood as undermining the foundations of the secular education that was thought to be a foundation of the republican tradition. Some of the attempts

to modify the bill in a conservative direction as it passed through the political process would come from liberal academics who had voted stalwartly for the Left in the elections of June (Gérard Conac, interview, 23 March 1990).

18. Astre interview, 5 April 1990.

19. Although SNESup, under Alain Geismar, opposed compromise with the authorities even before May (Aubert et al. 1985, 204), the Syndicate National des Instituteurs (SNI) was quick to vote for a return to work after the general strike of May 20th, whereas SNES decided to continue the strike a while longer. FEN experienced contestation from insurgent teachers even before the end of the crisis: first on June 7, when some 200 radical *instituteurs*, opposing the organization's support for the end of the general strike, occupied the courtyard of the federation in Rue de Solferino (Barbet 1988, 12). Although its leaders' basic instinct was to defend its members' professional interests, the FEN developed in May a strategy of political mediation (Barbet 1988, 15) that made it difficult for the federation to act when its constituent national unions were divided.

20. Although the SNI pushed for a platform on the school-leaving age and problems of curriculum and professional mobility for teachers, the SNES "insisted on the development of socioeducative activities, on the need for dialogue between parents and teachers, and on the reorganization of students' employment of their time" (Aubert et al. 1985, 207) and the SNESup opposed the reform altogether as a *"reformette"* (205).

21. In an early stage of his ministry, Faure and his collaborators wanted to include participants in the former movement in the early stages of participation. In fact, Faure's first plan for the election of the councils of the future university— bodies that would also draft their statutes—was to create informal bodies—which in many cases would, in fact, end up to be the instances de fait that had emerged in May and June—to act as the bodies that would elaborate the new statutes for the universities (Chalendar 1970, 174). But this was too much for the government, which feared the influence of the instances de fait of May on the future universities (117), and the idea of provisional committees had to be abandoned. As we shall see below, this defeat turned out to be crucial in the creation of the new university structures during the 1968–69 academic year.

22. Gérald Antoine, interview, 21 March 1990; Chalendar, interview, 17 March 1990. Between his appointment in early July and the end of the summer, Faure and his collaborators reportedly saw over 4,000 individuals interested in one way or another in educational reform (Michel Alliot, interview, 2 April 1990).

23. Gérald Antoine, interview, 21 March 1990.

24. Astre, interview, 5 April 1990.

25. The haste was not accidental. Alliot was of the opinion that "in France, the only decisions that are taken are taken quickly" (interview, 2 April 1990).

26. Because several of these new units would continue to share the same facilities, the task was far more delicate than the creation of provincial universities (Gérard Conac, interview, 23 March 1990).

27. The first was that the law left a number of substantive gaps to be filled in later. Some of these would be dealt with in supplementary legislation in 1971 and 1975, whereas others—for example, the provision for regional councils—

remained a dead letter. A large number of details were also left to be dealt with by administrative negotiation. The most crucial issue that the law left open was the nagging problem of selection—a problem that no one, either in the delicate atmosphere of l'après-mai or since, has been willing to broach (Gaussen 1990, 10). Another result was that an enormous number of amendments was proposed to deal with the ambiguities of the project. From Faure's original draft of nine pages, a document of thirty-nine pages finally emerged, "codifying a large number of situations and mechanisms, balancing general and generous principles with precise and numerous restrictions" (Passeron 1986, 385).

28. Alliot reports that on the morning after the law's passage, he was congratulated by a member of the prime minister's cabinet for its passage without a single dissenting vote. The same official promptly confided to him that now it was time to decide how to avoid its implementation (interview, 2 April 1990).

29. Under French constitutional procedure, although the minister could effect the arrêtés necessary to create new units within the universities, only the prime minister or the president could effect the décrets necessary to create new établissements publiques, which is what the universities would become.

30. I am following Michel Alliot's reconstruction of these events (interview, 2 April 1990).

31. Faure was aware of the danger. As Chalendar (1970, 75) noted, he warned at the time that "simply transforming the existing units into UER's will carry the risk of quickly denuding the reform of its content."

32. As Salmon (1982, 79) judiciously wrote, "there were many anomalous collections of disconnected UERs." The biggest problem was in Paris. Here the overgrown university had to be divided into thirteen units, and the process was so complicated that discussions and conflicts lasted up until the rentrée of 1970. Many of the "universities" that emerged were pluridisciplinary in name only, with odd collections of UERs existing cheek-by-jowl in uneasy cohabitation and frequently offering no more of an interdisciplinary training to their students than had the old faculties (Chalendar 1970, 177). In some cases, different universities had to share the same premises—for example, in the Sorbonne—which could lead to territorial disputes over wings of the building, rectorial apartments, even corridors. The UER of history ended up with 6,000 students; that of English literature more than 10,000 (Salmon 1982, 177). Although changes were later made, the quality of university education in the capital never recovered.

33. Fomerand reported that 77 percent voted in the university institutes of technology and 68 percent in the former medical faculties, but only 53 percent in law, 43 percent in sciences, and 43 percent in liberal arts. Fomerand—and Faure—regards these as successful figures, but it is difficult to know what to compare them to. What was certainly true was that the extreme Leftist groups were soundly defeated (Formerand 1974, 241–43).

34. Consider the principle of the autonomy of the universities. Although the reformers achieved the liquidation of a priori administrative tutelage of the university's budgets, the autonomy of the new institutions would continue to be restricted by a ministry of education that had the power to define "programs of study leading to national diplomas" (Passeron 1986, 387) and continued to exercise a posteriori control over their budgets.

36. The one *universitaire* was Gérard Conac, himself a member of the Paris Faculty of Law and Economic Science.

37. Fomerand (1974), whose careful study is the most dispassionate one around, shared this view. He wrote: "Often described as a mere political 'mesure de circonstances,' the Orientation Act, in several respects, was also an epoch making event" (Fomerand 1974, 232).

3

Social Movements and Cultural Change

William A. Gamson

> *I shall not attempt further to define it . . . and perhaps I could never*
> *succeed in intelligibly doing so. But I know it when I see it.*—Justice
> Potter Stewart, struggling with the problems of a legal definition of
> obscenity, in *Jacobellis v. Ohio,* 1964.

Is cultural change the latest candidate for the "it" in the above quote?
How can we possibly assess the impact of social movements when we can
not answer the question of impact on *what?* Various writers call upon us
to consider changes at the level of personal identity and consciousness, in
the lifeworld of the household and neighborhood, in our daily life in the
workplace, in making the unthinkable thinkable, in the supplanting of
one "moral-intellectual" universe with another. In fact, the referents for
cultural change are all around us, diffused through the civil society in a
thousand ways, but this does not tell us where to look to assess impact.
If the changes are everywhere, then one can look anywhere. One is left
to wonder whether, in observing the cultural changes around us through
the myriad ways in which people in different social locations live their
lives, we will have any common referent at all by which we can assess
movement impact.

Perhaps this is one reason why, to quote McAdam, McCarthy, and Zald
(1996, 6):

> The literature is long on ringing programmatic statements regarding the ne-
> cessity for "bringing culture back in," but short on the kind of cumulative
> scholarship that we now have on political opportunities or mobilizing struc-
> tures in the emergence and development of movements.

Furthermore, this weakness seems most acute on the issue of impact. In contrast, detailed specification of cultural processes in movement mobilization have helped us to understand why symbolic processes and identity processes are central. But, as Polletta (1996, 483–84) observes in reviewing a recent collection of essays on cultural politics and social movements, there is considerably less success "in demonstrating the *impacts* of cultural challenge."

Fortunately, a solution is at hand and is already well begun—*assess movement impact on cultural change through public discourse.* This has several advantages. For one, it differentiates a cultural level of analysis from social psychological processes such as personal identity, political cognition, public opinion, and political socialization. The conflation of these levels of analysis invites the-culture-is-everywhere-so-look-anywhere confusion. If we want to know whether one moral-intellectual universe has been supplanted by another, we look at particular forums of public discourse to see if it has been supplanted in that forum. Whether it has been supplanted in the hearts and minds of citizens is a separable issue involving the complex ways in which people use public discourse in combination with other resources in making sense of issues raised by social movements.

A second advantage is the way in which the study of public discourse lends itself to the Swidlerian view of culture as a tool kit (Swidler 1986). We ask what has happened to the tool kit available to people through public discourse and whether any changes reflect an input from social movements that is in some sense distinguishable from that of other social actors. By not making culture everything—and by recognizing the ways in which people use their personal experience and popular wisdom as well as public discourse—one can specify the referent and make manageable the assessment of cultural impact.

Finally, it enables us to extend the well-known typology of outcomes used in *The Strategy of Social Protest* (Gamson 1990, herein referred to as *Strategy*). In doing so, it highlights the problems of using the outcome measures in *Strategy* for assessing *cultural* change. But by looking to public discourse to find outcome measures, we can use the same typology, thereby helping to integrate cultural change into studies of movement impact on social policy and power alignments.

Constructing Public Discourse: A Working Model

The focus on public discourse also has some limits, as I hope to make clear in proposing a working model of the construction of public discourse.[1] Public discourse means public communications about topics and actors related to either some specified policy domain or to the broader symbolic interests of some constituency. It includes images as well as information and argumentation. The production of images rather than information or argumentation is worth emphasizing because this more subtle form of meaning construction is at the heart of measuring cultural impact. It is useful in reminding us to attend to the visual, to verbal imagery, and other modes of conveying a broader frame—through music, for example. It encourages us to look beyond conventional discussion of public affairs to advertising and entertainment as additional sites where images are communicated. But the distinction between images and factual information can be overdrawn: facts as much as images take on their meaning by being embedded in some larger system of meaning or frame.

Public discourse is carried out in various forums. A forum includes a site or arena in which meaning is being contested plus an active audience or gallery. The contributors or players in any given forum are aware of the gallery, some of whose members may themselves become active players at other times or in other arenas. We define the public sphere as the set of all forums in which public discourse takes place.

Every forum has its own norms and practices governing both the form and content of expression and who has standing to participate. The model does not assume that any given forum is "fair" in the sense of providing a level playing field for all participants. On the contrary, the rules and practices of the gatekeepers in any forum are part of the explanation of cultural impact or its absence. Not only do the assemblers of discourse provide opportunities and constraints for cultural challengers, especially around issues of access, but they actively participate as important sponsors of meaning in their own right.

The *mass media* are the most important forum for understanding cultural impact since they provide the major site in which contests over meaning must succeed politically. First, they provide a master forum in the sense that the players in every other forum also use the media forum, either as players or as part of the gallery. Among the various forums of public discourse, it provides the most generally available and shared set of cultural tools. Social movements must assume that their own constituents are part of the mass media gallery and the messages their would-be supporters hear cannot be ignored, no matter how extensive the movement's own alternative media may be.

Second, the mass media forum is *the* major site of contest politically, in part because all of the would-be or actual sponsors of meaning—be they authorities, members, or challengers—*assume* pervasive influence (whether justified or not). The mass media often become the critical gallery for discourse carried on in other forums, with success measured by whether a speech in the legislative forum, for example, is featured prominently in the *New York Times* or the *Frankfurter Allgemeine Zeitung.*

Finally, the mass media forum is not simply a site where one can read relative success in cultural contests. It is not merely an indicator of broader cultural changes in the civil society but influences them, spreading changes in language use and political consciousness to the workplace and other settings in which people go about the public part of their daily lives. When a cultural code is being challenged, a change in the media forum both signals and spreads the change. To have one's preferred framing of an issue increase significantly in the mass media forum is both an important outcome in itself and carries a strong promise of a ripple effect.

Political Interest Mediation

This dual role of the mass media as both sponsor of meaning and site of a meaning contest emphasizes its role in a complex system of what Schmitter (1977) and Rucht (1995) call "political interest mediation." Various actors in this system—political parties, corporations, associations, and social movements—attempt to generate, aggregate, transform, and articulate the interests of some underlying constituency. Social movements are only one of several potential *carriers* of the interests of a given constituency in this larger system of interest mediation. To assess their impact on any kind of change—be it cultural or institutional—one must consider their relationship to the other carriers.

To call this a mediation system, as Rucht (1995) reminds us, implies the linking of at least two external elements that, for a variety of reasons, cannot or do not communicate directly. They "obey conflicting logic and principles which permit no direct link" (Rucht 1995, 105) or, more metaphorically, they do not speak the same language. But the mediation system discussed here does much more than simply translate inputs and outputs into a common language. It takes on a life of its own with its own operating logic and interests and transforms and shapes what is being communicated; indeed, its processes often override the intentions of actors in the external systems being linked.

If social movements are part of a complex mediation system, what are the external systems being linked? On the one hand, we have constituencies. One may think of these as solidarity groups or, to borrow Anderson's (1991) useful concept, "imagined communities." Examples would include women, workers, Christians, greens, conservatives, Latinos, the "left," and many others. Since people have multiple identities, they are potentially part of many constituencies. A given solidarity group may provide a lead identity for some people that they use on all or most issues, while for others it may be one of several which vary in salience from issue to issue. The degree of solidarity or personal identification with a particular imagined community is an empirical question, with the operation of the interest mediation system providing most of the explanation.

The other end of the mediation system is more problematic and forces us to take a closer look at what is meant by "interests." Consider, for example, that the constituency whose interests are being mediated is "farmers." The term "interests" conjures up images of crop subsidies, regulations, and other agricultural policies that will operate to the advantage or disadvantage of this group. Or perhaps of power arrangements that will increase or decrease the political influence of those who carry the political interests of farmers. In this narrow sense of policy interests, the other end of the mediation system is the system of authorities who are able to make binding decisions on policies and how they are implemented.

In considering cultural change, however, the term "interests" seems too narrow and restrictive. Farmers also have certain "interests" in the nature of public discourse and these include both interests in promoting desired policy frames in various forums and also more subtle ones that do not relate to any specific policy contests. As an example of the former, support for policies favoring farmers is likely to be greater if the image of farmers in public discourse emphasizes the small, independent family farm rather than the agribusiness that is, in fact, the dominant "farmer" in the production and distribution of most crops. But aside from this instrumental and strategic use of public discourse to further policy interests, some groups of farmers may have concerns about the degree of respect they receive in the broader culture—for example, about the disparaging depiction of white farmers in the South as "rednecks" or "hillbillies" in movies and in television entertainment forums. In short, the various constituencies whose interests are being mediated have *symbolic interests* and these should be the focus of an assessment of cultural impact.

For the mediation of symbolic interests, the other end of the mediation system is less clear. Authorities do not make binding decisions about language use nor does anyone else. Their decisions about usage may or may not be adopted by others and often authorities may simply follow the lead of various parts of the mediation system—especially the dominant usage in mass media discourse. Hence, for symbolic interests, it is the outputs of the mass media system, rather than the decisions of authorities, that are being linked to constituencies via the mediation system.

Both authorities and the mass media, then, play a dual role in the system of interest mediation. For power and policy interests, authorities function as the external system being linked—that is, as the target of the carriers in the mediation system. But at an organizational level, some official agencies may function as carriers of the interests of some constituency, as an inside voice for these interests in the internal discussions of decision-making bodies. In this role, they are part of the mediation system rather than the external system being linked. The Department of Agriculture, for example, may be less a producer of binding decisions than a carrier of a particular definition of farmers' interests within internal government forums.

To complicate matters further, we cannot assume that the state is merely a target system that produces outputs but must recognize that it has systemwide interests of its own. These may or may not be engaged on a given issue but cannot be ignored. On abortion, for example, state interests may involve the maintenance of a given population level, thereby providing a link to the abortion issue and reproductive policies more generally. Certain carriers in the mediation system may also be carrying these state interests. Clearly, those who do will enjoy advantages in any contest with rival carriers.

Similarly, when the media are a site in which various carriers compete to further the symbolic interests of their constituencies, they are the external end of the mediation system. But when we examine how their structure and practices shape the outputs and how journalists articulate the symbolic interest of particular constituencies, we are considering them as part of the mediation system in their own right.

The mass media system, like the state, can also be assumed to have autonomous interests of its own, beyond the varying organizational interests of the field of actors that comprise it. Again, these systemwide interests may or may not be engaged on a given issue but cannot be ignored. We do not assume that the mass media system is neutral among different types of carriers—for example, between members and challengers—but that the openness varies from issue to issue and must therefore be part of any assessment of cultural impact.

Nature of the Mediation System

The political parties, corporations, associations, and social movements in the interest mediation system are each *fields of actors* that may overlap. Green interests, for example, may be mediated by a movement or party that is simultaneously part of the political party and movement subsystems and is variously linked with associations as well. One cannot assess the impact of movements independently of their role in this broader system. The symbolic interests of a given constituency may be shared by a field of actors who pursue them in different ways—including a movement sector.

If we find an improvement in the salience of preferred frames in public discourse, we cannot attribute it to the movement component in particular unless we can differentiate the symbolic interests it emphasizes from those that are common to the network of carriers. Since the internal decisions of this network are typically the site of a contest about what are the best frames and policies to pursue, one can often use this internal discourse to distinguish the particular symbolic interests being articulated by social movement organizations and advocacy networks.

The mediation system as a whole structures the opportunities and constraints in which carriers of particular interests must operate. Different opportunity structures may make it easier or more difficult to mediate any given set of interests. Movements may have more or less opportunity for influence within the mediation system, compared to parties and associations. For cultural change, we should focus on the *media opportunity structure*—that is, the linkage between the mass media subsystem and the various carriers of symbolic interests. The political economy of the mass media, as well as their norms and practices, affect the rules of access for whose ideas and which ideas are taken seriously. Any comparative assessment of the success of movement symbolic strategies must reflect differences in media opportunity structure, lest we underrate success in movements challenging more fundamental aspects of cultural codes and, hence, face more formidable obstacles to change.

Public Discourse and Public Policy

Success in having an impact on public discourse is important, but it does not necessarily translate into impact on either public policy or a broader set of practices in everyday life. With respect to public policy, decision makers in the political system are clearly an attentive part of the gallery and may be directly influenced by the metaphors, images, and arguments that they watch and read. But other forums may be more important—including a policy forum where the gallery is less the general public and more those with professional work interests and responsibilities in the policy domain.

Most of the impact of the media forum on public policy is indirect—mediated by the perceived or actual impact of media discourse on the distribution of individual opinion among the voters. To the extent that media discourse shapes these opinions on issues that are electorally relevant, it will constrain political decision makers or induce them to follow dominant tendencies to avoid defeat at the next election. This argument can be seen as a version of the two-step flow of influence—in this case, from the media to voters to policymakers. But the opinions of voters—whether in the form of sample surveys or the words of one's taxi driver—

are open to interpretation with various carriers competing to give their spin on what the "public" really thinks. For advocates in the policy arena, media discourse may be primarily a cultural tool whose content they can use in their own efforts to garner support rather than something by which they are influenced directly.

Policy processes, however, are not driven only or even primarily by ideas. Decision makers may be influenced by many other factors that operate with substantial insulation from public discourse—for example, the exchange relationships and deal making of political insiders, the maintenance of support from influential political supporters who may have substantial material interests engaged, and the demands of party discipline. It is quite possible to win the battle of public discourse without being able to convert this into the new advantages that flow from actually changing public policy.

But doing badly in mass media discourse creates vulnerability in pursuing policy interests. Political parties and individual politicians looking for issues that will attract voters for themselves and embarrass or divide their opponents may make the issue electorally relevant. For supporters of existing policies, the success of challengers in the mass media forum puts supporters on the defensive and complicates their work. They are left consistently vulnerable when their would-be allies are worried that their policy choices will become an issue that opponents are likely to use against them in the next election. If challengers are sufficiently successful in defining the terms of debate in media discourse, the support of a powerful but discredited interest group may stigmatize those who carry its water in policy disputes.

The link between cultural success and policy outcome is further mediated by the complicated relationship of media discourse to public opinion. In their attempts to make sense of the world of public affairs, ordinary people are only partially dependent on media discourse and dependency varies widely among different issue domains. *Talking Politics* (Gamson 1992a, 179) likens people's efforts to make sense of issues to finding their way through a forest. "The various frames offered in media discourse provide maps indicating useful points of entry, and signposts at various crossroads highlight the significant landmarks and warn of the perils of other paths."

On certain issues, media discourse may be a first resort and the primary resource for making meaning, but even on such issues, they typically will find multiple frames available. The openness of the media text requires that they use other resources as well to complete the task. People control their media dependence, in part, through their willingness and ability to draw on popular wisdom and experiential knowledge to supplement what they are offered. If media dependence is only partial when media discourse serves as the starting point, it is even less so where experiential knowledge is the primary resource for finding a path through the forest.

However, lack of dependence does not imply lack of use or influence. Most people on most issues construct meaning by different combinations of media discourse, experiential knowledge, and popular wisdom. They integrate these sources of meaning with varying degrees of success into a coherent cognitive schema for those issues that are important to them; for many policy domains, they may never have thought or talked about it, or ever felt the need to have any opinions about it. The flow of influence from media discourse to public opinion is itself heavily mediated, indirect, and partial, further diluting the impact of success in the mass media forum on policy outcomes.

Finally, success in public discourse also fails to guarantee that broader cultural and institutional practices will necessarily change. One may win the battle of words while practices remain unchanged or even change for the worse. Here, the abortion issue will serve well as an illustration. Most studies of media discourse on abortion, including the one in which I am currently engaged, suggest that—in the United States, at least—the proponents of frames emphasizing rights of individual privacy and women's self-determination do very well. At the same time, access to abortion is not increasing and has significantly declined in some areas. Some states have only a single abortion provider, requiring women to travel great distances. The symbolic contest over the framing of abortion may be very far from the minds of potential abortion providers who are deterred by the fear that they may become the target of anti-abortion violence—regardless of whether the violence is roundly condemned in media discourse.

Nevertheless, there is solid evidence that abortion access is heavily influenced by public support for abortion rights. In Wetstein's (1996) quantitative study of abortion rates in the fifty American states, he examines the percentage of counties within a state that have one or more abortion providers. Using a multivariate LISREL analysis to estimate a path model, he found that two primary factors can account for 63 percent of the variation in abortion access. "Greater support in the mass public translates directly into greater levels of access to abortion (B = .32). The only other significant variable to influence the level of providers is the socioeconomic variable" [a combined measure using median income, median education, and other similar indices] (B = .53) (Wetstein 1996, 120). Wetstein included no measures of media discourse in his analysis, but his results certainly suggest that the cultural climate on the issue in a given state is one of the most important predictors of abortion practices.

Measuring Success

Cultural social movements are sustained and self-conscious challenges to cultural codes by a field of actors, some of whom employ extra-institutional means of influence. Extra-institutional means refers to everything other than the use of the electoral system, the judicial system, and the peaceful petitioning of public officials (lobbying, testifying at public hearings, presentations, letters, petitions). In the case of cultural challengers, the extra-institutional means may include guerrilla theater or other dramatic displays, demonstrations, vigils, marches, burning of effigies, graffiti, and other norm-violating symbolic politics.

ACT UP, an AIDS activist organization, has been especially inventive in this regard, using such venues as a Mets game at Shea Stadium to denormalize taken-for-granted codes. Josh Gamson (1989, 351) describes their slogans, which use baseball themes: "No glove, no love," "Don't balk at safer sex," and "AIDS is not a ballgame." He quotes a straight fan who complained, "AIDS is a fearful topic. This is totally inappropriate," suggesting that the fan has inadvertently summed up the point of the action. The opportunity to challenge invisibility and what is taken-for-granted is there for those challengers willing to use unconventional forms of collective action.

Many movements seeking structural change also challenge cultural codes. The civil rights movement, the women's movement, and the environmental movement, for example, are cultural movements by the above definition. Rather than classifying movements, it seems more useful to ask how any movement that has a cultural challenge as one component can measure success in this realm, even if it is not their primary emphasis.

The Strategy of Social Protest (Gamson 1990) offers an approach to measuring success that can be adapted to measuring cultural impact as well. *Strategy* suggests that we think of success as a *set* of outcomes, recognizing that a given challenging group may score differently on equally valid measures. However, it divides the outcome measures into two basic clusters: one concerned with the fate of the challenging group as an organization and one with the distribution of new advantages to the group's beneficiary. The central issue in the first cluster focuses on the *acceptance* of a challenging group by its targets as a valid representative for a legitimate set of interests. The central issue in the second cluster focuses on whether a group's constituents gain *new advantages* during the challenge and its aftermath.

By combining these two questions, as in figure 3.1 below, we can specify four possible outcomes: full response, co-optation, preemption, and collapse. The full response and collapse categories are relatively unambiguous successes and failures—in the one case, the achievement of both ac-

FIGURE 3.1
Outcome of Resolved Challenges

		Acceptance	
		Full	None
New	Many	Full response	Preemption
Advantages	None	Co-optation	Collapse

ceptance and new advantages; in the other, the achievement of neither. The remainder are mixed success categories: co-optation refers to acceptance without new advantages and preemption to new advantages without acceptance. *Strategy* operationalizes these variables with a strong structural bias, inadequately meeting the challenge of measuring cultural impact. But with appropriate modification, the same outcomes can be used.

Acceptance

Acceptance in *Strategy* assumes the existence of a visible antagonist or set of them. "This antagonist necessarily begins with a relationship of active or passive hostility toward the challenging group or, at best, indifference. Acceptance involves a change from hostility or indifference to a more positive relationship" (Gamson 1990, 31). As indicators of a more positive relationship, *Strategy* focuses on consultation, negotiations, formal recognition, and inclusion in positions of authority in the antagonist's organizational structure.

This operationalization of acceptance ignores the fundamental dilemma of those who challenge cultural codes—the invisibility of the antagonist. Much of what ACT UP is fighting, for example, "is abstract, disembodied, invisible: control through the creation of abnormality" (J. Gamson 1989, 352). The premise of a visible antagonist who can grant acceptance is violated, requiring a different type of operationalization. But by focusing on media discourse, there is a ready solution to a cultural definition of acceptance.

Acceptance, for cultural challengers, can be measured by media *standing*. In legal discourse, standing refers to the right of a person or group to challenge in a judicial forum the conduct of another, especially with respect to governmental conduct. The rules for according legal standing have been anything but fixed and clear. Former Chief Justice Earl Warren, in *Flast v. Cohen* (1968), referred to it as "one of the most amorphous concepts in the entire domain of public law." Rather than a matter of clear definition, legal standing is a battleground, and the environmental movement, in particular, has had considerable success in expanding who has standing to sue the government.

By analogy, media standing is also contested terrain. In news accounts, it refers to gaining the status of a regular media source whose interpretations are directly quoted. Note that standing is not the same as being covered or mentioned in the news; a group may be in the news in the sense that it is described or criticized but has no opportunity to provide interpretation and meaning to the events in which it is involved. Standing refers to a group being treated as an agent, not merely as an object being discussed by others.

From the standpoint of most journalists who are attempting to be "objective," the granting of standing is anything but arbitrary. Sources are selected, in this view, because they speak as or for serious players in any given policy domain: individuals or groups who have enough political power to make a potential difference in what happens. Most journalists would insist that their choice of sources to quote has nothing at all to do with their personal attitudes toward those sources. If they choose to call Operation Rescue and quote its erstwhile spokesman, Randall Terry, on his reactions to a Supreme Court decision on abortion, this has nothing to do with whether they like or dislike Operation Rescue or Terry. They are simply reflecting a reality that is out there—for better or worse, the group has enough power that it must be taken into account and Terry is able and willing to speak for them.

Croteau and Hoynes (1994) conducted studies of the guests on *Nightline* and identified some apparently significant sources who did not appear. Host Ted Koppel and his associates defended their choices. The authors quote *Nightline* executive producer Richard Kaplan who argued, "We're a news show, not a public-affairs show. Our job is to bring on guests who make the news—the players, in other words."[2] News, in this world view, is about those powerful enough to make a difference—this objective reality is the basis of standing for a news show.

Of course, sophisticated journalists such as a Ted Koppel or a David Brinkley are aware that an appearance on their show also enhances the claims of players to be taken seriously. Presumably, they are both flattered by their ability to influence who has standing with other journalists and made uncomfortable by the unwanted responsibility. They would like it to be true that they merely reflect rather than create standing and their awareness that this is only half true is disquieting. In the end, they content themselves with trying to pursue the idea of objectivity as best they can in an imperfect world.

In the model offered here, media standing is the end point of a contest over which sponsors of meaning will have an opportunity to appear in a mass media forum *that defines membership in terms of political power.*

Defining *acceptance* in these terms emphasizes standing as a measure of achieved cultural power. The model here assumes that journalists operating in a news forum try to reflect their perceptions of who the key players are, but that, in practice, they are influenced by various other factors in choosing sources and quotes. Choice of sources—at least in the U.S. media—is often driven by the need for spectacle and drama; sources are used who give good sound bites or provide footage of people with fire in the belly.

In cultural contests, sources are often chosen because they are seen as representing a particular perspective. Rather than being seen as representative in the sense of typical, they are chosen as prototypes who represent a particular cultural tendency in a compelling and dramatic way. In this sense, standing still reflects a journalistic political judgment about which cultural movements make a difference or are players.

Note that this discussion of standing operationalizes the concept for policy discourse; to assess some broader cultural acceptance, one must look beyond news forums to include such mass media forums as television entertainment, movies, talk shows, and advertising. It is especially problematic to ignore these when talking about cultural change because they may be more sensitive indicators. Standing, measured as who gets quoted in news accounts, does not capture this broader form of cultural acceptance. It does not deal, for example, with the portrayal of gay and lesbian characters in a sympathetic or matter-of-fact way in entertainment forums, which may say more about the acceptance of the homosexual constituency than quoting a person from ACT UP or the National Gay and Lesbian Task Force.

New Advantages

Much of the discussion of this variable in *Strategy* is relevant here in spite of the structural bias in operationalizing it. Did the potential beneficiaries of the challenge receive what the group sought for them? The challenger's perspective and aspirations are the starting point for assessment. We are left to judge whether the benefits sought were or would have been "real" benefits; they are benefits as defined by the challenger. On the issue of whether the benefits actually happened, *Strategy* supplemented the group's own assessment of success with that of the antagonist and professional historians, looking for consensus.

By using media discourse as the measure of new cultural advantages, we have a simpler and more quantifiable measure of success than perceived outcome by observers in different social locations. Challengers to cultural codes have an alternative way of framing the issues in some normative domain. Their preferred alternative frame calls into question the taken-for-granted assumptions of the code being challenged—for example, about the nature of what is normal and abnormal, visible or invisible, or what is appropriate behavior in work and family settings. Often such challenges focus on visual images, language and labels—whether on the abortion issue, for example, one uses the term "fetus" or "baby."

If one charts mass media coverage of some issue domain over time, frames and their associated idea elements and symbols will ebb and flow in prominence. Success in gaining new advantages in cultural terms is measured by changes in the relative prominence of the challenger's preferred frames compared to antagonistic or rival frames. Take, for example, a specific cultural practice challenged by the women's movement—the use of the generic "he" in English, to be replaced by various alternative forms of gender-inclusive language. To assess success, one compares media samples from today with those before the second wave of the women's movement began in the late 1960s. If gender-exclusive language is reduced or has disappeared, here is a clear measure of success.

Extending this measure of success to other non-news forums is less problematic than it is for standing. Frames can be extracted from cartoons, films, advertising, and entertainment as readily as from news accounts. The prominence of preferred movement frames can be assessed over time in such forums in the same way as in news forums.

Using these two measures, the four outcomes above are redefined for cultural challengers. *Full response* means that a challenger receives both media standing and a significant increase in the prominence of its preferred frame. *Collapse* means it receives neither standing nor increased prominence for its preferred frame. *Co-optation* means that the group receives media standing but no significant increase in its preferred frames. Finally, *preemption* means that the challenger's preferred frame has significantly increased in media prominence in spite of the absence of media standing for its sponsor.

Explaining Success

Cultural movements face a number of daunting obstacles in competing with public officials, corporations, political parties, organized interest groups, and other more resource-laden sponsors of meaning. Some do well anyway in spite of the uneven playing field. Why do they succeed? To answer this, we will examine each of the four major factors in determining the success of a frame in the mass media forum: sponsor activities, media norms and practices, cultural resonances, and narrative fit.

Sponsor Activities

Frames succeed, in part, because of sponsors who promote them through such tangible activities as speech making, interviews with journalists, advertising, article and pamphlet writing, and the like. Many of these sponsors are organizations who employ professional specialists whose daily jobs bring them into contact with journalists. The sponsor of a package is typically an agent who can draw on the resources of an organization to prepare materials in a form that lends itself to ready use. Professionalism abets sophistication about the news needs of the media and the norms and habits of working journalists.

Cultural challengers can rarely hope to compete with the full array of production assets that defenders of cultural codes can muster, but they can compete successfully in some realms. Production assets include not only material resources such as personnel and money that are available for sponsoring preferred frames in the media but also sophistication and know-how about how the mass media work in a practical way. Many cultural challengers can and do acquire this know-how.

The abortion issue in the United States is a ready illustration. Both pro-choice and pro-life movement groups have highly skilled professionals with a sophisticated understanding of what works in the mass media forum. They concede nothing in this respect to organized religious groups or political parties, for example. Many of the actors in the movement organizational fields have a relatively stable flow of resources although some, of course, struggle to survive. In this case, whatever general disadvantages movements face in production assets have been neutralized to a point at which they can compete on more or less equal terms with nonmovement sponsors.

The importance of production assets is mitigated by what Gamson, Fireman, and Rytina (1982, 87–88) call the *threshold hypothesis*. They suggest that the simple linear hypothesis—the greater the production assets, the higher the probability of success—is inadequate. It is more useful to specify a desirable threshold for different kinds of assets. "Those groups of potential challengers that fail to meet this threshold have a deficit with negative consequences [for success]. But enough is enough. Once a group has sufficient assets, no further advantage accrues from having more." By this argument, cultural challengers must overcome any deficits in production assets to succeed but, having achieved a certain threshold, increasing production assets will only add marginally to the probability of success.

Media Norms and Practices

Hallin and Mancini (1984, 841), building on Habermas's arguments about the structural transformation of the public sphere, note the replacement of a participatory, decentralized bourgeois public sphere "by a process of political communication dominated by large scale institutions:

political parties, unions, and other organized associations of the private sector, and the mass media." This public sphere is structured quite differently in the United States and in Germany, for example. Political interpretation in Germany is provided by the institutions that have traditionally dominated the modern public sphere: political parties, unions, industrial associations, and organized religion. In such a situation, the journalist does not need to play a very active role as an interpreter of meaning.

In the United States, in contrast, the institutions of the public sphere are weak. Political parties are loose coalitions organized to compete for public office, not for expressing unified frames. The meaning of events is often a matter of internal party contention; to sponsor any given frame is to risk a potentially costly internal division that may weaken the party in competing for electoral success. On the issue of abortion, for example, the best strategy for Republican Party spokespersons often is to say as little as possible rather than to promote the pro-life frame in the party platform. As a result of this relative institutional vacuum, the mass media become *the* primary institution of the U.S. public sphere in performing the function of providing political interpretation.

Partly because of this function of giving meaning to the events of public life, certain journalistic conventions have developed in the United States that are unusual in Europe. These include, Hallin and Mancini (1984) argue, a greater tendency to frame and interpret and the use of narrative structures and images. The result of these differences in journalistic conventions and the nature of the public sphere is a greater opportunity for social movements to shape media discourse in the United States. The relatively smaller importance of institutional actors leads journalists to seek other interpreters, including social movement spokespeople. The consequence is that movement actors are generally more likely to be given standing in the media as interpreters of meaning, even though they must compete with rival movement actors, public officials, corporations, and private interest groups to get their ideas across.

The operation of the journalistic *balance norm* also opens opportunities for challengers, albeit in a complicated way. In news accounts, interpretation is generally provided through quotations, and balance is provided by quoting spokespersons with competing views. The balance norm is vague and the practices that it gives rise to favor certain frames over others. Organized opposition to official views is necessary to activate the norm, which, once invoked, tends to reduce controversy to two competing positions—an official one and the alternative sponsored by the most vested member of the polity.

The balance norm is not generally interpreted to include challengers unless they have already achieved standing. But even those challengers without standing can open doors for allies. In the U.S. antinuclear movement, for example, access to the media was greatly enhanced by the 1977 site occupation of the Seabrook, New Hampshire, reactor by the Clamshell Alliance. This action helped to define nuclear power as controversial, thereby invoking the media's balance norm. The chief beneficiary in terms of enhanced media standing was not the Clamshell Alliance but the Union of Concerned Scientists (UCS). As Gamson (1988, 235) puts it, "When demonstrators are arrested at Seabrook, phones ring at UCS." Preemption is one likely outcome for cultural challengers who use extra-institutional means to draw the attention of the media—their preferred frame increases in prominence through the words of others even though they do not themselves receive standing.

Of course, internal rivalries between movement actors can undermine such convenient divisions of labor. As Gamson and Wolfsfeld (1993, 123) point out, movements frequently offer multiple frames, each identified with different actors. Those who increase movement standing through their unconventional actions may find that their particular preferred frame is poorly represented by those who become the media-designated spokespersons. They may attack and attempt to undercut these spokes-persons.

The internal movement contest can easily become the media's story, distracting attention from the issue and blurring the preferred frame. There is an underlying tension between the more pragmatic and cynical culture of journalism and the more idealistic and righteous culture of movements. Movements, of course, do not have a monopoly on self-righteousness, moralizing, piety, and the like. Conventional politicians frequently exhibit these traits as well, but they often privately share the journalists' culture of cynicism in off-the-record contacts. They are playing a public role with a wink to journalists—although this does not make them immune to discrediting accounts when their private behavior blatantly seems to contradict their public persona.

Only those who are true believers are operating counter to the culture of journalism, but they are also operating counter to the culture of conventional politics. Most movement participants believe in an injustice frame and *are* indignant rather than faking it for public consumption. Movements hector people, including journalists, and call them to account. This righteousness is unappealing to those who are living with the inevitable compromises of daily life. This means, suggests Gamson and Wolfsfeld (1993, 120):

> that internal movement conflicts and peccadilloes will have a special fascina-
> tion for journalists, giving them an opportunity to even the score from their
> standpoint. The fall of the righteous is a favored media story wherever it can
> be found and movements offer a happy hunting ground.

Hence, a division of labor is likely to work only if there is a common frame and a willingness to subordinate concerns about who gets credit for being the messenger.

Cultural Resonances

Not all symbols are equally potent. Some metaphors soar, others fall flat; some visual images linger in the mind, others are quickly forgotten. Some frames have a natural advantage because their ideas and language resonate with a broader political culture. Resonances increase the appeal of a frame by making it appear natural and familiar. Those who respond to the larger cultural theme will find it easier to respond to a frame with the same sonorities. Snow and Benford (1988, 210) made a similar point in discussing the "narrative fidelity" of a frame. Some frames, they wrote, "resonate with cultural narrations, that is, with stories, myths, and folk tales that are part and parcel of one's cultural heritage."

Talking Politics (Gamson 1992a) suggests that this level of analysis can best be captured by focusing on the dialectic between cultural themes and counterthemes. Themes are safe, conventional, and normative; one can invoke them as pieties on ceremonial occasions with the assumption of general social approval, albeit some private cynicism. Counterthemes typically share many of the same taken-for-granted assumptions but challenge some specific aspect of the mainstream culture; they are adversarial, contentious, oppositional. Themes and counterthemes are linked with each other so that whenever one is invoked, the other is always present in latent form, ready to be activated with the proper cue.

Discursive strategies, for challengers as well as for other players, center on the use of language, symbols, and images that resonate with cultural themes and counterthemes. The basic strategy is to invoke the resonances of themes and counterthemes on behalf of one's preferred frame and to neutralize the potential resonances of the most important rival frames. Framing contests often involve competition over a particular theme.

The battle over the symbol of "equal opportunity" in the United States is a good illustration. In the civil rights movement of the early 1960s, demonstrators carried signs demanding "Equal Opportunity for all Americans." The demand was that every individual be given a fair chance to succeed, regardless of skin color. The symbol of equal opportunity utilizes the resonances of a powerful self-reliance theme that invokes a world in which, with resourcefulness, pluck, and a few breaks, even a poor bootblack can become a millionaire. Rival frames, far from competing for the resonances of this theme, were vulnerable to the charge that they denied individuals the opportunity to succeed on the basis of their efforts and talents.

But during the 1970s, as policy controversy centered on affirmative action programs, the power of these resonances was effectively challenged and neutralized. The major vehicle, a *reverse discrimination* package sponsored by a neoconservative advocacy network, fought over the same resonances. Advocates embraced equality of opportunity and colorblindness, claiming that this is what they sought while opposing only those programs in which "some are more equal than others." The power of the original resonances was effectively neutralized since there is no effective resonance when discordant frames play the same note.

When dominant frames that are being challenged rely heavily on resonances with certain themes, challengers can sometimes compete by invoking the countertheme. The antinuclear movement, for example, found themselves confronting a dominant frame that invoked the theme of progress through technology. Existing alongside this theme is a countertheme that emphasizes harmony with nature rather than mastery over it and suggests that technology can sometimes develop a life of its own. To quote Emerson, "Things are in the saddle and ride mankind." The more we try to control nature through our technology, the more we disrupt the natural order and threaten the quality of our lives. Much popular culture reflects the countertheme: Chaplin's *Modern Times,* Huxley's *Brave New World,* Kubrick's *2001,* and countless other films and books about mad scientists and technology gone wild, out of control, a Frankenstein's monster turned on its creator.

Before there was an antinuclear movement, supporters of nuclear power handled the potential tension between nuclear energy as a symbol of technological progress and as a symbol of ultimate destruction by a strategy of nuclear dualism. Atoms for peace invoked the progress theme and the countertheme was safely compartmentalized in the nuclear weapons discourse. By invoking the resonances of this countertheme, the antinuclear movement was able to interpret events in ways that helped to destroy nuclear dualism and, with it, the resonances of nuclear power as a technofix for America's energy problems.

Narrative Fit

A theory explaining the success of frames must be based on an epistemology that recognizes facts as social constructions and evidence as taking on its meaning from the master frames in which it is embedded. The essence of frame contests is competition about what evidence is seen as relevant and what gets ignored. Does this social construction model force us to abandon all attempts to evaluate the implications of empirical evidence of the claims of competing frames? Does it reduce us to what Goodman (1978) calls a "flabby relativism" in which all frames have an equal claim in interpreting the world?

Clearly, there is an important and complicated relationship between the characteristics of events and the success of certain frames. The accidents at Three Mile Island and Chernobyl did not make life easy for those who frame nuclear power as technological progress. But neither did they provide empirical refutation of this frame. As its advocates will point out, Three Mile Island "proved" the "defense in depth" safety system works; even in this most serious of nuclear accidents, no one was killed and no significant amounts of radiation were released. And Chernobyl "proved" the wisdom of the U.S. nuclear industry in building reactors with the reinforced concrete containment structures that the Chernobyl plant lacked.

Frames provide a narrative structure that leads one to expect certain kinds of future events. No spin control is necessary when the frame already suggested that such events were likely. But when the narrative confronts unexpected events, some *ad hoc* explanation and special effort is required by advocates to sustain the frame. A poor narrative fit with unfolding events that cannot be ignored places the burden of proof on those frames that must make sense of them; with a good narrative fit, unfolding events carry the much easier message: "I told you so."

Conclusion

To assess cultural impact, this essay urges a focus on mass media discourse. This is the most important forum for understanding cultural impact because it is the major site in which contests over meaning must succeed politically. One can use the outcomes at this site to read relative success in cultural contests. More specifically, one can use it to define acceptance and new advantages in cultural terms—where acceptance is measured by standing and new advantages by relative success in having ones preferred frame and its idea elements displayed there. This allows one to redefine the outcome categories of full response, co-optation, preemption, and collapse in cultural terms.

Cultural challengers operate on a playing field that is rarely level and is tilted against them to various degrees, depending on the issue domain. However, even an uneven contest does not prevent some challengers from success. The ones who succeed do so by overcoming deficits in production assets and acquiring the necessary know-how; by using media norms and practices to their advantage; by the use of discursive strategies that resonate with broader cultural themes and counterthemes; and by providing an expected scenario that can anticipate and include unfolding events easily and comfortably in its narrative structure. Of course, challengers may still perform as skillfully as possible and fail because their rivals are equally skilled and have additional structural advantages as defenders of the status quo.

Cultural success is important, but winning the battle of words does not guarantee success in other realms. It is a necessary condition for success in changing policies and practices and one major factor in the set of sufficient conditions. But policy processes are political processes, and political influence does not operate only or primarily through persuading others through words and symbols. Nor are broader institutional and cultural practices determined merely by the outcomes in the mass media forum. Nevertheless, there is much evidence for ripple effects.

Success in media discourse is one important influence on public opinion and on which issues will be relevant for electoral politics. Losing the battle of words certainly adds to the difficulties of those who rely on other means of influence to shape public policy. Cultural and institutional practices are influenced by other factors as well, but the climate created by media discourse plays an important role in maintaining or changing them. Cultural impact is not everything, but it is a significant goal in its own right for cultural challengers.

Notes

1. This working model is a collective one, shaped by numerous discussions with my partners in research on the construction of abortion discourse in Germany and the United States—Myra Marx Ferree (University of Connecticut), Freidhelm Neidhardt (Wissenschaftszentrum Berlin für Sozialforschung), Dieter Rucht (University of Kent at Canterbury), and Jürgen Gerhards (University of Leipzig)—and by the participants in the Media Research and Action Project (MRAP) at Boston College. It is informed by a broad and eclectic literature. On the role of the mass media in framing issues, it draws especially on Tuchman (1978), Gans (1979), Gamson and Modigliani (1989), and Gamson (1992b). On the interaction of movements and media, the model draws on Gitlin (1980), Ryan (1991), and Snow and Benford (1988, 1992). On the role of public discourse in a democracy, it draws on Dahlgren and Sparks (1991), Entman (1989), Fraser (1995), Garnham (1986), Gerhards (1996), Habermas (1987, 1989), and Keane (1991). On the mediation of discursive interests, it draws on Rucht (1995). On movements as a field of organizations, it draws on Melucci (1989) and Klandermans (1992).

2. In the case of *Nightline*, this defense fails to deal with one of Croteau and Hoynes (1994) principal findings—that the most frequent guests were often *former* players, not those who were presently active.

Part II

Transformation

4

Contentious Politics in Complex Societies

New Social Movements between Conflict and Cooperation

Marco G. Giugni and Florence Passy

As several observers have pointed out (e.g., Luhmann 1982; Melucci 1996a; Willke 1991), complexity is a fundamental feature of contemporary societies. Social complexity stems both internally from a growing functional differentiation and externally from the emergence of a world system transcending national states (Willke 1991). As a result, unlike in traditional societies, the modern state has to act upon the social system to regulate the society. This intervention raises important problems, most notably that of governability: the state is always less able to warrant the governability of complex democracies (Crozier, Huntington, and Watanaki 1975) and to pilot the society alone. This new situation is a major challenge for the modern state. The classical regulatory media, such as the law, money, and the legitimate use of violence, are no longer sufficient for the regulation of complex societies (Willke 1992). To face such complexity, the state needs new sources of legitimacy, for in complex societies no one can anticipate the long run consequences of most decisions, which implies that the state does not have the authority for autonomous decisions (Willke 1991). In addition, information and knowledge become crucial resources for social regulation (Papadopoulos 1995). In brief, the modern state has lost its hegemony over the pilotage of society and is now engaging in a process of coregulation (Willke 1991).

As students of the so-called third sector have pointed out (e.g., Bütschi and Cattacin 1994; Evers 1990, 1993; Willke 1991), certain organized groups of the civil society play an important role in this joint regulatory process. Yet, few social movement theorists have examined the role of

81

movements therein, a lack of attention that stems from the very definition of social movements. Most recent research on social movements is based on the assumption that they challenge the political authorities and the state. According to this view, movements and their allies form a conflict system opposing political authorities. To be sure, this view of social movements as a specific form of contentious politics must not be abandoned, quite on the contrary. Nevertheless, we must acknowledge that various contemporary movements also engage in a series of activities that do not necessarily entail a conflicting relationship with powerholders. Apart from activities aimed at reproducing the sense of belonging and collective identity of participants or at raising citizens' consciousness about specific political issues, movements also cooperate with the state. In complex societies, where the solution of public problems as well as the elaboration and, above all, implementation of policies are particularly difficult tasks, certain movements tend to become integrated into the decisional, regulatory, or implementation phases of the political process. These activities are increasingly important and supplement, for certain movements, the range of activities that characterize them as a specific form of contentious politics. In particular, the new social movements undergo a process of incorporation in state structures and procedures. Thus, new social movements intervene in the political process in two ways: by challenging existing or proposed policies and by helping to elaborate and enforce government policies.

The integration of social movements aimed at the coregulation of complex societies is the result both of a bottom-up and a top-down process. On the one hand, movements try to expand the channels of access to the state in order to increase the chances to reach their political aims. One way for movements to do so is to become integrated into state structures and to address their claims from inside. At least in western democracies, social movements have constantly been knocking at the state's door in order to obtain, at a minimum, procedural impacts and, preferably, substantial impacts. Women's movements are a good example. Since their early days, women's groups have looked for institutional channels to influence the state from within. Women's organizations are nowadays invited to collaborate with the state to find solutions to inequality and discrimination. Thus, most western states have created structures (ministries, offices, etc.) jointly with the movements in order to improve the condition of women. On the other hand, states are also working to integrate social movements and their organizations. In various policy areas, they face an information gap and lack the knowledge needed for appropriate problem solving. As a result, they look for collaboration with actors and organizations in the civil society that possess such knowledge and may help them in the regulation of society. An area that is subject to this kind of coregulation between the state and social movements today concerns the AIDS epidemic. Several western governments have asked gay movement organizations to "lend" them knowledge and experience in order to respond to this plea in a more effective manner.

As we shall see below, certain institutional features of the state provide favorable opportunities for the creation of cooperation between social movements and the state. Although all western states are confronted with the complexity of society, not all of them share the same willingness to share their power with sectors of the civil society in the regulatory process. With respect to AIDS, Switzerland is a "school case," for the government has incorporated several movement organizations that have become real partners in the search for solutions to this social problem (Bütschi and Cattacin 1994).

In this chapter, we focus on the cooperation between social movements and the state. We argue that certain contemporary movements are following a path of incorporation in state structures that is nevertheless qualitatively different from the traditional path of institutionalization followed by labor movements. We address this new kind of incorporation both theoretically and empirically. First, we define cooperation and single out the main differences with three traditional models of interest-mediation: the pluralist, the corporatist, and the policy-network models. Second, we examine the conditions that make cooperation more likely. Third, we provide an empirical illustration of this process drawn from two policy areas: development aid to Third-World countries (targeted by the solidarity movement) and environmental protection (targeted by the ecology movement). Finally, we discuss several implications of cooperation both for social movements and the state. It is important to note that the focus of this essay is on the national level. We only marginally deal with cooperation taking place in the international arenas, which yet is a crucial aspect of the cooperative behavior of movements (Passy 1995; Smith and Pagnucco 1995; Smith, Chatfield, and Pagnucco 1997). It is also important to remark that, although we argue that what we are witnessing is conflictual cooperation, in this chapter we will stress its cooperative side rather than its conflicting side.

What Is Cooperation?

According to the definition given in the introduction to this volume, a social movement is a sustained series of challenges to powerholders (Tilly 1994; see also Tarrow 1994a, 1996; Tilly 1984).[1] This definition clearly sees movements as the expression of an existing social conflict. Virtually all scholars who are interested in the political aspect of movements follow this line of reasoning (e.g., McAdam 1982; McAdam, McCarthy, and Zald 1996; Tarrow 1994a; Tilly 1995a). In addition, some include in the definition the use of unconventional and/or disruptive actions (e.g., della Porta 1996; Tarrow 1994a, 1996). Also scholars working within a different sociological tradition, although they strongly criticize what they see as political reductionism in the above definition, view the essence of movements in the underlying conflict of which they are the carriers (e.g., Melucci 1996a; Touraine 1984). They argue that a definition in terms of overt protest activities ignores a whole range of activities aimed at the construction and reproduction of individual and collective identities, which are seen as a fundamental dimension of social movements. However, they do not point to the fact that movements may not only challenge the powerholders, but also establish a cooperative relationship with them. Even an author like Melucci (1996a, 28), who has made a useful attempt to plotting social movements in the context of a broader variety of forms of collective action, including cooperation, still sees movements as the overt expression of a latent social conflict. Yet, even a cursory look at the relation between several contemporary movements and the state suggests that it is made both of conflict and cooperation.

Generally speaking, by *cooperation* we mean a relationship between two parties based on an agreement over the ends of a given action and involving an active collaboration aimed at reaching such ends. In our case, the two parties involved are the state and a social movement or parts of it, such as an organization or a group of organizations. Cooperation must be distinguished from three other broad types of activity carried out by movements, as shown in figure 4.1. *Protest* actions represent the typical means that movements have at their disposal to reach their goals. But movements can also voice their *opposition* to state policies in a discursive manner, for example, through proclamations, resolutions, and the like. Although the kind of involvement differs, both types of activity stem from a disagreement with government priorities, decisions, and policies. On the other hand, interactions between social movements and the state can also take place on the basis of an agreement over the ends of a given action. This type of interaction takes two different forms. When the agreement is located at the level of discourse instead of that of action, we speak of *consensus*. When the agreement is a matter of action, we define the interaction as cooperative.

Thus far, we have spoken of cooperation to define the latter type of interaction between social movements and the state. However, there is seldom full cooperation. The distribution of power between actors in a cooperative relationship is uneven: social movement organizations (SMOs) have much less power than the state. This leads SMOs to use an

FIGURE 4.1
A Typology of Social Movement Activities

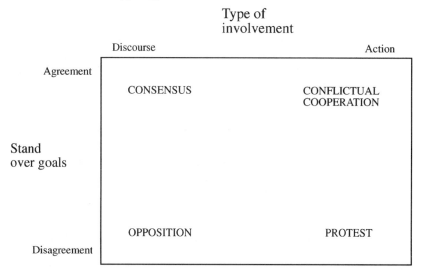

ambivalent strategy made of a combination of conflict and cooperation. Following Evers (1990), we call it *conflictual cooperation.*

Conflictual cooperation between social movements and the state occurs at different points in the political process. First, it takes place in the legislative arena and in the decision-making process. SMOs become integrated in the legislative process, for example, when a parliamentary committee needs specific competencies possessed by SMOs before an issue goes to the floor to be discussed and voted. Second, conflictual cooperation occurs in the administrative arena and in the regulatory process. Regulation refers to those state activities aimed at managing and problem solving through means that do not imply the adoption of new laws or the amendment of existing ones. This task is usually accomplished by state agencies. For example, the Environmental Protection Agency, created in 1970, is charged with the regulation of environmental matters in the United States. New opportunities stemming from the creation of agencies at the local, regional, national, and international level (in particular, on the European Union level), coupled with the need on the part of these agencies of specific knowledge about complex problems, have facilitated the integration of movement actors in the regulatory process. Third, we can observe conflictual cooperation still in the administrative arena, but with regard to policy implementation. Here the role of movement actors is particularly important, for the complexity of problems and tasks faced by the government is especially high in the implementation stages of the political process. In various policy areas, the state resorts to noninstitutional actors in order to implement the decisions taken on legislative and regulative levels. Often the state delegates certain tasks to these actors.

Similarly to what happens in the conflict system, social movements intervene in the collaboration system in various ways. Three broad types of cooperation can be distinguished in this respect. To begin with, the state can resort to noninstitutional actors in order to get information that may help reach certain decisions or realize them. Here collaboration takes the form of *consultation*. In this case, the movement has mainly an advisory role for the state. A deeper collaboration occurs when the movement becomes part of the structures in charge of taking or implementing a decision. In this case, we observe the *integration* of movements in panels, committees, working groups, or government agencies. Such integration is usually aimed at transferring information from the civil society to the state in order to help the elaboration of public policies. Finally, a still deeper cooperation implies a *delegation* of certain tasks, that is, a transfer of responsibility from the state to the movements on the operational level. This occurs above all in the phase of policy implementation, which in certain areas is becoming increasingly complex and difficult to be carried by state structures alone.

Each of these three types of cooperative interaction between social movements and the state can be carried at the *individual* or at the *collective* level. Although in this essay we focus on the collective level, it is important to make this distinction. In the first situation, for example, single members of SMOs are hired by the state to work in specific policy areas on the movement's agenda. A common instance of the second situation is the integration of certain SMOs in a committee created by the legislature or by the administration. In addition, within each type, regardless of its individual or collective nature, there can be different degrees of collaboration, which may be measured according to various criteria. Among these, the number of actors involved and that of contacts are certainly important ones for assessing the intensity of cooperation between social movements and the state.

On the empirical level, we may say that collaboration becomes stronger as we go from consultation to integration to delegation, as we shift from the individual to the group level, and as we get higher values on various indicators of intensity (number of actors, number of contacts, regularity of contacts, etc.). Figure 4.2 gives an overview of the types of cooperative behavior according to the three criteria we have just described.

Interest Intermediation and Conflictual Cooperation

If we go through the history of social movements, we can easily see that the incorporation into institutional structures and procedures is not a new

FIGURE 4.2
Types and Degrees of Cooperation

	Individual Level	*Collective Level*
Consultation	– ———— +	– ———— +
Integration	– ———— +	– ———— +
Delegation	– ———— +	– ———— +

phenomenon. In particular, labor movements have followed a process of institutionalization in the polities of western countries. In part, also the new social movements, which apparently are less willing to become incorporated in state structures, have nonetheless institutionalized (Giugni and Passy 1997; Kriesi 1996; Melucci 1996a; Roth 1997). The political science literature offers a number of studies that deal with the system of interest mediation and, indirectly, with the institutionalization of social movements. The study of the processes of interest mediation involving interest groups (employers' associations and labor unions) gives us some clues for analyzing the cooperative relationship between social movements and the state. In this respect, we can distinguish between three distinct models of interest intermediation. The pluralist model stresses the negotiation between a plurality of interest groups within the political system and maintains that even the less structured and powerful groups can influence the political decisions (Dahl 1971; Polsby 1985). According to this view, the role of the state is to balance and reconcile conflicting interests in the society. In contrast, the neo-corporatist model maintains that only the most powerful groups are able to influence the political decisions through peak agreements (Cawson 1986; Lembruch 1993; Schmitter 1981). In this elitist perspective, the state plays a role of regulator of opposing interests in a strongly structured and closed system of interest intermediation, thus offering an opportunity to the most powerful actors to negotiate. Finally, a policy-network model has recently been brought to the fore (Marsh and Rhodes 1992; Smith 1993), which stresses the existence of a community of actors organized around specific policy areas and trying to influence the political decisions. Each network is relatively closed, but might change over time through the inclusion of new actors and the exclusion of old ones.

We argue that conflictual cooperation involving new social movements differs from these three models of interest intermediation (and of institutionalization) in at least five respects. First, as regards the *content of the exchange,* cooperation implies that organized groups possess specific knowledge needed by the state to regulate the society. As we have previously pointed out, in complex societies information becomes a crucial resource and the state has to rely upon organized groups that can transfer their knowledge to the state for a more efficient regulation of society. Several SMOs, for example, are knowledgeable about the AIDS epidemic or other health-care, environmental, or development-aid matters. The nature of the exchange between these organized actors and the state is different from the one described in the three models of interest intermediation. Pluralist and neo-corporatist models focus on the exchange between labor movements and the state aimed at preserving a balance between conflicting interests and avoiding class conflicts. Conflictual cooperation with new social movements, on the other hand, involves an exchange of competencies and a transfer of knowledge aimed at problem solving.

Second, in conflictual cooperation nonstate actors and the state work together on a *common goal,* be it the protection of the environment, the aid to Third-World countries, the improvement of the conditions of women, or other goals. Unlike the pluralist and neo-corporatist models, here we are not in a situation of interest intermediation. SMOs and state actors try to find solutions to shared problems. Indeed, here lies the core of cooperative interaction. However, it still is conflictual interaction insofar as, although the goals are in common, there often is disagreement over the means for reaching such goals as well as over the extent of the proposed solutions. For example, labor unions cannot be said to act on the basis of an agreement with the state over the goal of a given policy. The asymmetry of power between employers' associations and unions reflects a difference of goals between the labor movement and the state (Offe and Wiesenthal 1980).

Third, conflictual cooperation has a *dialogical nature.* Social movements interact directly with state actors. In contrast, in the pluralist and neo-corporatist models, the state takes on a role of mediator, balancing and reconciling conflicting interests. In the area of industrial conflict, for example, employers' associations and labor unions negotiate in order to find compromises and the state regulates the negotiations. To be sure, the state is far from being a neutral regulator of conflicts (e.g., Kriesi 1980; Offe and Wiesenthal 1980) and generally facilitates the entrance of employers' associations, to which it provides more freedom of action. In the case of new social movements, we are in the presence of an unmediated interaction between organized groups of the society and the state. However, sometimes nonstate actors with divergent interests—for example, supporters of the economy versus those of the ecology—are involved in negotiations, whereby the state intervenes not as a mediator but as an actor directly involved. In such situation, negotiations form a policy network.

A fourth important difference between conflictual cooperation and the three traditional models of interest intermediation concerns the concept of *agency*. The space for action of social movements is greater in the former than in the latter. This is mainly due to the knowledge that certain movements have in comparison to state actors, knowledge that is a valuable resource and provides them with some power in the negotiations. If we accept the foucaultian argument that knowledge is power, in complex societies this is all the more true. Thus, knowledge opens a space for action that is much broader for new social movements than, say, for labor movements.

Finally, conflictual cooperation is typical of a *self-reflexive society*. The modern state is conscious of its own limits to pilot complex societies. According to Willke (1992), the state must regulate the society with more flexibility and adopt an ironic attitude to survive in complex societies. The consciousness by the state of its own limits represents a qualitative break that leads to a new attitude toward the organized sectors of the civil society. In this context, we are witnessing a shift toward a reflexive state (Willke 1991) or even a propulsive state (Morand 1991). This new kind of state has emerged in reaction to both the "authoritarian" way of piloting complex societies, promoted by the socialist tradition, and the autoregulation promoted by the liberal tradition (Willke 1991). The resulting new way of piloting the society relies upon organized actors of the civil society who possess specific skills, knowledge, and competencies that can be used in the coregulation of the complexity of modern societies.

The five aspects just mentioned clearly distinguish conflictual cooperation from the pluralist and neo-corporatist models. However, differences with the policy-network model are less obvious. In fact, sometimes collaboration between new social movements and the state forms a policy network, that is to say, a community of state and nonstate actors negotiating in a given policy area. The difference between conflictual cooperation and the policy-network model is analytical rather than empirical. The latter focuses on the form of negotiations, whereas the former looks at the nature of negotiations, which it defines as a combination of conflicting and cooperative strategies.

Conditions of Cooperation

A number of hypotheses can be formulated about the conditions under which cooperation between social movements and the state is more likely to occur. To begin with, the nature and outcome of a relationship based on collaboration depends on the characteristics and attitudes of the two parties involved. According to our first hypothesis, the type and intensity of cooperation vary as a function of the formal structure of the state. Here we can refer to the opposition between strong and weak states (Atkinson and Coleman 1989; Birnbaum 1988; Kriesi, et al. 1995; Waarden 1992). Strong states have concentrated (versus fragmented) structures of power, a coherent and effective public administration, and offer few points of access to external actors. These characteristics make them more effective in making and implementing public policies than weak states. Therefore, we expect them to be less likely to resort to external actors. For example, in a country such as France—the ideal-typical case of contemporary strong state—cooperation between social movements and the state should be less pronounced than in a weak state such as Switzerland.

A similar argument can be advanced for the prevailing strategies of the authorities to deal with challengers. Like the institutional structures, this is an aspect of the political opportunity structure, but referred to its informal side (Kriesi, et al. 1995). Our second hypothesis is that, in countries that are characterized by exclusive prevailing strategies of powerholders, cooperation with social movements is less likely to occur. The rationale for that is quite obvious: although cooperation is not identical to an inclusive strategy of the authorities, a cooperative relationship can only emerge to the extent that the latter accept movements as a legitimate and trustful partner. Thus, cooperation should be stronger in countries with inclusive strategies, such as Switzerland and the Netherlands, than in countries with exclusive strategies, such as France and Germany.

In addition to these two structural characteristics, there is a third, more conjunctural aspect of the state that partly influences the possibilities of cooperation between powerholders and social movements: the specific configuration of alliances at a given time (Kriesi, et al. 1995; Tarrow 1994a). When the main ally of a social movement is in the government, the chances of this movement to engage in cooperation with state actors should be greater. For instance, when the Socialist Party—the principal ally of the new social movements—leads the government, this movement family should tend to collaborate with the state to a greater extent than when right-wing parties rule the government. Thus, depending on the presence of movement allies in the executive power, the closedness of the state may become a relative openness. This hypothesis was verified in France when the Socialists seized the power and, despite the closedness of the state, several organizations belonging to the new social movements—in particular, anti-racist SMOs—suddenly became partners of the government. Once the Left lost the elections and was replaced by the Right, cooperation between these SMOs and the state faded away.

While the first three conditions refer to the state, the remaining ones regard social movements, the other party involved. In particular, we stress four relevant aspects in this context: the type of issue raised by the movements, their organizational structure, their strategies, and the knowledge they possess. To begin with, cooperation depends on the type of issue at hand. On the one hand, certain policy areas are more complex than others because they imply the consideration of a variety of technical issues. For instance, the area of environmental protection is particularly complex, due to the multiplicity of problems created by pollution and to the overlap of local, regional, national, and international levels of government intervention. In addition, the increasingly global character of environmental problems makes their management and resolution extremely difficult. On the other hand, certain issues are more threatening for the authorities than others (Duyvendak 1995; Kriesi et al. 1995) because they pose an electoral threat to powerholders or because they strike the core interests of the state. As they are a matter of strong disagreement, such issues are also less likely to become the object of cooperation. Thus, our fourth hypothesis is that cooperative interactions between social movements and the state are more likely to occur when the issues at hand do not pose a fundamental threat to the political authorities. In this respect, environmental protection and the aid to Third-World countries are certainly two domains that present a potential for collaboration. In these domains, there is a high degree of consensus, among political elites and among the general public, about the need to find feasible solutions to given problems.

A further condition of cooperation refers to the organizational characteristics of social movements. The state often looks for collaboration with sectors of the civil society. However, it does not do so at random, but it selects carefully its partners according to their characteristics. As the institutional approach to organizations suggests (Meyer and Rowan 1977; Zucker 1987), organizations with formalized and professionalized structures have greater access to the state, for governments and public administrations prefer to deal with groups that have working procedures reflecting their own routines. Thus, according to our fifth hypothesis, we expect cooperation to be facilitated by the internal structuring of SMOs, in particular, when the latter display a high degree of formalization, professionalization, centralization, and bureaucratization (Kriesi 1996).

The emergence of a cooperative relationship is also facilitated by the strategic and tactical choices made by social movements (Staggenborg 1988). SMOs that make use of radical or violent actions have fewer chances to become part of a cooperation system than those that opt for moderate and conventional forms of action. In fact, strongly formalized and professionalized SMOs prefer to adopt institutional means because the latter are more compatible with a formal structure and with the routines of a professional staff. Hence, our sixth hypothesis is that cooperation is more likely to take place with moderate movements (in terms of forms of action) than with radical movements.

Finally, as we have hinted above, cooperation depends on the knowledge possessed by social movements and their organizations. Public administrations increasingly rely on external actors (often in their capacity as experts) to manage and regulate public policies. However, in order to be considered by the authorities, these actors must have specific competencies in the domain in which they are asked to intervene. Knowledge may be theoretical as well as practical and gives SMOs the capability to find solutions in a specific domain. For instance, several environmental organizations hold theoretical knowledge on specific ecological issues, such as the destruction of rainforests, the impact of pollution on the change of the climate, the disappearing of animal and vegetal species, and so forth. Theoretical knowledge stems from their own research or from scientific studies that they politicize by interacting with the state. In addition, SMOs also have practical knowledge coming from their experiences in the field and from the elaboration of concrete projects. Movements may thus become part of an epistemic community (Holzner and Marx 1979), that is, a community of experts who share a given set of beliefs and values over policies to be applied (Haas 1989). Therefore, our seventh hypothesis maintains that cooperation between social movements and the state is a function of the amount of knowledge possessed by the latter in given policy areas and on given issues.

Conflictual Cooperation in Solidarity and Ecology Movements: An Illustration

The hypotheses proposed above represent several avenues for research into the causes and mechanisms of the conflictual cooperation between social movements and the state. In order to provide a preliminary test, we have conducted an empirical investigation on the basis of official documents of state agencies, interviews, and a structured questionnaire sent to a sample of SMOs of the ecology and solidarity movements in France and Switzerland, two important new social movements.[2] The goal of the questionnaire was to provide a picture of conflictual cooperation by comparing two different movements in two different political contexts over time. It included a series of questions about cooperation with government institutions (national, regional, or local), such as its origins, nature, and form (consultation, participation in committees, etc.), changes in the cooperative relationship, and the margin for action of SMOs. The empirical material we have in our hands is not sufficient for a strong test of our hypotheses, but gives us some interesting insights into the kind of state-movement interaction we focus on in this chapter. In particular, it suggests that conflictual cooperation between certain new social movements and the state is becoming a central feature of western societies and that it varies according to the type of state as well as to the type of movement.

The Solidarity Movement

As of today, the solidarity movement has reached perhaps the strongest degree of cooperation with state institutions. This holds less for issues pertaining to the national context, such as immigration and political asylum, than for matters related to the international context, particularly development aid. Traditionally, noncontentious interactions between the state and social movements have taken the form of subsidies granted to some SMOs. In France, this type of interaction became institutionalized in 1959, at the peak of the decolonization process, with the creation of the ministry of cooperation and the aid and cooperation fund (FAC). The latter was aimed at funding the development of former colonies in Africa. The entire public aid to development amounted to 42 billion French francs in 1995 (including large shares from other ministries) and made France the second highest contributor to public aid in the world. However, only a small part of this budget is devoted to the funding of nonprofit organizations. In 1994 SMOs received 49 million French francs from the FAC (that is, for the cofinancing of specific projects).[3] France ranked fifteenth among the eighteen Organization for Economic Cooperation and Development (OECD) countries as to the share of public aid to development generated by SMOs. Furthermore, as table 4.1 shows, the share of financial resources of organizations dealing with international solidarity issues coming from public funds has increased steadily in the nineties, both in relative and absolute terms, after a decline in the late eighties.[4]

TABLE 4.1
Financial Resources of French SMOs
International Solidarity Issues

Year	Total Resources	Resources from public funds	% resources from public funds
1985	1342	376	28
1986	1355	379	28
1987	1607	434	27
1988	1828	402	22
1989	2101	462	22
1990	n.a.	n.a.	n.a.
1991	2274	773	34
1992	2534	887	35
1993	2753	1019	37
1994	3197	1279	40

Notes: Absolute figures are in millions of French francs. Figures for 1990 are not available.
Source: Commission Coopération Développement

Already at this stage, which is not an indicator of cooperation *per se,* state agencies and bureaucrats prefer to deal with relatively formal and professional SMOs that have working procedures similar to their own (Meyer and Rowan 1977; Zucker 1987). For example, we can read in a joint document of the ministry for foreign affairs and the ministry of cooperation in France that, in order to be eligible for obtaining state funds, an association, among other organizations, must have been created at least three years before and hold general assemblies as well as regular reunions.

Besides the rise in funds granted by the French state to various SMOs of the solidarity movement, in recent years the cooperation between the two parties has turned toward a growing consultative role of SMOs and toward their integration in the the state's structure. Several bodies have been created in order to facilitate the dialogue and collaboration in the policy area of development aid. The most important is the committee cooperation development, created by the ministry for foreign affairs in 1983, an institution within which government representatives and organized groups of civil society participate on equal terms. In general, the latter participate as members of groups of SMOs (*collectifs,* in the French jargon), which the state recognizes as legitimate partners in various advisory bodies. The committee cooperation development has a consultative role on issues pertaining to international solidarity; in addition to gathering and diffusing information about and sensitizing toward Third-World issues, it suggests policies and interventions to the competent state bodies, mainly (but not solely) the ministry for foreign affairs and the ministry of cooperation.

The integration of the solidarity movement is further facilitated by several institutions that have been created with the aim of facilitating the links and coordination with state agencies. The office of associative life, which has recently replaced a number of previous bodies, is the most important one. This office is linked both to the ministry for foreign affairs and to the ministry of cooperation. It is in charge of managing the relations with SMOs that deal with development issues and functions as the interface between these SMOs and the state, in particular the two aforementioned ministries. In addition to the office of associative life, the other bodies further facilitate the interface between the SMOs of the solidarity movement and the ministry for foreign affairs with regard to issues related to development aid.

The committee cooperation development itself has promoted other opportunities for the coordination between SMOs and government agencies. For example, a number of thematic networks have been created in 1983 with the aim of integrating into several sectoral policies the reflection of a series of other actors in the field of development, SMOs among others.

Here we have a clear indication of the significance of knowledge possessed by social movements for them to establish a cooperative relationship with the state. The goal of these networks is precisely to take advantage of the know-how of nonstate actors for the elaboration and implementation of policies in the domain of development aid. A similar function is fulfilled by the two existing solidarity programs: the solidarity program water, created in 1984, and the solidarity program habitat, launched in 1988. However, these programs are, in principle, open to a wider range of collective actors, both public and private.

The process of incorporation sped up during the nineties. In 1991, for example, a discussion began, aimed at creating a new contractual relationship between the state and the SMOs and at reaching a better coordination of activities, as well as a simplification of the existing procedures. At the beginning of 1995, in addition, the joint programming committee was created in which both sides are represented on equal terms. As the term indicates, this device provides for a joint programming of interventions in the nongovernmental sector and helps the integration of SMOs beginning in the conceptual phase of cooperation policies.[5]

The situation in Switzerland displays both similarities with and differences from that of France. As in France, in the early years, the collaboration between the state and the SMOs of the solidarity movement was based mostly on the provision of financial resources. From the point of view of the state, the Swiss government, unlike that of France, has never had a strong and well-defined foreign policy. The small size of the country, the internal fragmentation of power, the absence of colonial tradition, and, above all, the neutrality principle have prevented the formulation of a clear policy in this domain. As a result, development-aid policies also had a slow start. But, at the same time, they were carried out almost exclusively by private institutions (Schild, n.d.) In this context, the intervention of the state was mostly limited to providing financial help to private initiatives and organizations. This situation has changed starting from the sixties. The Swiss agency for development and cooperation (SDC), the governmental agency in charge of policy elaboration and implementation in this domain, was formed in 1961. Since then, the role of the state in development aid has sensibly increased. Today, cooperation between the Swiss state and SMOs dealing with Third-World issues is very strong on all dimensions, but especially on the operational level.

As far as financial resources given to SMOs are concerned, at first glance Switzerland seems to be less generous than France. If we compare the total financial resources given to SMOs by the SDC in 1995, shown in table 4.2, with the share of public funds of French SMOs in 1996 (table 4.1), we see that the latter are more than six times larger than the former.[6] If we subtract international public funds in the French case (about three

TABLE 4.2
Financial Contributions to SMOs
Swiss Agency for Development and Cooperation

Year	Contributions to programs	Credits for small projects	Programs for volunteers	Total
1995	37.7	1.5	10.6	49.8
1996	41.6	1.8	8.5	51.9
1997	42.5	2.0	8.6	53.1
1998	43.5	2.2	8.8	54.5
1999	44.4	2.2	9.0	55.6

Note: Projected figures in millions of Swiss francs.
Source: Operationelles Organisationshandbuch DEH (15 November 1995)

quarters of the total), the funds of internal origin are still higher than those provided by the SDC. However, if we take into account the different size of the two countries and the consequent larger state revenue in France, we see that Switzerland does not seem to invest less than France to support SMOs in the domain of development aid. Furthermore, the figures for Switzerland do not include all the contributions to SMOs. In 1995, for example, the SDC gave 187 million Swiss francs to private organizations of development.[7] Hence, it is reasonable to say that the Swiss government has given more support to SMOs than France. According to a recent survey, the share of public funds amounted to 47 percent of the total budget of private institutions of development in 1994 (42 percent from the central government).[8] Yet, the contributions by the French government display a steady increase in recent years, while those by the Swiss government are expected not to rise in a dramatic way.

With regard to consultative procedures, cooperation in the area of development aid is noteworthy. The SMOs of the Swiss solidarity movement (specifically, those devoted to mutual aid) take part in policy formation in this domain. The SDC provides a number of channels for the institutional dialogue with SMOs, both with respect to the significance in terms of development policy of various political issues and with regard to specific issues of development policy on the operational plan, mutual information, and negotiations about financial contributions to SMOs. Such institutionalized dialogue sped up in the nineties, particularly in the aftermath of the United Nations conference on environment and development held in Rio de Janeiro in June 1992, which gave a decisive boost to the collaboration between governments and SMOs in various countries. Today, several organizations have access to the Swiss state in extraparliamentary committees, both temporary and permanent, created by the government, such as the committee for development aid.

Although incorporation in consultative procedures, unlike in France, is a typical feature of the Swiss political system in general, much like in France, it is facilitated by the gathering of SMOs in peak organizations. The so-called Working Community, which gathers five among the major SMOs that deal with humanitarian and development issues, is the privileged interlocutor of the government and the SDC for matters related to development aid. SMOs are often consulted by the government as experts on development matters. The case of Intercooperation is quite instructive. Largely supported by the government (39 million Swiss francs in 1995), it was created in 1982 with the aim of providing the government with a tool for the implementation of projects in the area of development. It gathers seven among the major SMOs and functions as the interface between SMOs and state institutions, a role similar to that played by the nine collectives in France.

If a dialogue exists in Switzerland between the SMOs and the state in connected but distinct policy areas such as development aid, humanitarian aid, human rights, aid to refugees, and, as we describe below, environmental protection, cooperation on the operational level is particularly strong in the first of these areas. It is here that a genuine cooperation takes place. The traditional policy, based on the provision of funds to SMOs so that they can carry out specific projects in Third-World countries or educational initiatives in Switzerland, has been complemented with a policy of operational collaboration, particularly starting from the early eighties. Indeed, development aid is the policy area in which sectors of the civil society actively intervene in the enactment of political decisions, not only in the elaboration of those decisions. This cooperation occurs in two basic ways. On the one hand, the government contributes financially on an institutional basis to projects developed by the SMOs by means of the SDC. The share of funds thus granted usually covers between 30 and 50 percent of the costs (59 million Swiss francs in 1995). On the other hand, the Swiss government can also delegate the execution of projects or programs elaborated on the state level to one or more SMOs through the so-called *mandats de régie* (65 million Swiss francs in 1995).[9] In this case, the government keeps control over operations. In this division of tasks, SMOs are responsible for the operational planning, the execution, and the monitoring of the project, but they often intervene in the project's conceptual phase as well. The SDC is responsible for the general policy, the project's general planning (though, as we have seen, SMOs are consulted on this level as well), and the project's evaluation.

With the *mandats de régie*, cooperation between social movements and the state reaches its peak. SMOs that are seen as being of public utility become an instrument of the state in order to reach its goals in a given policy area. SMOs are chosen according to their specific skills and knowledge, get funds, and are responsible for the implementation of the planned projects. In fact, some private organizations were active in development aid before the Swiss government became involved in this domain. Afterwards, development aid has become increasingly centered around the state and put under its control. But, as compared to the French situation, which is mostly based on a subsidizing state, the Swiss case reflects the model of the inciting state (Bütschi and Cattacin 1994), whereby the latter invites and stimulates the intervention of organized groups of the civil society, in particular social movements. In the case of development-aid policies, this relationship is becoming so close that we may ask whether certain SMOs of the solidarity movement are not becoming part of the state. Is it the same in the ecology movement?

The Ecology Movement

The complexity of environmental problems in contemporary society forces the state to search for forms of cooperation with the ecology movement. SMOs such as the World Wide Fund for Nature (WWF), both in France and Switzerland, or the Swiss League for the Protection of Nature, have long established collaborations of various kinds with the political authorities at different administrative levels. However, in comparison to the solidarity movement, the cooperative relationship of the ecology movement is not only less pronounced but also more decentralized, bearing on the regional and local levels, in addition to the national one (although these administrative levels are not absent from development-aid policies, both in France and Switzerland). Various environmental SMOs collaborate with local authorities (municipalities, local councils, communal committees, etc.). This cooperation may consist of occasional or regular consultation and expertise, participation in local committees, or intervention in specific projects (planning, monitoring, evaluation, etc.). For example, the Movement Defense of the Bicycle is regularly consulted by the city of Paris since 1986, and has participated in a local committee and a working group since 1996; the Swiss Foundation for the Protection and Planning of Landscape is officially consulted on environmental issues by the government since its creation in 1970, and collaborates at the cantonal and communal level as well. The Swiss Society for the Protection of the Environment (SPE) is occasionally consulted by local authorities, such as in Geneva, and collaborates with other cities as well. In addition to national SMOs, various local SMOs have established a cooperative relationship with the political authorities on the communal level.

Most typically, however, SMOs display a multilevel intervention. Thus, the French National Movement of Struggle for the Environment has established different forms of cooperation with the ministry of the environment, as well as with several regions, department, and communes since 1981. The forms of cooperation range from regular consultation to participation in committees and working groups. Similarly, the SPE in Switzerland cooperates with the Swiss Agency for the environment, forests, and landscape, with the federal office of energy, with the canton of Geneva, and with several cities. Some SMOs, however, tend to concentrate on the national level. This seems to be the case of Pro Natura, an old organization of the Swiss ecology movement, whose collaboration with the Swiss Agency for the environment, forests, and landscape goes back to the midsixties, when it was charged with the management of a national park. Later on, the relationship with this regulatory agency came to include several consultative tasks and, most important, the delegation of specific projects to the SMO. In addition, during the eighties and nineties, this SMO has engaged in some kind of cooperation with other governmental bodies that deals with environmental or energy issues and even with the SDC. The cooperation with the latter also includes the delegation of projects.

A second difference between ecology and solidarity movements lies precisely in the kinds of activities undertaken by SMOs in a cooperative relationship. Less involved in the operational aspects of specific projects, environmental SMOs often intervene in the political process as consultants. Thus, their role consists mainly of providing information and expertise to state actors. At the beginning, they were consulted only occasionally. Later on, consultative procedures on a regular basis were created. Finally, participation in extraparliamentary committees has become more common. The origins of the incorporation of parts of the ecology movement in decisional and regulative processes is twofold. On the one hand, the growing complexity and global character of environmental problems force the authorities to look for support from SMOs that have specific knowledge about these as well as related matters. The emerging concept of sustainable development, which the 1992 conference in Rio de Janeiro has brought to the fore, clearly calls for the collaboration of various state and nonstate actors, on both the national and international levels. On the other hand, environmental issues are increasingly dealt with through a problem-solving behavior based on cooperation among various actors (Amy 1990; Wälti 1993; Weidner 1993). This holds true above all in a country such as Switzerland, where the search for consensus is a general feature of the political system (Linder 1994; Lijphart 1984; Neidhart 1970). This would explain, at least in part, why cooperation between the ecology movement and the state is more pronounced in Switzerland than in France.

However, the clearest examples of cooperation between environmental SMOs and the Swiss state can be seen on the international level. On the one hand, the scope and complexity of international problems require the intervention of knowledgeable external actors. On the other hand, it is in this domain that the ecology movement has pushed the collaboration with state agencies and bureaucracies farthest in order to put into practice the concept of sustainable development. Some SMOs acting in the international arena work so closely with state powers that they can hardly be seen as parts of a social movement. One of the most powerful among them is the World Union for the Nature, a peak organization whose members are states, public bodies, and SMOs that work in partnership to protect the natural world and its resources.

Just as in the area of development aid, cooperation between the ecology movement and international administrative and regulatory bodies has increased after the 1992 United Nations conference on environment and development. Indeed, the Declaration of Rio includes explicit references to the participation of the civil society in the management of environmental problems. In addition, the so-called Agenda 21, also a result of the conference, calls for a partnership between SMOs and the political authorities for its execution, not only on the international level, but also on the national level. Thus, in the nineties, cooperation between the ecology movement and the state has strengthened in various European countries, including France and Switzerland. A publication of the Swiss department of foreign affairs, for example, mentions eighteen SMOs that cooperate with the Swiss government on environmental matters, including several SMOs of the solidarity movement. This also shows the growing interconnection between environmental and development issues on the world scale.

Discussion

Our empirical illustration shows that social movements do not only challenge powerholders, but establish a cooperative relationship with state actors and structures, and that collaboration between the state and the two movements studied here has increased, beginning in the eighties. The illustration also reveals that collaboration between SMOs and the state is not a homogenous process, but varies across countries as well as across movements. In this respect, the seven hypotheses that we have proposed find some support. To begin with, we observe a striking difference between the two national contexts under study. In France, collaboration between social movements and the state remains strongly based on the provision of financial resources to SMOs and on sporadic consultation. In other words, collaboration between SMOs and the French state exists, but its intensity is rather low. Cooperation is much more widespread and intense in Switzerland, where the political process is characterized by the joint action of state agencies and social movements in several policy areas, especially on the operational level (that is, delegation of tasks) in the case of the solidarity movement. This difference is partly a result of divergent state structures and prevailing strategies of the authorities toward challengers. Switzerland is a paradigmatic case for the favorable opportunities offered to social movements to influence the state (Kriesi et al. 1995). A strongly decentralized and open state, coupled with a long tradition of integration of nonstate actors, facilitate the emergence of conflictual cooperation as a type of interaction. France is also a paradigmatic case, but in the opposite sense, making collaboration with social movements more difficult.

The characteristics of social movements also influence the interaction with powerholders. In particular, conflictual cooperation depends on the type of issues. While both ecology and solidarity movements can collaborate with the state because they raise issues that do not threaten the political authorities in a fundamental way, we can nevertheless make a distinction between these two movements. As our illustration suggests, the solidarity movement has established a stronger cooperative relationship with the government, as compared with the ecology movement. This holds true above all for the SMOs that intervene in development-aid policies. Policy implementation and task delegation involve SMOs of the solidarity movement to a greater extent than environmental SMOs. This difference, at least in part, is due to the type of issues raised by the two movements. Development aid is less threatening for the political authorities than environmental issues. Challenges regarding certain environmental issues, such as nuclear energy and the building of national routes, do threaten the core state interests and, therefore, are subject to opposition and protest rather than consensus and cooperation.

The other hypotheses concerning the influence of social movement features on the emergence of conflictual cooperation also found some support. First, SMOs that collaborate with the state, such as the WWF, Caritas, or Swissaid, are more formalized and professionalized than those that are excluded from this kind of interaction. Second, SMOs that collaborate with the state tend to have moderate goals and to adopt moderate forms of action. Third, SMOs that collaborate with the state display specific knowledge, both theoretical and practical, that is often instrumental in bringing solutions to new emerging problems in given policy areas. In sum, although the quality, scope, and intensity of cooperation are substantially different in France and Switzerland, the examples of solidarity and ecology movements suggest that social movements engage in cooperative interactions in addition to contentious interactions.

Implications

The emergence of cooperation—specifically, conflictual cooperation—between social movements and the state has a series of implications for both these collective actors. Repercussions for social movements are threefold. First, with regard to the organizational structure of movements, cooperation presupposes the existence of well-structured and competent SMOs, but, in turn, it induces the concentration and conglomeration of movement resources. To engage in collaborative interactions with the state is very demanding in terms of resources (Bütschi and Cattacin 1994). Thus, movements that enter a cooperative relationship with the state tend to become bigger in size, more professionalized, and more bureaucratized.

Second, regarding the nature of movements, cooperation implies a social recognition of SMOs by the state, but one that can also change their characteristics and role. On the one hand, in order to engage in a cooperative relationship with the state, SMOs need to moderate their actions and goals, for the state tends to avoid collaboration with radical SMOs. Cooperation, in turn, produces moderation. Cooperation means that a compromise must be reached. Therefore, the actors involved need to moderate their goals. The distribution of power among the various actors will determine who has to grant more concessions. Social movements, even when they are integrated in the structures of the state and even if they possess knowledge useful for state agencies, obviously have much less power than the state. This does not mean that the latter will not have to make concessions, but it will do so to a lesser extent.[10] Thus, SMOs in a cooperative relationship tend to moderate their goals. On the other hand, incorporation into the state challenges the movements' identities. Even when they collaborate with the government, SMOs are critical toward official policies. They try to promote their goals and find new opportunities to influence existing policies, but the state makes the rules of cooperation. This provokes not only a moderation of movement goals, but also the shifting away from a critical role toward the action of the state. SMOs carry a social conflict that they help to politicize and bring a critique of the action (or inaction) of the state in given areas; once they begin to cooperate with the state, their identity as social movements changes. The search for a compromise becomes the underlying logic of movements that look for cooperation with state agencies and bureaucracies. Two options are available at this stage. SMOs can adapt to their new function and alter their identity, to the point of becoming semistate organizations (Linder 1987) or, alternatively, they can keep their movement identity and take part in a form of collaboration with the state that, following Evers, we have called conflictual cooperation.

Finally, cooperation with the state affects the levels of mobilization of social movements. If collaborating opens up new institutional channels for SMOs, it also has a negative impact on the amount of protest events produced by movements and the volume of participation in those events. On the one hand, SMOs tend to shift from mobilization to interest representation. In other words, they concentrate their energy and resources toward the obtainment of their goals within institutional arenas, thus neglecting their typical means (street demonstrations, political campaigns, etc.). In doing so, they lose public visibility and the potential for recruiting new members, who provide them with legitimacy and negotiation power to be used in collaborative interactions with the state. In the worst situation, this will lead them to be cut off from their social support. On the other hand, cooperation with the state may deepen the fragmentation within the movement. The incorporation of the movement's moderate wing may increase the conflicts with its radical wing. In fact, integration is often used by political authorities as a strategy to weaken a social movement (Karstedt-Henke 1980). The moderates become even more moderate due to their integration within conventional arenas, while the other wing radicalizes even further. This worsens the internal conflicts and eventually leads to the movement's demobilization.

Conflictual cooperation also has a series of implications for the state. A first set of repercussions has to do with the internal organization of the state. To begin with, cooperation affects the efficacy of the state in two opposing ways. On the one hand, negotiations with social movements slow down the decision-making process. Consultation and the search for compromise with external actors makes the decisional process longer and more complex, hence also less efficient. Switzerland is a good example (Linder 1987). However, the efficacy of policy implementation increases, especially in states that have a weak administrative body. When the state delegates the implementation of programs to external actors, administrative costs diminish and the effectiveness of implementation carried by more knowledgeable actors increases. The Swiss state's delegation of the implementation of development projects to the solidarity movement provides an illustration of this process. In the area of development aid, state actors often are less competent than SMOs, some of which had projects in the Third World long before the creation of the SDC. Therefore, they have developed valuable skills and knowledge, an experience in the field, and structures in Third-World countries, allowing for a better implementation of programs. The Swiss state still lacks these capabilities. Therefore, the delegation of tasks represents an important advantage in terms of efficacy of policy implementation.

Second, conflictual cooperation affects the legitimacy of the state. Following the participatory approach to democracy (Pateman 1970), according to which citizens are "ideal citizens"—that is, we-thinkers (Barber 1984) naturally oriented toward the production of the public good—cooperation between organized sectors of the civil society and the state can be seen as contributing to a more legitimate democracy. In this perspective, states that have created structures (relational programs, in Willke's terminology) to promote or facilitate cooperation with external actors, such as SMOs, add to their legitimacy by inciting participatory democracy. In contrast, following the liberal approach to democracy, according to which citizens have their own definition of the public good, are free agents making free choices (Gould 1988), and are not naturally oriented toward "the" public good, an increase in the number of external actors raises the problem of the balance between private or particular interests within the state and the definition of the public good. In this perspective, states ground their legitimacy on neutrality and on the existence of institutional procedures that allow for the regulation of private interests (Gianni 1994). The intrusion of various private actors who pursue their own interests within the state raises the problem of the redefinition of institutional procedures in democratic states in order to define the public good. If, at least in theory, democracies must provide for universal access (Willke 1991), in practice, access is not the same for everybody. Certain organized actors have more resources and greater access than others. Moreover, the distribution of power among these actors when they are in a relationship of collaboration with the state varies. Swiss democracy provides a good illustration of that to the extent that neo-corporatist arrangements not only exclude certain actors but are also unbalanced with regard to the actors who participate (Kriesi 1980). The problem of access raises the question of the legitimacy of decisions taken by state actors. The state no longer is the defender of the public good. Furthermore, with the intrusion of private actors, the state runs the risk of fragmentation. Due to the incorporation of organized groups of the civil society into the state aimed at pursuing sectoral interests, the state risks becoming more fragmented, losing a global view of the society, and, as a result, modifying its action.

Third, cooperation with social movements entails some organizational adaptations by the state. The political authorities develop several structures aimed at controlling the implementation of programs and public policies and at institutionalizing the cooperation with external actors. As we have seen, both the French and the Swiss administrations have developed structures of coordination in the areas of development aid and environmental protection.

Finally, and perhaps most important, conflictual cooperation produces a transformation of the role of the state. As we have pointed out at the outset, modern democratic societies are increasingly complex and differentiated. The state is less and less capable of warranting the governability of complex democracies. As Willke (1991) has underscored, the civil society includes many organized actors who compete for the piloting of society. Social movements participate in this competition. In order to face the growing complexity and differentiation of society, the state relies on these actors. Their incorporation and the cooperation thus established improve the flexibility and adaptability of the responses to the complexity of society (Willke 1991), but, at the same time, change the role and nature of the state. Its traditional role, whereby the state has the upper hand over the piloting of society, is transforming, and this task tends to be shared with other actors. In addition, collaboration between the state and organized groups in society—that is, an increasing interpenetrating of the state and the civil society—helps to stabilize the conflictual relations between them (Evers 1990). This calls for a different way of ruling the power and a different type of state, which becomes a regulating state that looks for compromises, or even consensus, in order to pilot an increasingly complex society.

Conclusion

This implication suggests to us some final considerations about the impact of movements on social change. First of all, the emergence of cooperative interactions between social movements (particularly, new social movements) and the state in certain policy areas raises the question of whether we are witnessing a traditional process of institutionalization of challengers, or, on the contrary, whether this is a qualitatively new form of incorporation of noninstitutional actors into the political system. As we have hinted in our discussion of the differences between the traditional models of interest intermediation and conflictual cooperation, we think there are good reasons to see the outline of a new type of incorporation. Differences between traditional trajectories of institutionalization and conflictual cooperation as to the content of the exchange, the sharing of goals, the dialogical nature of the exchange, the place of agency, and the self-reflexive character of society suggest that new social movements have undergone a process of incorporation into the political system that is substantially distinct from the one labor movements have followed decades before. Whether this is only a temporary condition of movements or a permanent trait of the contemporary society is impossible to ascertain. It could well be that, once the knowledge of social movements has been transferred to the state, the latter will not need them anymore and the process described here will come to a stop. Or maybe it will continue even in the absence of a practical need of knowledge and expertise by the state.

Only the future can tell us which way will eventually be followed. The important point, however, is that, at some point in the history of modern societies, important sectors of a family of social movements that see their *raison d'être* in contentious political actions have begun to engage in co-operative interactions with political authorities and state structures. This has had two main consequences. On the one hand, it has expanded the range of actions displayed by social movements. In a way, in addition to a repertoire of contention, one could now speak of a repertoire of cooperation when referring to new social movements. Just as somewhere around the mid-nineteenth century the old action repertoire was replaced by a new action repertoire that gave birth to the modern social movement (Tilly 1986, 1995a), perhaps the end of the twentieth century will have witnessed a second broad transformation in the modalities of interaction between the political power and the civil society.

Thanks to the example of conflictual cooperation, we can see the role that social movements play in the transformation of society. Far from simply being a result of large-scale social changes, movements contribute to its transformation through their presence and actions. In our case, their impact is on the structure of the state and on the political process itself. However, we cannot draw a firm causal arrow in one or the other direction. As della Porta (forthcoming) has shown in the case of the public discourse over the policing of protest, there is no simple causal nexus between movement actions and social change. Rather, social movements and change go hand in hand, mutually influencing each other, as in conflictual cooperation, whereby movements are part of a process of change that might result in a transformation of the nature of the state and its relation with the civil society.

Notes

We would like to thank the participants of the Think, then Drink seminar held by the Committee of Historical Studies at the New School for Social Research and those of the staff seminar held at the Department of Political Science at the University of Geneva, where we presented previous drafts of this paper, for their comments and suggestions. We especially thank Hanspeter Kriesi for his detailed criticism.

1. For a similar definition, see Tarrow (1994a).

2. Of the 48 questionnaires we sent out in the two countries (20 in France and 28 in Switzerland), 12 were returned with enough information to be included in the analysis (4 in France and 8 in Switzerland). We supplemented this small dataset with interviews conducted with 6 other SMOs in both countries and with official documents about the collaboration of state agencies with SMOs in the development-aid and environmental policy areas.

3. The entire financial help by the French state to SMOs on international-cooperation matters amounted to more than 300 million French francs in 1992. This figure includes support to associations of volunteers, cofinancing of projects, and information activities.

4. These figures include both national and international public funds. The latter comes above all from the European Union (75 percent) and, in 1994, amounted to 76 percent of the total public funds.

5. Despite our focus on the national level, SMOs dealing with Third-World issues have established a dense network of relationships with international institutions. In the case of the solidarity movement, the European Union, the United Nations, and the World Bank are three crucial points of intervention for SMOs. Each has specific bodies for the exchanges between SMOs as well as between them and official institutions. In addition to putting pressure on the international administrative bodies with the aim of increasing and improving the institutional support to development aid, SMOs acting on the international level operate as consultants and help the implementation of policies.

6. To make a gross comparison of the two tables, figures for France must be divided by a factor of four, which is more or less the exchange rate between the French franc and the Swiss franc.

7. Reported in *La Suisse* + *le Monde*, no. 3, 1996.

8. Reported in *La Suisse* + *le Monde*, no. 3, 1996.

9. Four organizations currently receive the *mandats de régie:* Helvetas, the Graduate Institute of Development Studies, Intercooperation, and Swisscontact.

10. We should note, however, that the state is not equally strong in all policy areas. For example, it is generally weaker in the economic domain than in the areas of development aid and environmental protection.

5

To Move Mountains
Collective Action and the Possibility of Institutional Change

Elisabeth S. Clemens

> Men make their own history, but they do not make it just as they
> please.
>
> —Karl Marx (1978, 595)

Human agency is limited, Marx's caveat reminds us, by the constraining, obdurate character of the social world, by those "circumstances directly found, given and transmitted from the past" (595). For all that men and women have tried to secure far-reaching reorganizations of their collective existence, the object of these efforts resists, often successfully. The potential of collective action to produce significant social change, therefore, is shaped in large part by the character of what may be changed. Whether a mountain can be moved depends as much on the character of the mountain as on the resources, strategies, and commitment of the would-be mover.

If social movements matter in part because they produce social change, then a theory of movement outcomes must be a theory of the relationship between protest or insurgency and those durable aspects of social organization. Yet efforts to trace the connections between the characteristics of challenge and those of change have been discouraged by theoretical formulations in which extensive *indeterminacy,* often in the form of state breakdown, is identified as the most salient outcome of successful challenges to sovereign institutions and the proximate condition for significant social change. Protest is portrayed as producing opportunities, openings, or vacuums within which new forms of social organization may be constructed. Developed most explicitly in the analysis of social revolutions, this form of argument makes it difficult to attribute social change to collective action in nonrevolutionary settings.

This difficulty is evident in the very restricted conceptions of social change that have been linked to movement activities. Typologies of movement outcomes have focused on the ability of movements to secure access or additional advantages from political systems (e.g., Gamson 1975; Amenta, Carruthers, and Zylan 1992), neither of which necessarily entails a more fundamental reordering of existing institutions. In contrast to successful revolutions, which are portrayed as profoundly disruptive of social order, social movements at most appear to alter the roster of participants or to secure marginal changes in the distribution of benefits. Such explanations do not address the relation of insurgency or mobilization to the less-than-catastrophic but still profound alterations of social order that constitute a goodly portion of what we recognize as social change.

"Institutional change" provides a useful label for this category of noncatastrophic transformation of the basic rules of the game or principles of order that characterize a particular society at a particular point in time. The contrasts among familial, communal, and bureaucratic authority suggest what is at stake in such change—alterations in the basic procedures for making collective decisions can transform relations of power and the distribution of valued goods. The past centuries have seen sustained, if not always successful, efforts to diminish the roles of race and gender as principles of hierarchy in social life. But if so much is at stake in existing institutional rules, how is it possible to transform a part of the social order without disrupting the whole, producing the cascade of indeterminacy that figures prominently in classic accounts of revolution? After posing this dilemma, this essay draws on recent developments in institutional theory to characterize sources of more bounded indeterminacy, moments and social locations in which not everything is possible, but more than one thing is. The various new institutionalisms provide a vocabulary for identifying different dimensions of social durability and for locating organizational alternatives in situations unmarked by widespread institutional breakdown.

Discontinuities in Theory

How, and under what conditions, do social movements change political institutions? What is surprisingly difficult about this question is not the construction of an answer—a difficult task, but not surprisingly so—but the location of precedents for this task. Surveying Marxist, revisionist, and modernization accounts of the French Revolution, Lynn Hunt

(1984, 3) argued that "the revolution merely serves as the vehicle of transportation between long-term causes and effects; as a result, the emergence of a revolutionary politics has become a foregone conclusion." For all their theoretical differences, she argues, these traditions share "a preoccupation with origins and outcomes" that precludes granting a significant causal role to underdetermined political agency and, therefore, to the actions of central interest to the study of social movements. In such accounts, the mobilizations, strategies, and tactics that concern social movement theorists appear as mere surface ornamentation, obscuring the more muscular forms of structural social change.

One response to this implicit denigration of social movements and political agency is exemplified by the work of Charles Tilly (1993) and Jack Goldstone (1991), both of whom make a fundamental analytic distinction between the possibility and the process of revolution, between revolutionary situations and revolutionary outcomes, between state breakdown and revolution. These distinctions identify points of heightened indeterminacy in the flow of social reproduction. Wars, population pressures, and fiscal crises all contribute to an expanded space for political agency. And then, history happens. One party to a conflict suppresses or outmaneuvers the other. Revolutionary outcomes are shaped by the intentions, interests, and ideologies of the contestants under conditions of societal indeterminacy, but things would have turned out differently had the roles of winner and loser been reversed. Thus large-scale social change generates conditions under which politics may be not only contentious but consequential.

This analytic strategy of distinguishing opportunity from political process effectively reestablishes the role of political agency—and therefore of movement activity—in the study of revolution, although at the cost of presuming a degree of disconnection between the sources of breakdown and the determinants of change. But when transposed to the study of nonrevolutionary social movements, the problem reappears. If nonrevolutionary contention is defined by the absence of competing claims to sovereignty, then existing political elites are by definition always the winners. The presence of political challengers may make it more difficult for elites to pursue their interests, but movements do not change the fundamental shape of the outcome. Without the indeterminacy of state breakdown, social movements would seem to lack the opportunity for exercising political agency *except* insofar as it is allowed by existing institutional rules (e.g., movements may be able to secure new types of government funding, an exercise of agency practiced also by a multitude of other claimants). Access and advantage define the range of possible movement outcomes insofar as they are the forms of change most easily conceptualized within this theoretical framework. The possibility of institutional change, of a nonrevolutionary transformation of the prevailing rules of social order, is obscured by the presumption that widespread institutional breakdown or contested sovereignty is a necessary precondition for more fundamental social change.

Understanding the links between collective action and institutional change requires a theoretical account of how social movements act as agents of change *in the absence* of the profound indeterminacy that is attributed to moments of state breakdown or revolutionary situations. To do so, let us return to Tilly's claim that revolutionary situations are distinguished from other moments of contention by multiple sovereignty, when "two or more blocs make effective, incompatible claims to control the state or to be the state" (1993, 10). Revolutionary politics does not constitute a distinct form of action but is the product of existing repertoires of contention played out in a revolutionary situation. But if it is possible to imagine a continuum of contention, one may also define revolutionary situations as one end of a continuum of indeterminacy. Just as there may be multiple claims to control the state, there may be multiple contenders to sovereignty over family, church, workplace and so on.

One way to restore a claim to the determination of social change by collective action is to argue that contradictions among social institutions generate sufficient indeterminacy to allow a space in which collective action may produce significant change. This involves a modification of the predominantly temporal understanding of indeterminacy that has informed studies of revolution, apparent in the use made of Ann Swidler's argument about "unsettled times" (1986; e.g., Goldstone 1991, 445). If state breakdown or revolutionary situations are marked by the contemporaneous "unsettledness" of large portions of a society, in nonrevolutionary times we may distinguish between relatively settled and unsettled social locations.

In this construction, movements are seen as exploiting locales of indeterminacy generated by the conflicting logics of adjacent social spheres. In the nineteenth-century United States, for example, organized labor mobilized in response to contradictions generated between a growing capitalist economy and a body of labor law premised on medieval relations of master and servant (Orren 1991). This formulation repeats the logic of the distinction between revolutionary opportunities and processes: "structural" social change generates contradictions or indeterminacies that constitute arenas for conflicts among challengers and established elites. Change, insofar as it happens, does not take the classic revolutionary form of a fundamental breakdown and subsequent reordering of the polity but rather of a realignment of various institutional orders, a moving of boundaries, and in some cases, the subsumption of one institution by another. To the extent that contradiction is in the eye of the beholder, however, movements may take a more proactive part in generating or expanding indeterminacy. If agency is enhanced by the intersection of multiple social structures, then part of the cultural work of a movement may be to heighten awareness of such intersections, to increase the salience of institutional contradictions, and to expand the sense of indeterminacy surrounding a particular social locale. Faced with these opportunities, movement actors may seek either to exploit recognized indeterminacies or to discover them.

Dimensions of Institutional Durability and Instability

To understand when and how collective action can produce significant institutional change, we must attend not only to the characteristics of movements but also to the character of that which they seek to change. This task is eased by the development of "new institutionalisms" in many of the social sciences. Although grounded in distinctive intellectual lineages (for overviews, see Powell and DiMaggio 1991; Scott 1995; Steinmo, Thelen, and Longstreth 1992), the various institutionalisms all seek to account for durable or regular aspects of social life, including those regularities that are central to such processes of social change as scripts for collective action. To simplify a complex set of literatures, three basic foundations of such regularities can be identified: the distribution and normative salience of practices, beliefs, and sanctions (see Crawford and Ostrom 1995).

Rather than pitting these arguments against one another as competing theories of societal durability, it is useful to conceptualize the various institutionalisms as potentially complementary accounts of the production and reproduction of regular patterns of social action. Understood as potentially autonomous sources of societal durability (Tilly 1998), each type of institutional effect may afford more or less potential for disruption by challengers, and, taken together, the various dimensions may either reinforce or undermine one another. By dissecting the multiple sources of societal stability, one may discern not only the capacities of collective action to disrupt that stability but also the conditions under which challengers will have the capacity to institutionalize alternatives of their own.

The discussions that follow elaborate on a single model of institutional change. Rather than portraying a sequence of social breakdown, indeterminacy, and reconstruction, this analysis links challengers' capacities for disruption to the character of their contributions to a transformed social order. Certain movements, I argue, demonstrate repeated affinities for distinctive types of institutional alternatives that, if those movements succeed, may become the templates for new institutions. Yet the threat presented by a particular institutional alternative is itself shaped by the character of societal durability at a particular place and time. In a social order structured by relations of dependence, domination, and exploitation, the capacity to articulate ideological alternatives is of less consequence than the ability to escape interdependence. Just as round pegs may not fit into square holes, different movements may be required to move different mountains.

The Interdependence of Practices

What are the sources of societal durability? Perhaps the most basic form of institution is rooted in habit, particularly in those habits upon which others come to depend, the "reciprocal typification of habitualized actions" that Berger and Luckmann identify as the origin of institutions (1966, 54). For those economic historians who have embraced the banner of institutional analysis, the development of webs of interdependent practices is a primary source of durable, even though potentially inefficient, social arrangements. The classic example is provided by the relations among typewriters of both the mechanical and human variety. A particular arrangement of keys, designated QWERTY by the upper left-hand letters, was adopted to minimize the frequency of jams caused as hammers criss-crossed one another in the early machines. Typists then learned this arrangement, some investing the time and effort to learn to type by touch. Consequently, even though mechanical hammers are long gone and the old arrangement has been repeatedly demonstrated to slow typing speeds, the widespread distribution of the skill of touch-typing on QWERTY keyboards has locked-in this particular arrangement (David 1985; North 1990, 93–94). Such widespread interdependence of habits and practices cements social relations.

Social life is rife with comparable examples. The distributions of potentially interdependent practices not only entrench durable patterns of interaction but also shape relations of power and dependence. Given general knowledge of the practices of raising a crop or building a barn and the resources necessary to perform these activities, a community may be capable of supporting itself; absent such practical knowledge and necessary resources, members of that community will be dependent on the expertise of outsiders or the opportunities to earn the means with which to purchase their subsistence. As de Tocqueville (1955, 38) recognized throughout his analysis of prerevolutionary France, shifts in the distribution of the capabilities to act were entwined with changes in the distribution of power. The increasing dominance of the central government was visible in the changing map of social competence and the inequities that dependence generated:

All the great highways and even the local roads from one township to another were maintained by the public funds and it was the Council that drew up plans for them and made the contracts. The Intendant supervised the work of the engineers, while the subdelegate recruited the forced labor it involved. The activities of the local authorities were confined to the upkeep of parish roads, which gradually fell into a shocking state of disrepair.

By comparison, the capacity of New England townships to build their own bridges signaled their greater autonomy with respect to the central government.

To the extent that the interdependence of practices undergirds societal stability, there are at least two methods for social movements to disrupt these regular patterns of interaction and to challenge the relations of power that are built upon them (movement may also exploit disruptions produced by exogenous forces). The first seeks to develop alternatives to unequal relations of interdependence. In its most extreme form, this may involve withdrawing from the broader web of social interaction through formation of self-sufficient utopian communities (Kanter 1972). Short of such exits from interdependence, movements may strive to develop alternative patterns of interdependence that generate fewer relations of inequality or domination. In the U.S. labor movement, for example, numerous unions organized their own factories to hire their members, their own banks to collect savings and provide loans, and their own newspapers to inform the working class. Employers' associations, not surprisingly, forcefully opposed many such worker-led efforts to exit from the web of market exchanges (Clemens 1997, chap. 4; Frank 1994). Similarly, second-wave feminism fostered woman-owned and operated bookstores, garages, health clinics, and cultural festivals, organizing the provision of goods and services in ways that obviated the need to engage in exchanges with men (Ferree and Martin 1995, Part III). The by-laws for one feminist organization in Ohio specified its dedication "to build a cooperative community of women with free space where we can learn to depend upon one another, work together, and live an alternative free of sexism" (quoted in Whittier 1995, 190). In European history, the links between withdrawing from interdependence and constituting a political challenge are clearly evident in both the development of socialist "ghetto parties"— tendentially separate worlds constituted through clubs, recreational groups, housing arrangements, and social services (Esping-Andersen 1985, 4–5)—and the effort of the Polish Solidarity movement to "turn its back on the state" in an effort to build an alternative or parallel society (Kumar 1993, 386). In both these cases, to use Albert O. Hirschman's terms (1970), exit may be a prelude to voice.

The second strategy is more closely linked to protest itself: to the extent that collective action can be based on scripts shared among challengers but unfamiliar to elites with their habitualized methods of containment, that protest has the potential to be far more disruptive of habitual relations of political conflict. As Charles Tilly observed, "even government officials and industrial managers of our own time generally behave as though they preferred demonstrations and strikes to utterly unconventional forms of collective action" (1986, 391; Tarrow 1994a, 25, 116). Routine protest, it follows, can be distinguished from truly disruptive protest. An unanticipated innovation in protest techniques may elude standard methods of repression. In the 1930s, for example, the invention of the sit-down strike by factory workers stymied police forces whose strategies were designed to contain or disperse picket lines at the factory gates (Fine 1969). Decades later, tactical innovations within the civil rights movement altered the forms and dynamics of contention within the American South (McAdam 1983). More generally, much of the social history of democratic political participation has involved the uses made of nonpolitical organizations—whether friendly societies, fraternal orders, unions, churches, reading clubs, or business enterprises—to forge collective identities that were not precommitted to existing political alignments and, thereby, to establish the basis for mobilizing challenges to dominant political institutions (e.g., Clemens 1997). Francesco Alberoni (1984, 20) captured this link between the construction of alternative solidarities and mobilization for social transformation in the concept of the "nascent state," which is "a proposal for reconstruction made by one part of the social system" at moments of "failure of those forces which constitute social solidarity." When durable social relations are not reproduced, alternative visions may be realized in these openings and then generate more far-reaching challenges to existing patterns of social order.

To the extent that societal durability is generated by webs of interdependence, it is possible to assess the disruptive potential of a particular social movement or subculture. Such an analysis would begin by identifying critical points of interdependence and would then inquire to what extent that movement is able to circumvent or substitute the ties that constitute the framework for existing forms of social order. Where most individuals have come to depend on wage labor to secure their subsistence and where this economic tie is the basis of social order, exit from domination centered on employment relations will require a movement to provide either alternative employment or some means of exit from the labor market altogether such as the development of self-sufficient, communal farms. In such a society, a movement lacking this capacity probably does not pose a serious threat to social order, no matter how heated its insurgent rhetoric.

These discussions of interdependent practices and non-routine protest also identify the macrosocial characteristics that enhance the probability that collective action will produce significant institutional change. As with so many theoretical discussions of social movements, a familiar curvilinear relation is evident. In societies where control of the methods and resources necessary for sustenance is highly centralized, withdrawal from these webs of unequal interdependence will be difficult; in societies where these methods and resources are widely distributed such that individuals or households can sustain themselves, withdrawal will be easy but there will be less reason to organize collectively. In societies with a very limited organizational repertoire, it will be difficult to coordinate protest in forms that are unfamiliar or uncontained by existing political institutions; in societies where repertoires are highly fragmented or idiosyncratic, it will be costly to coordinate large numbers of actors in some form of social protest. Where control of resources is somewhat dispersed, where necessary practices are widely known, and where those practices require the development of systems of coordination, social movements are more likely to succeed at organizing for exit or mobilizing to voice grievances effectively.

Uncertainty and Belief

The interdependence of practices is, however, only one potential source of social durability. A second line of institutionalist argument emphasizes the role of shared beliefs, values, or forms of thought rather than the web of relations among differentiated practices. From this second perspective, durable or regular patterns of social life reflect deeply embedded, at times sacralized, cultural components. Exemplified by the work of John Meyer and his many collaborators, this variant of institutionalist analysis portrays the diffusion of beliefs or normatively valued practices as a process of conformity (whether voluntary or coerced) to dominant logics of appropriateness. Such logics may be located at the level of "Western cultural myths" (Meyer, Boli, and Thomas 1987) or of particular organizational fields or industries shaped by exemplary firms, professions, or regulatory agencies (DiMaggio and Powell 1983; Meyer and Rowan 1977). In either case, the advantages (psychic, material, or otherwise) of conforming to already dominant logics of appropriateness facilitate the reproduction and extension of these core beliefs or values.

Given durable patterns of action and domination grounded in deeply held and widely shared values, under what conditions and with what strategies might collective action effectively challenge the existing order? As with the interdependence of practices, the critical issue is the availability of alternatives. In isolated groups, beliefs may be maintained in the face of seemingly contradictory experience because "competing explanations for events are not readily available and members reinforce one another's beliefs" (Babb 1996). Consequently, social durability grounded in shared beliefs may be undermined to the extent that the inevitability of those beliefs is challenged. Doug McAdam's analysis of the role of "cognitive liberation" in the process of mobilization underscores the power of subjective perceptions and evaluations of social arrangements, particularly oppressive arrangements: "Before collective protest can get under way, people must collectively define their situations as unjust and subject to change through group action" (1982, 51). While part of this process may be driven by perceptions of divisions among elites or the resources available to would-be challengers, the envisioning of alternative social arrangements or values is also a force for change.

Much of the work of social movements entails linking alternative values or visions to the experiences or grievances of potential constituencies. These processes have been captured by David Snow and his colleagues in their discussions of "framing." Of the four basic modes of framing work evident in micromobilization processes, the first two suggest possible indirect paths to institutional change through raising the visibility of alternatives and changing the distribution of shared scripts or interpretive schemas. In these terms, "frame bridging" discovers latent or passively shared frames and creates the basis for active sharing or cooperation by raising awareness of these common schema, while "frame amplification" alters the salience of existing values or of the ideational elements by which those values are linked to models of action in the world. The last two modes involve higher-order work that alters the relationships among cultural elements. "Frame extension" incorporates new problems in existing frames, while "frame transformation" links novel frames to meaningful activities, established beliefs, or recognized problems (Snow, Rochford, Worden, and Benford 1986; see also Babb 1996). In this way, new relations are crafted among diverse sources of belief and value:

> Out of a cultural toolkit of possible symbols, movement entrepreneurs choose those that they hope will mediate among the cultural underpinnings of the groups they appeal to, the sources of official culture and the militants of their movements—and still reflect their own beliefs and aspirations. (Tarrow 1994a, 122)

To what extent may processes of micromobilization also be processes of institutional change, altering the cultural frameworks that inform everyday life and core concepts of legitimacy in a society? Two recent studies of abolitionism cogently illustrate the capacity of movements to reorganize culturally available frames or discourses to alter prevailing understandings of a particular social issue. Examining the British movement to abolish the slave trade in the late eighteenth century, Leo d'Anjou (1996) argued that abolitionists were able to secure a rapid and widespread shift of public opinion in favor of abolition (if not legislation itself) by instantiating the problem of slavery within an Enlightenment discourse on human liberty, a religious reform discourse that valued benevolence, and the free-market claims of economists such as Adam Smith who denounced as unnatural exchanges based in either coercion or official state mercantilism. Anti-abolitionists were left with only the culturally thin claims of economic expediency and remained on the defensive until the slave trade was eventually abolished in the nineteenth century. A similar sensitivity to the multiplicity of frameworks that may be linked to a grievance or goal is evident in Stephen Ellingson's work on abolitionist debates and riots in antebellum Cincinnati. Defining discourse as "a relatively bounded set of arguments organized around a specific diagnosis of and solution to some social problem" (1995, 107), Ellingson argued that the eruption of anti-abolitionist violence undermined discourses that claimed slavery was compatible with either economic prosperity or the maintenance of law and order. Unintentionally, therefore, the violent actions of anti-abolitionists polarized local debate, allowing abolitionists to adopt "the arguments of the law and order group in a bid to define the movement as the champion of constitutional liberties instead of as the champion of the more unpopular ideas of emancipation and racial equality. They changed their argument to gain legitimacy, win new supporters, and forestall additional mob violence directed at them" (1995, 136).

Common to both accounts is the recognition that the multiplicity of cultural frameworks available for making claims to legitimacy constitutes the ground for strategic action and conflict on the part of movements, countermovements, onlookers, and political elites. Movements generate cultural indeterminacy by undermining established frameworks for understanding a social issue (e.g., slavery as the basis of economic prosperity), but that indeterminacy is itself structured by competing frameworks that have been deployed in the challenge. Again, this argument points toward macrosocial characteristics that will both facilitate movement-driven institutional change and set priorities for movement entrepreneurs. The more univocal and systematically integrated the prevailing cultural framework, the fewer alternative frameworks available for reinterpreting the experiences or grievances of a potential constituency. If alternative frameworks are available, but are highly personalized or idiosyncratic, it will be more difficult to construct a case for *collective* action. To the extent, however, that there are multiple, highly legitimate, cultural frameworks—democratic principles, religious faith, and personal loyalty, for example—the terrain will be far more favorable to social movements that seek not only to undermine but to replace dominant interpretations or prescriptions for action.

The history of abolitionism, however, provides an important caveat to any celebration of the institutional change that is possible under conditions of cultural heterogeneity. Even after slavery had been considerably discredited in cultural terms and eliminated in terms of formal law, relations of extreme racial inequality persisted. Perpetuated by webs of interdependence that sustained exploitative economic relations, the sharecropping system reconstituted racial hierarchies over those ex-slaves who remained. Forty acres and a mule was a necessary, but far too often unrealized, accompaniment to the ideological work of the abolitionists.

Sanctions and Rewards

To the extent that collective action can generate both exits from existing systems of interdependence and alternative ideological or cultural frameworks for living, the conditions for significant changes in patterns of social life are established. But while change may be possible, it may still be costly, painful, or difficult. Thus, in mobilizing to transform institutions, social movements must also confront a third source of social durability: the systems of rewards and sanctions that provide incentives to reproduce existing social relations and patterns of action. Among these, some are unavailable to challenging groups by definition, most notably the power of formal legal systems and the established police powers. Yet, in many other respects, challenging groups or oppositional subcultures can constitute alternative systems of rewards, status, and sanction in order to attract potential adherents and to discipline or entice current members who might be tempted to backslide toward conformity.

The capacity of a social movement to provide an alternative system of material rewards is closely linked to the establishment of alternative webs of interdependence. Reflecting on how movements or charismatic groups sustain their autonomy, both Max Weber and Robert Michels underscored the ability of these groups to provide a living at least for their leadership. The "staff" of such groups, according to Weber (1978, 246), have:

> an interest in continuing it in such a way that both from an ideal and a material point of view, their own position is put on a stable everyday basis. This means, above all, making it possible to participate in normal family relationships or at least to enjoy a secure social position in place of the kind of discipleship which is cut off from ordinary worldly connections, notably in the family and in economic relationships.

Although these mechanisms have long been criticized as enemies of charisma and genuine insurgency, such arrangements do contribute to another form of success that is often critical to a movement's ability to secure its goals: organizational survival. (See also Michels 1962, 138–40; Clemens 1993, 764–66.)

The use of rewards may reinforce alternative patterns of interdependence. The provision of selective incentives to members is another common tactic (Olson 1967); sickness benefits, funeral arrangements, and access to cooperative stores or housing have all been used to cement the ties of members to movements through the provision of material benefits as well as to escape from any monopolistic controls over these goods. Movement groups may also increase the dependence of members on the collectivity by requiring them to donate personal resources to a common pool; exit, thereby, is made much more costly and difficult.

Parallel strategies are evident in the ways that movements work to reinforce the advantages of ideological heterogeneity. Challenging groups and subcultures may construct alternative systems of status or recognition. Schismatic movements or religious heresies often generate distinctive models of virtuous behavior that contrast sharply with those of the established church and value actions that are more easily attained by those who are excluded by the recognized system of advancement within the clergy (Kaelber 1995). In modern societies, associations that might be viewed primarily as means to secure material benefits appear, upon closer inspection, as purveyors of status to their members. In the United States for example, fraternal orders provided elaborate hierarchical systems accessible to most white men who would undergo the sequence of initiations and organizational service (Carnes 1989; Clawson 1989). Somewhat less colorfully, early bar associations served to guarantee a small measure of immortality to their members by publishing obituaries or conducting memorial rituals (Espeland 1996).

What is given, however, may also be taken away. Just as challenging groups may be able to generate their own sources of status as a reward, adherence to the oppositional creed may be enforced by negative sanctions, particular when directed at those who already have made considerable sacrifices in rejecting dominant practices or beliefs. Members of a movement organization may be criticized for failing to shift their own beliefs to match developments in the official ideology or for "falling away" from a critical stance toward conformity with mainstream beliefs and practices (Whittier 1995, 196; see also Echols 1989, chap. 5). In this respect, the relationships across multiple strategies for securing change are evident. To the extent that members of a challenging movement have become embedded in alternative webs of interdependence controlled by that movement, the capacity of insurgents to punish their own is greatly enhanced. Insofar as challenging groups successfully establish alternative standards for evaluating behavior, their capacity to enforce actions that do not conform to mainstream values or rules is greater. In either case, a movement's ability to distribute rewards and sanctions enhances the robustness of those alternatives that are developed to existing patterns of societal order.

The Possibilities of Institutional Change

In certain respects, the use of institutional theory does no more than translate recent elaborations of the concept of opportunity structures into a different theoretical language. Where institutional analysis makes a distinctive contribution, however, is in providing the tools to determine whether and how much that opening matters. Beyond the dimensions of stability/volatility and cultural/institutional identified by Gamson and Meyer (1996) in their valuable elaboration of the concept of opportunity structures, the *centrality* of whatever it is that affords those opportunities is also of critical importance. In a social system in which shared beliefs are the mainstay of durable relationships, order is not threatened when members leave centers of settlement to colonize new regions or when missionaries head to foreign lands to secure new adherents for their faith. Under these conditions, ruptures in the webs of interdependence are likely to be less promising for would-be challengers than the development of genuine schism within core cultural institutions. Colonials may eventually take up arms to gain their independence and missionaries may be seduced by strange gods, but these developments need not act back upon the societal order of the metropole.

In other places at other times, however, durable social relations may be constituted primarily through webs of interdependence, even in conjunction with high levels of cultural fragmentation. Modern global capitalism, it may be argued, is precisely such a system. Consequently, the concern with oppositional identities that is so central to much of the work on the new social movements may have less prospect of producing significant institutional change than do the efforts to maintain tariffs, to protect domestic industries, or to redistribute landholdings in developing nations. These economic policies threaten a trans-societal system based on the continuous expansion of interdependence in ways that far exceed the elaboration of cultural critiques and oppositional identities. Indeed, movements based on cultural critique may be co-opted by consumer capitalism as the raw material of fads and fashions (Gottdiener 1985; Hebdige 1979). Without an assessment of the contribution of existing practices to societal durability, profoundly threatening forms of protest or withdrawal are not easily distinguished from collective action, which, from the perspective of institutional change, is little more than "sound and fury, signifying nothing."

This point must be tempered, however, by an argument that is woven through the preceding discussions of institutional change: the possibilities of change are increased by the presence of alternatives, and alternatives are transposable from one domain of action to another (Clemens 1997, chap. 2; Sewell 1992). Consequently, the development of oppositional practices or beliefs that, in their own right, may be no more than irritants to established systems of social life may prove to be seedbeds for collective actions that have the capacity to pose profound challenges to those dimensions of societal durability that are most important to the reproduction of particular societies at particular places and times. Absent the development of significant alternatives—whether of values, patterns of interdependence, or distributions of rewards—the indeterminacy of revolution is likely to be followed by reconstruction rather than transformation. As de Tocqueville (1955, vii) observed of those who are our very models of modern revolutionaries:

> they took over from the old regime not only most of its customs, conventions, and modes of thought, but even those very ideas which prompted our revolutionaries to destroy it . . . though nothing was further from their intentions, they used the debris of the old order for building up the new.

Without the elaboration of alternatives, indeterminacy leads to instability rather than institutional transformation. By developing alternatives, however, challengers may produce increments of the indeterminacy that they can then exploit to change their world.

Notes

For their comments and suggestions, I am grateful to Doug McAdam, Kelly Moore, Nella van Dyke, and the members of the Social Movements Seminar in the Department of Sociology at the University of Arizona.

6

Social Movements or Revolutions?
On the Evolution and Outcomes of Collective Action

Jack A. Goldstone

A major consideration in understanding the outcomes of contentious collective action is understanding the goals of the collective actors. If their goal is to overthrow the state, then, *ipso facto,* we are dealing with an attempt at "revolution." If their goal is to change a policy of the state or to influence the attitudes of some social group or society in general, we are dealing with a "social movement."

The Relationship between Social Movements and Revolutions

This distinction seems to make a clear demarcation between revolutions and social movements. Yet analysts of collective action have recently realized that the demarcation line may, in fact, be rather fuzzy. In a recent landmark article, Doug McAdam, Sidney Tarrow, and Charles Tilly (1996) have sought to redefine the spectrum of events that includes revolutions, social movements, and collective protests by bringing them under the single rubric of "contentious politics." Recognizing that processes of recruitment and mobilization, identity formation and goal articulation, confrontation with states and other collective actors, framing of situations and opportunities, and choosing from a (largely shared) repertoire of collective actions are common to social movements, revolutions, and other social protests (e.g., strikes), McAdam, Tarrow, and Tilly have laid out a path toward a synthetic analysis of a wide range of collective actions.

McAdam, Tarrow, and Tilly's definition relies on two elements to define contentious politics: "(1) it involves contention: the making of interest-entailing claims on others; and (2) at least one party to the interaction (including third parties) is a government" (1996, 17). Although I applaud their effort to underline the "continuities between movements . . . and revolutions" (1996, 27), in my view, this definition is both insufficiently specific and too narrow, thus leading us away from important issues in collective action.

First, this definition does not specify *who* is making the claims—whether it is another government, a set of scattered individuals, or even a single individual. Thus the actions of the Unabomber, who sent mail-bombs to government officials to make claims entailing renouncing technological progress, or of a terrorist who hijacks a plane and demands the government pay a ransom, fit this definition of "contentious politics," without being—in my view—either a social movement, a revolution, or collective action. Having a group or groups of cooperating individuals making claims seems to me an essential part of collective action; to fail to specify that wipes away the whole range of issues that arise regarding the cooperation of individuals and the coordination of their actions raised by public choice theory (see Lichbach 1996).

Second, I believe the definition is too narrow by specifying that government must be a party to the interaction. In many social movements, government enters late, or reluctantly. For example, in many confrontations of workers with employers, government is not a party to contention as much as a reluctant referee or negotiator among the contending parties. And while government may have triggered the recent U.S. struggles over abortion with the Supreme Court's *Roe v. Wade* decision legalizing abortion, the antiabortion movement has been mainly a direct struggle for the "hearts and minds" of the general population, with the antiabortion movement using TV commercials, sermons, and attacks on abortion clinics to discourage people from seeking abortions. But they have not targeted government as much as they have targeted the supporters of abortion. In other words, I believe that for much "contentious collective action," government may be a bystander or neutral party. Indeed, specifying in advance that government *must* be a party to "contentious politics" obscures some of the enormous problematic of government action—when and why *does* government enter into confrontation with social movements? How does the advent or terms of government entry into confrontation affect the evolution of the social movements?

The McAdam, Tarrow, and Tilly effort to define "contentious politics," however useful as a starting point, thus has major deficiencies. It may be preferable to speak of "contentious collective action," to denote the social movements/revolutions/collective protest spectrum of events, where "contentious collective action" is *any sustained effort at making claims on a society, or on other social actors, by a cooperating group (or groups) of individuals that provokes resistance.* This definition raises key issues regarding the genesis and maintenance of cooperation in collective action, and makes problematic the role of government in the resistance to collective action. Both of these are complex topics. I have explored the first issue elsewhere (Goldstone 1994); the second issue—the role of governments in the resistance to collective action—is the focus of this essay.

To return to the demarcation discussed earlier, how should we distinguish between social movements and revolutions? Despite the apparent clarity of the definition suggested at the outset, focusing on the *goals* of the collective actors is not enough. Odd though it may be, for many of the major revolutions of European history, the collective actors did not have the overthrow of the government as a major goal. In the English Revolution of 1640, Parliament sought to limit the scope of the King's action and defend religious fundamentalism; Parliament never sought to overthrow the government until the King took up arms to overthrow the Parliament. In the French Revolution, the representatives who assembled for the meeting of the Estates General sought to reshape the conditions of social status, financial exemption, and military and administrative service, as well as the royal tax system. But they did not seek to overthrow the king until the king's actions, and the population of Paris, forced them to those actions to defend their right to meet.

Conversely, some "social movement"-type goals may become revolutionary in contexts where the government adopts a stance of severe resistance to those goals. Thus the same goals that characterize social movements in some contexts characterize revolutionary movements in others. Is the human rights movement a revolutionary movement, or a social movement? You may get different answers in eastern Europe and China than in western Europe or the United States. Is the movement for racial equality a revolutionary goal? It was in South Africa, and sometimes seemed so in the United States in the 1960s, but is spoken of mainly as another social movement (along with women's rights, gay rights, disabled rights, etc.) in Europe and the United States today.

There are two dominant views of the relationship between social movements and revolutions. One view is that social movements and revolutions are wholly distinct. That view was enunciated most clearly by Theda Skocpol in her classic *States and Social Revolutions* (1979). Skocpol argued that social revolutions were a distinct phenomena that need a *sui generis* mode of explanation, a state-centered analysis that differed from the general analysis of collective action.

A second view, the one that Skocpol was contesting, argues that social movements and revolutions are similar, but differ in scale and scope. In this view, enunciated in Neil Smelser's (1963) *Theory of Collective Behavior* and given a more structural foundation in Charles Tilly's (1978) *From Mobilization to Revolution*, revolutions are the "extreme value" on a scale of social mobilization that reaches from protests to social movements to revolutions. This view is echoed in the recent McAdam, Tarrow, and Tilly 1996, 24) essay when they remark that "Revolutionary situations resemble extreme cases of social movement cycles." These are the two most widely held views of the relationship; they are depicted graphically in figures 6.1 and 6.2.

I wish to suggest a third image of this relationship, shown in figure 6.3. In this view, social movements and revolutions originate in similar processes, but evolve to different forms. In the social movement, the collective action of a particular group or groups remains focused on specific policy or attitudinal goals; the state may resist mildly, cooperate, or be neutral, but makes no effort to eliminate the movement or interfere with its actions. But in the case of a revolutionary movement, while it may begin as a movement to achieve certain policy or attitudinal goals, it evolves into a collaborative effort linking diverse groups with diverse policy goals into a movement that aims to overthrow the state. It evolves in that direction precisely because the state adopts a repressive stance of resolute resistance; it prohibits or sharply circumscribes movement actions, strongly opposes all who ally with the movement, and may seek to eliminate the movement and its supporters.

This last view of social movements and revolutions, therefore, suggests that both kinds of collective action start out with much in common—

FIGURE 6.1
Distinct Phenomena View of Social Movements and Revolutions

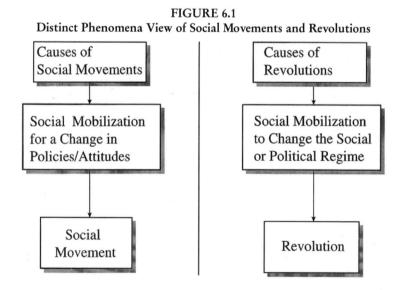

FIGURE 6.2
Continuous Phenomena View of Social Movements and Revolutions

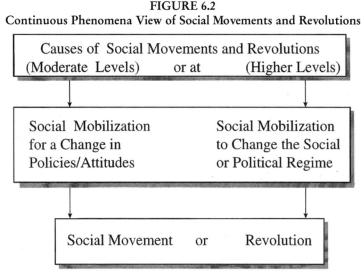

Causes of Social Movements and Revolutions
(Moderate Levels)   or at   (Higher Levels)

Social Mobilization   Social Mobilization
for a Change in   to Change the Social
Policies/Attitudes   or Political Regime

Social Movement   or   Revolution

FIGURE 6.3
Divergent Phenomena View of Social Movements and Revolutions

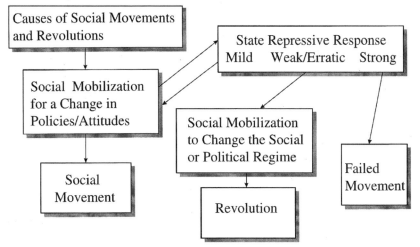

Causes of Social Movements
and Revolutions

State Repressive Response
Mild   Weak/Erratic   Strong

Social Mobilization
for a Change in
Policies/Attitudes

Social Mobilization
to Change the Social
or Political Regime

Social
Movement

Failed
Movement

Revolution

indeed, it is often not possible to tell whether a movement will or will not become revolutionary. The initial processes of grievance definition and framing, identification and mobilization of movement supporters, choices from a repertoire of collective actions, and relations with other supporting or resisting groups and institutions may be similar or even identical. But what happens next depends on the evolution of the movement in response to its interactions with supporters and opponents, particularly the government.

Acceptance of the legitimacy of the movement is likely to influence the framing, mobilization, and actions of the movement in a direction of limited protest, negotiation, and focusing its efforts on changes in legislation or attitudes to support its cause. However, rejection of the legitimacy of the movement by the government and/or opponents, and attempts to eliminate the movement and its supporters, are likely to shift framing, identification, mobilization, and action in a different direction. The nature and effectiveness of government tactics will determine what that direction will be. Where the government is able to focus its repressive measures squarely on the movement supporters, and use violence and imprisonment to curtail their actions, repression is likely to either end the movement or drive it underground and undermine its effectiveness. But where government responds with unfocused repression that terrorizes a wide range of civilians and groups either unconnected or only loosely connected to the movement supporters, or where repression is inconsistent and arbitrary, or where repression is limited by international or domestic pressures, the movement is likely to attract supporters while becoming more radicalized in its goals and actions. Framing, identification, mobilization, and action are then likely to veer in the direction of revolutionary mobilization, with the intent to overthrow the government that has, in effect, declared "war" on the movement.[1]

In examining the relationship between social movements and revolutions, it is worthwhile to first examine some interesting parallels in the prevailing theories of the origins of these two phenomena. It is remarkable that Skocpol's theory of revolutions, despite being developed in opposition to the generalized concept of collective action, nonetheless has striking similarities to the "political process" theory of social movements. Once these similarities are clear, it can be seen that the sharp demarcation between revolutions and social movements that Skocpol has drawn is illusory, and indeed not borne out by her own theory. At the same time, because these similarities are clearly parallels in similar paths of event-development, and *not* merely differences in degree or magnitude, the presumption behind the political process and resource mobilization view that revolutions are just an "extreme value" of social movement mobilization is not borne out either. Thus a close comparison of Skocpol's theory of revolutions and the political process theory of social movements will make clear the need to depart from the models shown in figures 6.1 and 6.2; and to move toward a synthetic but dynamic model such as that sketched in figure 6.3.

Social-Structural Models of Revolution and Political Process Models of Social Movements

Despite significant criticism, the dominant model of the origins of revolution in the social sciences remains that of Theda Skocpol as developed in her *States and Social Revolutions*.[2] She argued that social revolutions develop from the confluence of three distinct "social-structural" elements: (1) the weakness of a state relative to its external, international competitors, which either forces the state to seek to expand its resource extraction or, in extreme cases—such as defeat in war—weakens the state so that it cannot defend itself; (2) an elite that has leverage to effectively oppose the state because of its control of key resources that give it autonomy; and (3) structures of rural mobilization in peasant villages that enable coordinated action against landlords and state agents by the rural populace when state weakness is revealed. When, and only when, all three elements are present a social revolution is likely to occur. Although not developed to the same degree, Skocpol also noted the role of a fourth social-structural element: a marginal elite. A "marginal" elite is a group or groups who consider themselves entitled to a political role in society, but are denied that role by ascriptive characteristics used by the state to exclude certain groups from power. When state weakness, elite resistance, and popular mobilization create a social revolutionary situation, marginal elites act as the key players in reshaping the new political and social order, as they have not only the enmity to the old regime to lead a revolution against it but also the ambitions, education, and vision to create a new order.

At first glance, the political process model of social movements, developed first in Doug McAdam's *Political Process and the Development of Black Insurgency, 1930–1970* (1982), and since elaborated by David Snow, Rochford, Worden, and Benford (1986), Sidney Tarrow (1994a), and many others, seems strikingly different. Where Skocpol focused on the state, McAdam spoke more broadly of the "structure of political opportunities;" where Skocpol ignored agency and downplayed ideology, McAdam emphasized the importance of "cognitive liberation;" and where Skocpol spoke of "structures," McAdam spoke of "processes." Yet these distinctions mask deeper conceptual similarities.

In fact, each of the components of Skocpol's model of revolutions, despite the claims she made for its distinctiveness, can be "mapped" onto one of McAdam's conditions for the emergence of social movements. There are three main elements in McAdam's political process model of the emergence of social movements: (1) expanding political opportunities; (2) indigenous organizational strength; and (3) cognitive liberation. The first implies some combination of state weakness and elite divisions or rivalry that opens the way for opposition to the established order to develop; this is analogous to Skocpol's positing some external pressure on the state that weakens it as a prerequisite to the emergence of a revolutionary situation. McAdam's second condition implies some combination of elite leadership and popular mobilization that facilitates coordinated collective action against movement opponents; this is analogous to Skocpol's second and third conditions—elites and popular groups that have the autonomy and organization to challenge state authority. And finally, McAdam's third condition, cognitive liberation, is exactly what is supplied in Skocpol's model by the presence of a "marginal elite." While McAdam focused on the mental cognitions, and Skocpol focused on the social carriers and advocates of those new cognitions, the role of both cognitive liberation and marginal elites in these theories is the same—to supply and communicate a vision of a new order, whose justice and potential is greater than that existing under the status quo.

To put it slightly differently, comparing the Skocpol and McAdam models, we can see that precisely the same conditions are claimed in *both* theories as necessary for the emergence of a social movement or a social revolution, namely, (1) some pressures on the state that force it to depart from the status quo, either because it must reform to offset challenges or because those pressures demonstrate severe weakness; (2) effective organized opposition to the state, in the form of autonomous elite and popular organizations that can stand up to state authorities; and (3) articulation of an alternative vision of a better social and political order, and the belief that such an order is obtainable, here and now, as voiced and spread by a "marginal elite" and evoking a popular response of "cognitive liberation." In briefer terms, a shift in state control, an organizational base for effective opposition, and the belief that change is necessary and possible can, in combination, produce either a social movement or a social revolution.

We can flesh out this comparison further by looking at the precise historical elements cited by Skocpol and McAdam in their cases. In Skocpol's revolutions, pressure from external states led financially weaker states to seek internal reforms. In McAdam's study of the U.S. civil rights movement, it was the federal government that acted as an "external pressure" on southern state governments, forcing them to seek reforms regarding racial inequality. In Skocpol's social revolutions, autonomous and emerging elites—landed nobles or monied bourgeoisie—opposed their kings, while popular actions based on the preexisting communities of the peasant villages forced the elites to adopt more radical social policies. In McAdam's analysis of the civil rights movement, it was also autonomous and emerging elites—black professionals, particularly lawyers and ministers—who opposed government policies, while popular actions based on the preexisting communities of the black church congregations forced white elites to adopt more radical social reforms. Finally, in Skocpol's social revolutions, the old regimes lost legitimacy because their own reforms exposed the need for change, while the frustrations of marginal elites led them to highlight the injustice of the arbitrary class-status labels that excluded them from political leadership. In McAdam's discussion, the "Jim Crow" regime lost legitimacy because federal decisions such as that in *Brown vs. Board of Education* showed the need for southern reform, while the aspirations and frustrations of the black elite led them to articulate a vision of racial equality in direct opposition to the injustice of prevailing law and practice.

In short, if we look only at the causal conditions leading to the emergence of social revolutions and social movements, there seems little to distinguish them. Indeed, it is not too much to say, as some scholars have, that the fight for racial equality in the Jim Crow south *was* a revolutionary movement.[3] And the Puritan movement in seventeenth-century England, as well as the movement for "a career open to talents" in eighteenth-century France (which was actually partially implemented in the French army reforms after the Seven Years' War), were not, for decades after their emergence, avowedly revolutionary. Yet clearly, even if its outcome was revolutionary for the politics of the South, the outcome of the U.S. civil rights movement was reform, not a revolution (e.g., the overthrow of the institutions of governance). And just as clearly, in both England and France the outcome of those movements just mentioned *was* full-blown revolution. We therefore must move beyond both Skocpol's and McAdam's theories to understand the differences between revolutions and social movements. It appears that their emergence has much in common; it must therefore be something in the evolution of these movements after they emerge that determines whether the outcome will be revolution or something else.

State, Social Environment, Culture, and Process: Evolutionary Dynamics of Collective Action

The idea that state responses shape the evolution of collective action is not new. The notion of the "U"-shaped repression curve in studies of political violence has a similar idea at its core. In this view (Gurr 1969; Muller 1985; Muller and Seligson 1987; Weede 1987), political violence in societies depends nonlinearly on the state's repression—where repression is mild, there is no political violence because protest can be channeled into legitimate nonviolent forms; where repression is extremely strong, there is also no political violence because protest is suppressed; but at middling levels of repression, protestors find it both necessary and possible to challenge the state with violent protests, and substantial political violence occurs. However, these analysts speak generically of "political violence," making no distinction between social movements and revolutions.

McAdam, Tarrow, and Tilly (1996) have suggested that nondemocratic regimes are more likely to give rise to rare but revolutionary mobilization when opportunities arise, while democratic regimes are more likely to give rise to common but social-movement type mobilization. This certainly is true, and suggests a fruitful direction to follow. And it is certainly the case that the "home" of the modern social movement is the democratic state that emerged since the eighteenth century. Yet there have been social movements in nondemocratic societies (the monastic movement was certainly a social movement in medieval Europe, as the Enlightenment was in many respects a social movement for its first fifty years, as was Puritanism in England, and as were many utopian movements in Europe throughout the sixteenth to the eighteenth century; in China, the academy movement under the late Ming was a social movement as well). And there have been revolutionary movements in democratic ones (the U.S. Civil War is one example, the U.S. civil rights movement in southern states was, in the view of many, another; the student revolt of 1968 in France yet another). So the nature of the regime is not sufficient to determine the nature of contentious politics.

A provocative and detailed view of movement responses to state repression has been suggested by Sabine Karstedt-Henke (1980), although her focus was on the origins of terrorism in a democratic state—West Germany. In Karstedt-Henke's analysis, terrorism emerges from a cycle of protest and state response. Initially, the state overreacts to protest, but represses poorly and ineffectively; this provokes further protest. However, as the state gains more knowledge of the protest, it is able to split the protestors by offering moderate concessions. These attract the moderates in the movement to legitimate action, but frustrate the radicals who seek greater change. The radicals therefore press their fight, but now isolated, are more easily targeted by state repression. The radicals then strike back with more extreme violence, creating a spiral of terror and counterterror that ends with the radical extreme suppressed or driven underground.

While one must be skeptical of the determinism of this cycle, and the ability of the authorities to split protest movements seems more a particular characteristic of German politics in the 1970s than of contentious politics in general, Karstedt-Henke's basic point that different state responses conduce to different tactics by protestors appears sound, and has been borne out by empirical studies of European and U.S. protest waves investigated by Ruud Koopmans (1993).

Indeed, there is a wealth of empirical evidence on the evolution of contentious collective action in both democratic and nondemocratic contexts, and with both revolutionary and nonrevolutionary outcomes. A brief review of some cases may be helpful in clarifying the dynamics of this process.

Protest, Revolution, and Reform in Early Modern England

England experienced two major waves of contentious politics between 1500 and 1900. The first, from 1550 to 1660, beginning with reactions to Henry VIII's Protestant reform of the Anglican Church and culminating in the Revolution and Civil War of 1640 to 1660, focused on issues of royal power and religious authority. The second, from the 1760s through the 1860s, focused on issues of the incorporation of the working and industrial classes into political power. In *both* waves, contentious politics took forms that were alternatively "social movement" and "revolutionary," with state responses determining the outcome.

Although space does not allow a full account here, we may focus on the Puritan movement of the early seventeenth century on the one hand, and the period from the Peterloo riots to the Second Reform Act as contrasts. In the early seventeenth century, Puritanism arose as a movement to advocate stricter morality among the nobility and bourgeoisie, stricter supervision of the morals of laborers, and stricter demarcation of practice between the Anglican Church and the Church of Rome. Early Puritan preachers, such as Thomas Adams, Robert Bolton, and John Dowmane, made their reputations on public sermons that urged people to be more godly, *and to respect their King* (Woolrych 1968; Richardson 1973; Hunt 1983). Only in the 1620s and 1630s did Puritanism become allied with political radicalism, and it did so precisely because Charles I and his ministers attacked Puritans—and Puritanism—with a fervor that stigmatized its followers. As Lucy Hutchinson wrote in her memoirs, "if any were grieved at the dishonor of the Kingdome . . . he was a Puritane, . . . and if a Puritane, then enemy to the King and his government" (cited in Lamont and Oldfield 1975). The Parliamentary leaders of the 1620s wanted to rein in the king and halt what they perceived as the Romanization of the Anglican Church; they thus railed against abuses of power and popery. But

Parliamentarianism and Puritanism became a revolutionary tandem only when both were driven underground in the 1630s, as Charles ruled without Parliament and William Laud fought Puritanism in the Church. When in 1640, Charles's war with Scotland forced him to reconvene Parliament, he faced a more extreme and united opposition, which reluctantly moved into open revolution when Charles again sought to suppress their demands.

In the early 1800s, England suffered from a combination of rapid population growth and a shift in its economic engine from agriculture to industry. While those who worked in factories actually did better than most, they were a tiny percentage of the population. Those who labored in traditional crafts and services, from weaving to leatherwork to retailing to construction, who formed the overwhelming majority of the urban working population, saw their real wages plummet. Judging this effect to be the result of a conspiracy of landowners who were boosting the price of corn and a corrupt regime, urban workers and employers agitated for reform. Radical leaders such as Cobbett, Cartwright, and Hunt aroused a powerful response with their diagnoses that "the sufferings of the people were due to the inadequacies and extravagance of government, and the remedy lay in annual parliaments and universal suffrage" (Gash 1979, 93).

Was the radicalism of the 1820s the last wave of revolutionary action? Or the first wave of social movements? In October 1831, after the peers rejected the Second Reform Bill, the Duke of Newcastle's castle was put to the torch. At the same time, middle-class political unions organized massive demonstrations (Evans 1983, 210). Had William IV acted like Charles I and defied the House of Commons, could revolutionary movements have occurred? At least some analysts think it possible (Thomis and Holt 1977, 85–99). But William IV called a new Parliament in 1832, pressured the Peers to comply with Grey's reform ministry, and the Reform Bill passed, a monument to the power of social movements to spur reform.

While we think of the seventeenth century as revolutionary, and the early nineteenth as the age of reform, there was thus no obvious way that the Puritans of the seventeenth century and the radicals of the nineteenth differed when their popular mobilizations emerged. Instead, the responses of government, and particularly of the kings and their ministers, resulted in the one case in revolution, and in the other in reform.

Protest, Riot, and Reform in the American South in the 1960s

Aldon Morris (1984) and Doug McAdam (1982) have clearly shown that part of the success of the U.S. civil rights movement lay in provoking a repressive response from local southern authorities. Because that response was widely perceived as excessive and illegitimate, it reinforced the sense of solidarity of civil rights protestors, and won them sympathy and support throughout the nation.

This suggests that it is not merely the severity of repression, but also its *character,* that makes a difference in the evolution of a social movement. This point has also been forcefully made by Karl-Dieter Opp and Wolfgang Roehl (1990) in studying opposition to nuclear power in West Germany; by John Walton (1992) in his study of the Owens Valley struggle against Los Angeles over water rights; by Anthony Oberschall in his analysis of the demonstrations that ended the communist regimes in East Germany and Czechoslovakia; and by James DeNardo (1985) in his analysis of rational choice models. These authors argue that while repression clearly imposes material costs on protestors, the *perception and meaning applied to* repression also has an impact on potential activists and their supporters. Repression that is widely viewed as targeting innocents, or as being disproportionate to the offense, or as being imposed by a government of questionable authority, can work to undermine the legitimacy of that government, and arouse a more general opposition to it (Goodwin 1993; Gerlach and Hine 1970; White 1989).

In the case of the U.S. civil rights movement, protestors met with two kinds of response from state authorities. As Stephen Barkan (1984) has demonstrated, in Montgomery, Albany, and Danville, authorities used legalistic means to suppress the movement. Frequent arrests, high bail, and questionable injunctions and court proceedings held protestors at bay, disrupted the movement, and imposed high costs; yet these semilegitimate methods did not provide a high-visibility negative profile for the authorities. In these towns, civil rights activities were substantially damped out. But in Selma and Birmingham, local authorities responded to civil rights demonstrations with ostentatious violence. Captured on camera, the brutalization of peaceful marchers helped destroy the legitimacy of the southern authorities in the eyes of the nation, and forced the federal government to intervene on behalf of the protestors. The civil rights movement engaged in revolutionary battles—and won what amounted to revolutionary victories—because it exploited a highly repressive, yet highly illegitimate, response from the local state.

The role of northern and federal pressures points to yet another feature of the evolution of social movements—outcomes depend significantly on the degree to which a movement is supported by others groups or movements in society at large (Meyer and Staggenborg 1996). And that degree of support can be substantially influenced by the nature of state actions. Let us turn to one more set of examples that drive home that point: the evolution of rebellious and revolutionary movements in contemporary developing nations.

Revolution in Iran

Resistance to the absolutist rule of the Shah of Iran was nothing new in the 1970s. Nationalist and constitutionalist critics of the regime, led by then-prime minister Mohammad Mossadegh, had briefly seized power in the early 1950s. Leftist organizations, particularly the Mujahedin, had previously attempted to mobilize peasants and workers against the government. And fundamentalist Islamic leaders, of whom the most radical was the Ayatollah Ruhollah Khomeini, had long opposed the secularization imposed by the regime.

Yet only in the late 1970s did these various opposition movements coalesce into a single revolutionary movement; this was largely a result of state responses to particular protests. In the early 1970s, diverse groups in society nursed their separate grievances against the Shah's regime, but showed no signs of joining together to mobilize a revolutionary movement. Indeed the liberal constitutionalists and the Islamic fundamentalists had little in common. Similarly, the educated students and the technical intelligentsia shared little common ground with the bazaar merchants who dominated the traditional sectors of Iran's economy.

The chain of events that began the revolution started with a specific state action to deflect criticism and discontent, an action that boomeranged. The early 1970s were marked by oil shocks, as the Organization of Petroleum-Exporting Countries (OPEC) suddenly doubled the price of oil. The resultant flood of money into Iran was not managed well, but was drawn on to underwrite ever-larger debts incurred for military equipment and economic modernization. This fiscal disarray led to substantial inflation. Instead of attempting to deal responsibly with this inflation, the state decided to blame the bazaar merchants for rising prices, making them a scapegoat. After 1975, Abrahamian (1982, 491) reported that up to 8,000 shopkeepers were jailed, 23,000 were exiled, and 250,000 were fined. This repression, widely perceived as arbitrary and illegitimate by the entire bazaari community, drove the merchants and their financial resources into the arms of the fundamentalist Islamic leaders who sought to use the mosques and bazaars to mobilize the masses against the Shah.

In 1978, perceiving the clerical-sponsored critique of the state as a threat, the state responded by publishing a severely critical and demeaning article on Ayatollah Khomeini in a major daily; but more important, it prepared to use the army against demonstrators who gathered and marched in support of Khomeini. When the clerics organized a demonstration in the city of Qom in response to the critical article, the Shah's army used deadly force, killing hundreds, thus initiating "a cycle of violence that ended in the overthrow of the government" (Moshiri 1991, 128). The next eight months saw a series of demonstrations, protests, and strikes expressing outrage at the Qom massacre spread throughout the country, assisted by the Carter administration's pressure on the Shah to show regard for human rights. More important, the bazaar merchants, in cooperation with the clergy, would shut down the bazaars on designated protest days, and mobilize whole neighborhoods for demonstrations. Frustrated at increasing disorder, the Shah declared martial law on September 7; the next day the military launched new attacks and killed thousands of demonstrators.

Yet the result of this renewed and intensified repression was not to subdue the opposition—just the reverse. The disproportionate violence further spread the conviction that the Shah's government was wholly illegitimate and could not be tolerated. Secular liberals, and non-Shi'a Kurdish and Arab groups (the latter working in the critical oil fields) threw their lot in with Khomeini and the fundamentalist movement, as the best hope of defeating the Shah. From September through November, strikes spread to the oil-fields, a Kurdish revolt commenced, and demonstrations continued, culminating in nationwide general strikes in December. Army desertions increased, and officers decided to hold their troop in their barracks, leaving the streets of Tehran to Khomeini's followers. On January 16, the Shah fled Iran, having, by his own government's actions, forged a revolutionary alliance among previously disparate and ineffective opposition movements.

The Iranian revolution is a case where the government's efforts at repression so undermined its own legitimacy and expanded its opposition that revolution succeeded. But the widespread and rapid growth of support for the anti-Shah movement was rooted in real grievances that affected many elements in society: clergy who resented secularization; bazaaris who resented the emergence of an increasingly dominant industrial-technological economy; technical and middle-class workers and students who resented the Shah's monopolization of power; and civil servants and officers who resented the corruption practiced by the Shah's family and cronies. Without such extant and widespread discontent, the opposition movement would not have responded to the Shah's repression with increased mobilization. Nonetheless, even where revolutionary efforts have failed, one can clearly discern the same pattern of state repression turning various opposition movements into revolutionary organizations.

Failed Revolts in the Philippines, Colombia, and Kenya

John Walton's (1984, 29) excellent study of national revolts—the Huk Rebellion in the Philippines, La Violencia in Colombia, and the Mau Mau revolt in Kenya—revealed a consistent pattern in the development of each movement. "Each national revolt was immediately preceded by a sharp reversal in the economy *coinciding with* an abrupt cancellation or repression of political gains that the popular movement had achieved *within* the legal norms of conventional politics. Under this counterpunch from the 'system,' the popular movements reeled into a revolutionary situation." In other words, none of these violent revolutionary movements emerged in that form. Instead, they began as social movements, and only a combination of worsening conditions *plus* a severe state response turned them onto revolutionary paths.

Why did these revolts fail? The answer is that, unlike in Iran, where the Shah's repression was indiscriminately aimed at economic, religious, and technical elites, thus creating a national cross-class coalition against him, rulers in the Philippines, Colombia, and Kenya, after initially miscalculating their use of repression and reaping a whirlwind of opposition, moved to win elite allegiance and to separate the elites from agrarian and urban working classes. Violence was increasingly turned on the lower classes and vulnerable ethnic groups, while bargains were made with key elites. Violence aimed at those vulnerable groups seemed increasingly legitimate in the eyes of the elite, and reinforced, rather than undermined, state power.

We can sum up the preceding arguments in a simple table (shown in Figure 6.4), bringing together the various factors that we have argued, to shape the form and outcome of contentious collective action. One key dimension is the "cultural valuation" that individuals and groups throughout society place on the protest movement, and on the state's response. Where the state's response is viewed as legitimate, and the protestor's actions as questionable, we can deem the broad social environment faced by the protest movement as "not supportive." In contrast, where the state's position and actions are deemed questionable or illegitimate, and the protestors have broad sympathy, the social environment is "supportive."

A second key dimension is the nature of the state's response. Where

FIGURE 6.4
Forms and Outcomes of Contentious Action

Valuation of Protest Movement by Society	State Response		
	Legalistic	Weak/Inconsistent Repression	Strong/Consistent Repression
Supportive	Protest Cycle	Revolution	Unstable Authoritarian State
Not Supportive	Isolated Social Movements	Guerrilla or Terrorist Groups	Extinguished or Underground Movement

the state accepts the legitimacy of the protest movement to a degree, and fights mobilization and protest only through legal actions, we are likely to see conventional social movements. In such cases, the state may be a neutral bystander or act as a referee while a movement seeks to sway social opinion, to compete with countermovement groups, or to influence a particular target actor, e.g., an employer or a local polluting firm. Or the state may be involved in prescribing and monitoring the procedures of a group's actions, taking no stand on its substantive issues, but imposing sanctions if the movement engages in activities that break existing laws regarding property, social disturbances, or conditions of assembly. Or, in some cases, the state may be opposed to the substance of the movement's claims, but acts moderately and through legal channels against it. In all these cases, the state's reaction ranges from neutral to mildly repressive, and is strictly legalistic, acting within the framework of existing rules and procedures to enforce order and seek a desired outcome.

In these cases, the range of protest activity depends largely on the cultural valuation placed on the status quo identified with the existing state policies. Where the existing regime and policies are widely viewed as undesirable, the environment for protest is highly supportive. Under such conditions, the emergence of a protest movement, and its mild handling by the state, is likely to encourage others. As Tarrow (1994a) has argued, this sequence tends to build to form a society-wide cycle of social protests; the most notable recent example occurring in the United States and Europe in the late 1960s. In contrast, if the status quo is widely viewed as desirable, and protest by specific groups is viewed as selfish and unnecessary, then even a mild and legalistic response to a protest movement is not likely to touch off a protest cycle. Instead, the largely unsupportive environment means that individual social movements are likely to come and go, but without a pronounced "wave" of events.

But where the state adopts overt repression, we may see divergent outcomes. If repression is weak, inconsistent, and arbitrary in scope, it is likely to inflame but not suppress its targets. Such repressive acts by the state draw a violent response. Where the state is seen as illegitimate and protestors have wide support, the state's response can precipitate revolt or revolution. But where the state has greater legitimacy and the opposition movement has little support, protest violence is likely to remain sporadic and take the form of guerrilla or terrorist actions. Finally, where the state's repressive response is consistent, powerful, and tightly targeted on protestors, as in strong authoritarian states, protest is likely to be suppressed. If the state is viewed as legitimate, the protest is likely to be extinguished or driven underground into tiny cells of supporters. But where the state is viewed as illegitimate, suppression creates an unstable situation of invisible but high potential for revolt. Thus in situations where a state suddenly loses legitimacy, or shifts from strong to weak repression, movements can burst forth in a sudden eruption of revolution or revolt as the configuration of key elements shifts from the far-right or middle-bottom cells to that of the top middle cell in the figure.

For example, in the Soviet Union, much of the immediate post–World War II period was one in which society operated in the far-right bottom cell—economic growth satisfied most individuals, and only a few bands of hardy dissidents and exiles seriously favored protest over acceptance of the communist regime. However, a series of events in the 1970 and 1980s, including a steep slowdown in economic growth, the defeat of the Soviet Union in Afghanistan, the widely perceived corruption of the Brezhnev regime, sharp increases in infant mortality due to severe pollution, and the catastrophic explosion and cover-up at the Chernobyl reactor in Kiev, seriously undermined the legitimacy of the communist regime. The situation by the mid-1980s had thus shifted to the far-right upper cell. The next five years saw a harsh debate within the Kremlin, with Gorbachev alternating sides, over whether the government should, while seeking reform, maintain a "harsh" or "moderate" level of repression against opponents of communist rule. Testing the waters, social movements that began as environmental movements or communist reform movements began to shift, becoming more openly anticommunist and/or autonomy-seeking. The key test occurred in the Baltic states, where Gorbachev or hard-liners responded to peaceful autonomy movements with violence. The international condemnation that resulted led Gorbachev to decide in favor of "the Sinatra doctrine" and a light hand with opponents. This suddenly shifted the situation from the far-right upper cell to the middle upper cell. Gorbachev himself then fell victim to an attempted coup by hard-liners, who—for all their other faults—correctly perceived that by emphasizing the flaws of the communist regime, while simultaneously loosening the reigns of repression, Gorbachev had created a situation ripe for the revolutionary overthrow of the communist regime.[4]

On the Evolution and Varieties of Contentious Collective Action

The preceding sections argue that successful revolutions, social movements leading to reform, cycles of protest, and guerrilla or terrorist activities are not different *genera* of social phenomenon, each requiring a distinct kind or basis of explanation. But neither are they simply the same phenomenon, differing only by degrees from mild to extreme. Instead, they are best thought of as a family of related phenomena, originating in a similar set of circumstances, but evolving and diverging in consequence of distinct patterns in the interplay between protest movements, state response, the broader social environment, and cultural evaluations of state and protest actions.

Contentious collective action emerges through the mobilization of individuals and groups to pursue certain goals, the framing of purposes and tactics, and taking advantages of the opportunities for protest arising from shifts in the grievances, power, and vulnerability of various social actors. But the *form* and *outcome* of that action is not determined by the conditions of movement emergence. These characteristics are themselves emergent, and contingent on the responses of various social actors to the initial protest actions.

While this essay has focused on the differences between revolutions and social movements, these are not the only forms of contentious collective action that may be brought into this framework. Although the task is best left for another setting, there is in principle no reason why ethnic conflicts and nationalist mobilization cannot also be seen as forms of collective action that result from a specific pattern of state, social, and cultural responses to the claims of a particular group. Nationalist mobilization, for example, is likely to result when a group seeking protection or greater rights (e.g., more autonomy or use of a local language) from a government faces repression, but gains supporters throughout a significant region because others perceive the group's claims as legitimate, while the government's repression is seen as illegitimate imposition by an "alien" regime. Ethnic mobilization will occur in the analogous case but where the government is perceived as illegitimate because it "identifies" with or against a particular ethnic group (Oberschall and Kim 1996).

To incorporate nationalist and ethnic revolts into our "family" of contentious collective action, we can add one more category to the "supportive/not supportive" variable in figure 6.5). Instead of a dichotomy, let us say that in addition to being "supportive" or "not supportive," corre-

FIGURE 6.5
More Forms and Outcomes of Contentious Action

Valuation of Protest Movement by Society	State Response		
	Legalistic	Weak/Inconsistent Repression	Strong/Consistent Repression
Supportive	Protest Cycle	Revolution	Unstable Authoritarian State
Narrowly Supportive	Autonomy/Civil Rights Movement	Regional Revolt or Violent Ethnic Conflicts	Unstable state with nationalist or ethnic tensions
Not Supportive	Isolated Social Movements	Guerrilla or Terrorist Groups	Extinguished or Underground Movement

sponding to our existing categories, a protest movement's environment can also be "narrowly supportive," drawing support only from a particular region or ethnic group within the larger society. In this case, depending on the state's response, we may again see a range of outcomes: a peaceful autonomy movement, a violent ethnic or regional rebellion, or a situation of suppressed and unstable ethnic-regional discontent.

Separate studies of social movements and revolutions had once, as John Walton (1992, 1) pointed out, created a situation in which "social movements and the state are seldom treated together as interacting dimensions of the same political process." The political process model of social movements overcame that divide by making political opportunities afforded by state action a key element of mobilization. But considering the state only in terms of "political opportunity structures" is to take too passive and static a view of state/social movement interactions. Instead, a wide variety of different forms and outcomes of contentious action—ranging from social movements to terrorism to revolutions—can be generated by specifying a more varied and active range of state responses to movements, and by recognizing that social support and cultural valuations of both protest actions and state actions play a key role.

Notes

The ideas expressed in this essay draw heavily on the works and thought of my University of California, Davis, colleagues, John Walton, John Lofland, and John R. Hall, and on those of the students and faculty in the Mellon Seminar on Contentious Politics, which have been an enormous stimulus to my thought on social movements. Portions of this essay were originally presented as the Pitrim Sorokin Lecture to the 1994 Midwest Sociology Association annual meeting.

1. On the role of focused repression in squelching revolts, and the role of gross human rights violations (unfocused repression) in sustaining them, see Goodwin (1993).

2. Major criticisms of Skocpol's model are that it underplays the role of culture and ideology (Sewell 1985); that its structural model is too static (Goldstone 1991); and that it gives insufficient weight to matters of agency and choice among historical actors (Emirbayer and Goodwin 1996; Goodwin 1994). Moreover, many historians, following the falsification of Marxist models of the major European revolutions, have abandoned structural models of all kinds, and focused on understanding the shifts in discourse and *mentalités* that prefigured the revolutionary events (Hunt 1984; Baker 1990). Nonetheless, no synthesis has emerged to replace that of Skocpol's as the leading theory of revolutions in the social sciences.

3. Both the *World Atlas of Revolution* (Wheatcroft 1983) and the forthcoming *Encyclopedia of Political Revolutions* (Goldstone forthcoming[a]) include the U.S. civil rights movement among their catalog of revolts and revolutionary situations.

4. The "revolutionary" character of the collapse of the Soviet Union is, of course, much debated, with some commentators seeing it as having more elements of reform than of revolution. I have laid out in Goldstone (forthcoming[b]) my arguments regarding the causes of this collapse, and why we should regard the events of 1989 to 1991 as a true revolution.

Part III

Democratization

7

Democratic Transitions and Social Movement Outcomes

The Chilean Shantytown Dwellers' Movement in Comparative Perspective

Patricia L. Hipsher

One of the most striking occurrences common to states undergoing transitions from authoritarian rule is the "resurrection of civil society" (O'Donnell and Schmitter 1986, 55). In most southern European and Latin American countries, the shift from military authoritarianism to civilian democracy in the 1970s and 1980s, respectively, was accompanied by large-scale mass protest by students, workers, urban poor residents, women, and human rights activists. The movements demanded a return to democracy and respect for human rights, called for improved funding of social services, and advanced group-specific claims, including academic freedom, better wages and working conditions, an end to sexual discrimination, and greater public housing.

Preferring to focus on the impact of movements in democratic settings, like North America and western Europe, social movement theorists have paid scant attention to the impacts of social movements during transitional periods. This is surprising when one considers the generalized nature of the "resurrection of civil society" during democratic transitions, not to mention the optimism that scholars initially had expressed about the democratizing potential of these movements. In this chapter, I will attempt to fill this research void by describing and analyzing the variable impacts of social movements during the transitions to democracy in Latin America and southern Europe. I do so with reference to a particular case study, the shantytown dwellers' movement in Chile, and, to a lesser degree, various other social movements in Spain, Chile, Brazil, and Portugal. This research indicates that transitions from authoritarian rule not only provide opportunities for social movements to mobilize and democratize the political process, but also may place certain constraints on movements' abilities to remain insurgent. Generally, in the early stages of democratic transitions, the impact of social movements is strongly felt as movements push transitions beyond mere liberalization. Thus, one of the most important outcomes of social movements during democratic transitions is democratization.

What is ironic is that one of the frequent outcomes of democratization is the demobilization of the very movements that help set the process of democratization in motion. Examples of this demobilizing trend include the Solidarity trade union movement in Poland, the urban social movements in Uruguay and Spain, and the Spanish labor movement. However, it should be noted that this process is variable. While some movements demobilize and become institutionalized following democratic transitions, others remain mobilized and contentious. The extent to which movements decline during the consolidation phase is determined by the following four situational aspects of political opportunity structure[1]: (1) the configuration of power among political groups; (2) elite orientations toward and responses to collective insurgency; (3) movement activists' orientations toward the use of insurgency; and (4) the strength and density of party-movement ties.

What we find in the case of the shantytown dwellers' movement and in other cases is that movements tend to demobilize and to pursue institutionalized forms of collective action following democratic transitions in countries where authoritarian elites still exercise a good deal of power and influence, where there is a close relationship between political parties and social movements, and where political elites have a strong commitment to stable, protected democracy. Additionally, movements that experience declining outcomes tend to be those with a previous history of engaging in threatening mobilization; these are often class-based movements.

I have chosen to highlight the Chilean case because it represents a crucial case. In Chile, high levels of protest mobilization helped set in motion the transition to democracy (1983–89). The shantytown movement was a key actor in this protest movement. At the height of these protests, new social movement theorists asserted that, in the new democracy, the shantytown dwellers' movement was "not going to be easily pacified by vacuous promises emerging from the negotiations between the right-centrist civilian opposition and the regime" (Leiva and Petras 1987, 119). However, the return of democracy was characterized by wholesale movement demobilization and institutionalization. Such an extreme case demands an explanation.

Social Movements and Democratization

Democratization processes almost always begin with liberalization, the opening of political spaces, and the extension of certain rights to individuals and groups. However, there is considerable debate among scholars over the relative importance of "reform from above" as compared to "pressure from below" in causing liberalization (Tarrow 1995, 157). Some scholars emphasize the role of elites in liberalization processes, conceiving of liberalization as the result of cleavages between soft-liners (*blandos*) and hard-liners (*duros*) (O'Donnell and Schmitter 1986, 19). Others view liberalization as a consequence of popular protest (Lamounier 1979). Still others argue that liberalization results from a combination of "reform from above" and "pressure from below"; that is, "Liberalization is a result of an interaction between splits in the authoritarian regime and autonomous organization of the civil society" (Przeworski 1991, 57).

Despite disagreement over how much weight to assign social movements as causes of liberalization, there is general agreement that social movement mobilization can shape the direction of the transition and the structures and processes of the emerging democratic regime. It may do so, first, by pushing transitions farther and faster than they otherwise might have gone. Once the regime has begun to liberalize the political process, protest mobilization "makes a strategy of 'mere liberalization' impossible" (Maravall 1982, 12). Adam Przeworski argued that mobilization pressures soft-liners to "get off the fence" and either join the growing forces for democracy and more fully commit themselves to a democratic transition by calling elections or rejoin the hard-liners and assent to a return to authoritarianism (1991, 61). He also indicated that, in most cases, soft-liners opt for greater democratization.[2] The soft-liners will have already broken from the hard-liners to support a transition; thus, if hard-liners successfully repress the movement and install a new narrower authoritarian regime, soft-liners are likely to be excluded from power by the hard-liners, appearing to them as traitors. On the other hand, if the renewed repression fails and political democracy comes, soft-liners are likely to be excluded from power by the democratic opposition, appearing to *them* as traitors (Przeworski 1991, 61). Thus, one of the most important outcomes that social movements may produce is the expansion of the democratization process by encouraging soft-liners to call for elections.

Movement mobilization may also shape the democratization process by reconstituting civil society. One of the consequences of military dictatorship in Latin America and southern Europe has been the political deactivation of civil society. Dictatorships centralize power, prohibit many forms of political participation and association, and create cultures of fear in which individuals are alienated from the larger community.

Social movements may overcome these atomizing tendencies in two ways. First, as Manuel Antonio Garretón notes (1989a, 155), they "reinject politics into society" by acting as schools of democracy, where individuals have the opportunity to be a part of a community, participate, and express themselves. Second, and related to this, the collective identity and political education acquired in social movement activity may generate new demands and place new issues on the political agenda (Alvarez and Escobar 1992, 326). In these ways, movements act as democratizing forces by restoring the public sphere, which had been absent under authoritarianism.

While movement mobilization can have important consequences for democratic transitions, democratization processes, in turn, may shape movement outcomes. One of the most common outcomes of democratization is movement demobilization and institutionalization. In the remainder of this chapter, I explain and illustrate this process of demobilization with respect to the case of the Chilean shantytown dwellers' movement and other Latin American and southern European cases.

Democratization and Demobilization

The decline of social movements following democratic transitions is a phenomenon that has been noted in numerous countries, including Russia, Poland, Uruguay, Brazil, Spain, and Chile (Pickvance 1992; Canel 1992; Maravall 1978, 1982; Wozniak 1990; Mainwaring 1986; Oxhorn 1995). Many of these countries experienced large-scale mass protest during the decline of authoritarian and autocratic regimes. However, since the restoration of democracy, these groups have tended to demobilize and pursue institutionalized forms of collective action. Fewer people participate in protest events, and the number of actions in which the movement participates or sponsors drops off. Additionally, the groups tend to use more moderate forms of collective action, which "implicitly convey an acceptance of the established, or 'proper,' channels of conflict resolution" (McAdam 1982, 57).

In the literature on democratic transitions, movement decline is generally explained with reference to the opening of channels for legal and peaceful participation following the restoration of democracy. According to O'Donnell and Schmitter (1986, 55), the popular upsurge that generally accompanies the opening of authoritarian regimes is ephemeral and usually passes once political parties return to the fore of political activity and formal democracy has been restored. However, the authors do not specify the process by which parties and "normal" politics come to replace movement activity.

Edward Muller and Mitchell Seligson (1987, 429) offer us one possible explanation. They argue that the opening of normal channels of political participation (legislatures, elections, political parties) reduces the incentives for engaging in protest and, in this way, the return of parties leads to movement demobilization. They theorize that in a democratic regime, dissident groups will not face significant restrictions on their ability to organize peacefully and their belief in the likelihood of achieving at least some success from peaceful collective action will probably be high. The costs of peaceful collective action are lower than those of protest; thus, we should expect actors to opt for institutionalized action over protest.

The opening of opportunities for conventional political participation may be one reason for changes in the level and forms of collective action following transitions. The revival of political parties generally offers citizens a more peaceful alternative to street protest practiced during authoritarian and transitional periods[3] and a broader range of political activities in which they may participate. However, I find this argument wanting, as it ignores the evidence presented by social movement theorists that "many of the same people who have a high propensity to vote also have the highest protest potential" (Tarrow 1991, 29; Barnes and Kaase 1979). In countries with a myriad of social, political, and economic problems, it seems unlikely that the return of parties and elections, by themselves, would effectively demobilize movements with unmet demands.

A more powerful explanation of posttransitional movement outcomes is suggested by the political process approach to the study of social movements, in conjunction with the transitions literature on pact making. The political process approach explains protest potential with reference to the political opportunity structure. Sidney Tarrow (1994a, 85) referred to the structure of political opportunities as "consistent—but not necessarily formal, permanent or national—dimensions of the political environment that provide incentives for people to undertake collective action by affecting their expectations for success or failure." Political opportunities are fluid and variable over time, which explains why social protest is not constant, but rather ebbs and flows, depending on the opportunities available to movement actors.

The main premise of the political process approach is that movements do not appear and disappear "only in direct response to the level of supporters' grievances," but rather to changes in configurations of power, resources, and institutional arrangements (Tarrow 1994a, 17, 18). Movements are likely to mobilize in protest when political institutions are divided and weak (Hobsbawm 1974; Tarrow 1989, 56), vulnerable to demands (Piven and Cloward 1977, 15–18; McAdam 1982, 82), and when the aggrieved populations have sufficient resources and support to press their claims (Gamson 1975; Jenkins and Perrow 1977; Lipsky 1970; Eckstein 1989, 35).

Cathy Schneider (1992) presents persuasive evidence from the case of Chile that economic grievances are insufficient for the mobilization of protest. More important for movement mobilization are the opening of opportunities, owing to changes in the configurations of power and in elite and mass orientations toward the use of insurgent collective action, and a history of collective action and solidarity (Schneider 1992, 1995).

If the opening of political opportunities supports the emergence and development of social movements, it seems reasonable to presume that a contraction of opportunities will lead to movement decline. I argue that, in the late stages of the transition and the early phases of civilian rule, when democratization is most vulnerable, the perceived costs and risks of collective action may rise, narrowing the opportunities for collective action. The following discussion of the literature on pact making demonstrates how transitional processes may cause changes in the structure of opportunities and the ideas held by political actors regarding the relationship between democracy and collective action.

Most studies of democratization have concluded that successful democratization largely depends on moderation on the part of opposition elites and compromise between authoritarian and opposition elites on institutions and rules of the game (Kaufman 1986; Cardoso 1986; Przeworski 1986). A common form of collaboration between opposition and authoritarian elites is pact making. O'Donnell and Schmitter (1986, 37) define a pact as "an explicit, but not always publicly explicated or justified, agreement among a select set of actors which seeks to define (or better, to redefine) rules governing the exercise of power on the basis of mutual guarantees for the 'vital interests' of those entering into it." Terry Karl (1986, 198) explains the importance of pact making in democratization processes: "They provide a degree of stability and predictability which is reassuring to threatened traditional elites."

While I am critical of this elite-oriented approach to transitions because it tends to ignore the role of social movements, the work on pact making is, nevertheless, useful in explaining movement demobilization. According to Michael Burton, Richard Gunther, and Jon Higley (1992, 23), an important element of elite settlements and pact making is prohibition on mobilizing ones' supporters, whether they be the military or the masses. "For opposition actors," they write, "this usually involves demobilizing mass organizations and social movements, so as to discourage the outbreak of polarizing incidents and mass violence."

The experience of dictatorship, in many instances, has not only made elites more moderate and prudent, but it has also made social movements and their members more likely to withhold demands, or to pursue strategies that will not threaten the democratic stability or the interests of authoritarian elites. Robert Kaufman (1986, 106) noted that in many countries:

> the trauma of bureaucratic authoritarian repression appears to have lowered the expectations of at least some of the excluded "popular sectors" and their political leaders, making them more amenable to self-limiting compromises over economic issues.

Popular sectors suffered the brunt of the repression under dictatorships in Latin America and southern Europe. As such, they, like elites, have come to esteem political democracy and are likely to practice patience and restraint to preserve it.

Social movement outcomes following democratic transitions are largely a product of the perceived costs of continued mobilization. These perceived costs may be raised or lowered by signals given out by political elites and potential allies to aggrieved groups. In Chile and elsewhere, following the return of democracy, the costs of protest were raised as a consequence of changes in the configuration of political power at the national level and opposition elites' decision to accept a limited democracy that, they believed, required protection from destabilizing forces.

Key in translating these perceptions of vulnerability into movement strategies is a close relationship between political parties and social movements. O'Donnell (1986, 12) hypothesizes that pact making and the demobilization of mass organizations is facilitated by a "strong and representative party system, especially in relation to the popular sector." This argument is supported by evidence from the Spanish and Italian transitions, where class-based, ideologically articulate parties were crucial in obtaining the acquiescence of the popular sector to social pacts (Tarrow 1991, 1995).

I now turn to the case of the Chilean shantytown dwellers' movement to demonstrate the way in which narrowed political opportunities and strong, dense party-movement ties led to the decline of contentious collective action following the democratic transition. I follow this case study with a brief discussion of movements in Spain that have experienced similar outcomes. I conclude by comparing these movements to those in Brazil and Portugal that have not conformed to this pattern of declining outcomes. In so doing, it will become evident that the approach put forth in this research can explain the variable outcomes of movements in democratizing settings.

The Shantytown Dwellers' Movement in Chile

Since the late-1950s, the Chilean shantytown dwellers' movement has been at the forefront of the national struggles against social, economic, and political injustices, making it one of the most active and combative social movements in the Southern Cone. The movement has traditionally organized the urban poor around housing, basic public services and utilities, and cost of living and employment issues. To achieve its goals, the movement has relied on both traditional grassroots forms of organization, including self-help construction projects, and more contentious forms of activity, such as land seizures, occupations, and demonstrations.

The shantytown movement began to organize politically in Chile during the 1950s. The first organized land seizure took place in 1957.[4] During the 1960s and early-1970s many more land invasions took place. They were usually organized or supported by left-wing political parties, such as the Movement of the Revolutionary Left (MIR), the Communist Party (PCCh), and the Socialist Party (PSCh). Most of these early land invasions were harshly repressed by the police and had a heavy toll on the *pobladores* (shantytown dwellers).

During the government of Salvador Allende (1970–73), the shantytown dwellers' movement exploded. Peter Winn (1986) argues that the more open political environment encouraged mobilization. In the shantytowns, this mobilization took the form of land seizures, street protests, occupations, and the development of revolutionary neighborhoods (Schneider 1995, 68–70). For instance, MIR organized eight revolutionary neighborhoods, each with its own health clinic, communal kitchen, and system of people's courts to deal with problems of drunkenness, domestic violence, and gambling (Pastrano and Threlfall 1974).

This wave of political euphoria and mobilization was brought to a sudden end, on September 11, 1973, when military officers, led by Augusto Pinochet, launched a bloody coup. During the first ten years of military rule, the government repressed social and political organizations, drove them underground and inhibited the formation of linkages between them.[5] Additionally, under Pinochet's neoliberal economic program, labor unions and labor rights were weakened, and unemployment soared to more than 30 percent.

During the early-1980s, social movement organizations and networks reemerged and formed the backbone of the popular protest movement. In the shantytowns, people engaged in collective forms of subsistence; they set up common kitchens, artisan bakeries, purchasing cooperatives, and vocational workshops. They also organized political organizations, educational groups, and collectives to solve social and economic problems. These latter groups included self-help housing organizations, human rights groups, and "homeless" committees (Campero 1987; Hardy 1986, 1988). Although the shantytown movement began a process of reorganization in 1979, it was not until 1983 that it mobilized a strong and sustained campaign of protest. Schneider (1995) indicates that the key elements in the development of an insurgent movement were divisions within the government coalition brought on by the economic crisis, a history of contentious collective action, and strong external support for protest by opposition political parties and the Catholic Church.

The mobilization campaign, which lasted from 1983 to 1987, was organized as a series of national days of protest, each one called by varying opposition groups. The main convoking groups were the Copper Workers' Confederation (CTC), the Democratic Alliance (AD), the Popular Democratic Movement (MDP), and the Civic Assembly (AC).[6] The protests were characterized by strikes, high levels of absenteeism, slowdowns, marches, and demonstrations. Cathy Schneider (1995, 4) describes the actions of shantytown dwellers:

> residents built burning barricades, drummed pots and pans, and organized marches. . . . protestors sprayed walls with political slogans, led mass marches, and cut electricity to large portions of the city. . . . when the armed forces attacked these seemingly defenseless communities, residents responded by digging trenches, erecting burning barricades, and pelting military tanks with rocks.

During this period, shantytown dwellers also revived the illegal land seizure as a solution to their housing problems. In September 1983, some eight thousand homeless families, organized by a communist-led shantytown organization, staged the largest illegal land seizure in the nation's history (Klaarhamer 1986). These actions were repressed by the police and armed forces. The police and special forces conducted neighborhood searches at all hours of the night, encircling the shantytowns and arresting all adult men.

From 1983 until 1987, community, labor, and party organizations sustained a high level of mobilization, challenging the dictatorship and calling for nothing less than the resignation of Pinochet and the return of democracy. The two main political alignments, the AD and the MDP, supported a strategy of mass protest and coordinated protest activities with one another on various occasions; however, the two groupings had different ideas as to the purpose of the protests. The AD, composed of centrist and center-right parties, viewed protest as the social pressure that should bring the government to the bargaining table to negotiate the transition timetable. However, the MDP, composed of leftist parties, saw protest as part of an overall strategy to bring the government to its knees (Garretón 1989a). This difference in goals remained obscure until the dictatorship offered to negotiate with the parties of the AD in late-1986 and actively sought to isolate the MDP.

The protests reached their peak on July 2 and 3, 1986, when the opposition launched a general strike. The AC forces managed to paralyze activities in Santiago for forty-eight hours. The government repressed the protest with unusually harsh tactics and tragic results. During the two days of protest, nearly a dozen people were killed by government forces, and two teenagers were covered with kerosene and set on fire by a military patrol.

In the wake of the protest, several events would cause a definitive break between the Christian Democratic-led and communist-led opposition groups, as well as a break within the Left between the Socialists and the Communists. The first event was the August 12, 1986, discovery of a clandestine arsenal of weapons brought into the country by the Manuel Rodriguez Patriotic Front (FPMR), an armed group associated with the Communist Party. The second was an assassination attempt against Pinochet by the FPMR on September 7, 1986, in which five of Pinochet's bodyguards were killed. Hundreds of political activists, suspected to be connected with the FPMR were arrested and twenty-five were sentenced to death. Pamela Constable and Arturo Valenzuela (1991, 294) commented that "although angered by the repressive excess that followed the assassination attempt, most politically active Chileans were equally horrified by the crime itself." As a result of these incidents and the general's own campaign to discredit the Marxist Left, the moderate opposition refused further collaboration with the Communists. The two socialist factions patched up their differences and began to work with the moderates for a negotiated return to democracy.

The government and the AD had attempted negotiations previously, in late-1983, but the dialogue had broken down because of government unwillingness to speed up the transition timetable. In 1987, however, the AD chose to negotiate a transition with the government within the strict parameters defined by the 1980 Constitution. The transitional process, which began in 1987 and culminated with the election of Christian Democrat Patricio Aylwin to the presidency in December 1989, represented a negotiated transition dominated by authoritarian elites. The regime change occurred as a protracted series of steps, delineated by the military regime's own constitution, and initiated and tightly controlled from above by the established regime. The authoritarian elites exercised control over the transition by regulating the timing of the reforms, structuring elections to benefit their supporters, and excluding certain policy areas from the agenda.

During the campaigns for the 1988 plebiscite to remove Pinochet from office and the 1989 elections, the shantytown movement remained relatively mobilized and the number of housing organizations increased. The campaign activity by political parties and the democratic election of neighborhood councils (*juntas de vecino*) encouraged a flurry of activity in the shantytowns and a spirit of optimism and hope for the future. Congressional candidates from the *Concertación por la Democracia*[7] went door to door organizing the shantytown dwellers into committees, promising them solutions to their housing problems. Leaders and activists of the shantytown movement, for the most part, accepted that a limited democracy, constrained by the institutional and juridical legacies of Pinochet, was better than no democracy at all, as they campaigned for the "No" vote in the 1988 plebiscite. However, they did not demobilize until 1990, when the *Concertación* took power.

Two changes took place following the 1989 elections that led to the demobilization and institutionalization of the movement. The first was the public proclamation of an antimobilization strategy by the government that singled out the shantytown movement and attempted to channel the movement into more institutionalized forms of collective action. The second was a change in the configuration of power among political parties, which ended leftist hegemony in the shantytowns and reduced the status of the Left nationwide.

The first development that encouraged movement decline was the *Concertación*'s harsh response to shantytown mobilization. The parties of the *Concertación*, which had once supported or at least tolerated insurgent activities by the shantytown movement and had defined democracy in terms of popular influence and political and economic rights, abandoned these strategies and goals to protect a limited democracy. In an attempt to preserve democratic stability, the government responded to mobilization with force and characterized protesters as antidemocratic and as endangering democracy. The view that confrontational politics is inimical to democracy has been widely accepted by shantytown organizations, which are led by political party activists of the *Concertación*. This view has been grudgingly accepted, not as truth, but as a widely held belief that informs the strategies of leftist shantytown organizations so as to avoid being labeled "extremists" (Hipsher 1994).

Beginning on February 12, 1990, following the elections and before the inauguration, shantytown dwellers across the country launched a series of illegal land seizures. Minister of Interior Enrique Krauss publicly condemned the seizures as not being "the appropriate way to resolve housing problems" and warned that under the new government such acts would not be tolerated (*Mercurio* 1990). The events, which in earlier times would have received the encouragement and moral support of at least some of the leading political parties, were rejected by all, save the Communist Party, which simply denied any involvement or responsibility.

In the months that followed the inauguration of the new president and legislature, there were a few more attempts at land seizures by groups of shantytown dwellers. Cabinet ministers and congressional members alike rejected and condemned the occupations. Luis Pareto, Santiago city official, told the press, "Breaking up a land seizure is painful, but it is fundamental to preserving the democratic regime that the legal norms are respected. Occupations lead to no-good ends, only to anarchy and disorder" (*Últimas Noticias* 1990). Christian Democratic deputies criticized the occupations for being inappropriate and illicit forms of pressure that endanger democracy and characterized those who participated in the seizure as "anti-democratic" (*Fortín Mapocho* 1990).

The *Concertación*'s rejection of mobilization was soon translated into a shift in movement strategies, partly owing to the close relationship between social movements and political parties in Chile and partly due to a commitment to democracy on the part of shantytown movement activists. Party strategies and power relations are important in explaining movement outcomes in Chile. Two important features of the Chilean political structure are a well-established system of strong, ideologically distinct parties and an interlocking pattern of relations between parties and social organizations (Garretón 1989b). Leaders of shantytown movement organizations are usually base-level leaders of political parties. One consequence of this "double militancy" is that social movements' strategies, tactics, and goals are often heavily influenced, if not dictated, by the position of the party with which they have ties.

The Left—in particular the Communist Party—was slow to adjust to changes in the national political environment during the transition, as it sponsored the assassination attempts against General Pinochet in 1986, failed to support the 1988 plebiscite until a few weeks before the elections, and continued to press for mass popular rebellion until 1990. As a consequence, the Communists lost considerable support and legitimacy among shantytown dwellers (Schneider 1995). The change in strategy by the Christian Democrats and Socialists to support a limited democracy and the decline in support among *pobladores* for the Left made sustained collective action increasingly difficult, opened the door for greater centrist and right-wing influence in the shantytown movement and ultimately led to the moderation of movement goals and strategies.

Movement leaders, who set the agenda of these organizations, came to oppose mobilization in the late 1980s and early 1990s. Leaders of centrist and center-leftist movement organizations cite a commitment to democracy and a stable transition as their reason for having rejected mobilization. In a 1991 interview with the author, Hugo Flores, president of the Christian Democratic-led Solidarity Shantytown Movement, stated:

> The protests are over now. We will not use land seizures anymore. We were involved in the 1983 occupation of Fresno and Silva Henriquez, and I used to work with Oscar Peña (vice president of the Communist-led Metro Housing Coordinator). There has been a lot of debate in our organization about land seizures, and historically this is not the moment. We must support this democracy.[8]

The vice president of Metro, Oscar Peña, expressed a similar commitment to democracy, underlying his organization's decision to refrain from inciting protest; however, he was clear that this is also a strategic decision:

> The fundamental problem of the shantytown dwellers' movement at this conjuncture is that it is very difficult to walk the line between supporting democracy and fighting for the rights that have not yet been given to us. The regime has changed, and we have to support the democratic process, even if it is not exactly what we had hoped it would be.[9]

This antimobilization strategy represents a dramatic departure from the movement's earlier strategy under the dictatorship. The president of a socialist-dominated shantytown organization in José María Caro, José Nancucheo, described the changes undergone by popular organizations since the return of democracy:

> Under the dictatorship, the housing committees and the shantytown movement, in general, in José María Caro worked on the basis of demands. With the democratic transition our work has changed. Now that we are part of the *Concertación,* part of the government, we try to encourage people to save and to work through the government subsidy program. Why provoke a land seizure if you know it is going to hurt you politically and if it could endanger what you've worked so hard to get—democracy.[10]

The reluctance of most shantytown organizations to support mobilizations has inhibited those that are ideologically disposed to protest from taking action, for fear of repression and being branded as "extremists." In Villa O'Higgins, a housing committee member, Sonia Marin, explained, concluding ironically:

> Within all of us, I believe, is the fear of threatening democracy. . . . We in our committee are disposed to occupying lands. But we have not done this because the Minister of Housing himself threatened that all the people who

participated in seizures would be removed from the subsidy programs. . . .
This is what democracy is. Long live democracy.[11]

Following 1987, when political events made a negotiated transition
more possible, movement leaders began to reevaluate their organizations'
strategies and objectives to conform with those of the major opposition
parties with which they had ties and to reflect their commitment to democratic stability. The result has been more moderate, institutionalized tactics and goals.

Movement Outcomes—Comparisons and Contrasts

The Chilean shantytown dwellers' movement is representative of movement sectors in other countries in that it has experienced a pattern of
demobilization and decline similar to that of other sectors. The Spanish
neighborhood and pro-amnesty movements are examples of movements
with similar developmental experiences. The opening of the political
process during the Spanish transition and the accompanying changes in
the political opportunity structure initially encouraged movement mobilization and the use of noninstitutionalized forms of action. However,
once the elections neared and the transition gave way to democracy, the
movements demobilized and their repertoire of collective action became
dominated by institutionalized forms. In both cases, mobilization capacity fell as a consequence of party conflicts over the appropriate strategy
to end the dictatorship and a desire on the part of the dominant coalition
to reduce tension by discouraging protest.

In Spain, the increasing influence of an elite opposition within the
Catholic Church and the government (Medhurst 1984), an increasingly
militant labor movement (Maravall 1982), and the death of Francisco
Franco in November 1975 (Medhurst 1984; Castells 1983) allowed the
emergence of neighborhood movement activity. In one Madrid working-
class neighborhood, the neighborhood association grew from six residents in 1970 to more than fourteen hundred families in 1977 (Castells
1983, 243). The neighborhood movement in Alcala-de-Henares experienced even more dramatic growth. The first neighborhood association
was started there in 1974 with fifty residents. By 1977 there were four
coordinated associations in the city, each one with a membership of more
than six hundred (Castells 247). By mid-1977, there were one hundred
and ten associations in Madrid, counting on some sixty thousand members with a core of about five thousand militants (Castells 247).

The close ties between neighborhood associations and the Spanish
Communist Party, which initially encouraged confrontation with the
government and called for a democratic "rupture,"[12] favored the move-

ment's use of contentious strategies. The movement used both institutionalized and noninstitutionalized forms of collective action; however, until the 1977 elections, its repertoire of collective action was dominated by the latter. It held mass marches and rallies, which drew between fifty thousand and one hundred thousand people, and dozens of public meetings calling for the legalization of the associations (Castells 1983, 229; Bier 1979, 1).

One could make a similar argument in the case of the Spanish movement for political amnesty. According to Paloma Aguilar (1995), the first pro-amnesty demonstrations took place at the end of 1975, shortly after the death of Franco, and in the months that followed, Communists, Socialists, and neighborhood organizations all mobilized separate pro-amnesty demonstrations. By mid-July 1976, the movement was in ascension. *El País* reported nearly one hundred protest events on behalf of political amnesty in the month of July alone, and more than forty events during the month of August.

However, as the elections neared, the number of neighborhood movement and pro-amnesty protest events declined and their forms of collective action became more moderate. Beginning in 1977, the Spanish neighborhood movement went into noticeable decline. The movement abandoned its former tactic of confronting the authorities directly through street protest and demand making. For instance, in one working-class neighborhood, La Vaguada, the movement had been fighting for over two years to stop the development of a metropolitan shopping center and a new motorway access that would cut across the neighborhood. During the two-year-long struggle, the residents had sent petitions to the town council and letters to the king, painted murals, clashed with police, and protested outside city hall in a strategy of direct confrontation. In 1977 the movement's leaders, most of them Communists, negotiated with developers to allow construction of the shopping center and access road (Castells 1983). This had the dual effect of creating conflict between activists and leaders, thus weakening the movement's ability to mobilize either residents or public opinion and of institutionalizing the movement and taking away its principal means of political recourse—protest.

Similarly, the pro-amnesty movement's decline can be traced back to mid-1977. In the Basque country, political mobilization and demonstrations had been intense throughout 1976 and early-1977. However, by June 1977, most opposition members had withdrawn their support for continued mobilizations. Aguilar wrote (1995, 29) that the "Pro-Amnesty Week" called for June 1977 "attracted very little support and took place in the midst of constant calls for calm and peace from the parties and unions in the region."

The movements' declines can only be explained by changes in the political environment at the end of 1976 and strategic changes by leftist political parties to support the consolidation of a negotiated democracy. Until December 1976, when Suarez held a referendum, the results of which overwhelmingly supported his proposed constitutional reforms, the opposition, particularly the Spanish Communist Party, had supported a "democratic rupture," as opposed to a pacted solution to authoritarian rule. In July 1976 Suarez initiated a dialogue with the opposition that brought the forces of "democratic rupture" into his camp. In the case of the pro-amnesty movement, he accomplished this by promising the opposition "that a much wider amnesty would be enacted after the formation of the first democratic government. . . . if the Left and Basque nationalists contributed to cooling down the political climate they would confer democratic legitimacy on the forthcoming elections" (ibid).

In this changed political atmosphere it became increasingly difficult for the Left to cling to a "rupture" strategy, and by January 1977, Kenneth Medhurst writes (1984, 32), the Spanish Communist Party had "dropped the demand for a provisional government and spoke instead of a *'ruptura pactada'* (a negotiated democratic break)." It was at this point that movement leaders began to demand restraint from their organizations in terms of their demands and forms of collective action.

Some social movements in other transitional countries do not conform to this pattern of movement demobilization and institutionalization. Deviant cases include the popular movements in post-Salazár Portugal and the Brazilian environmental movement. In the following section, I briefly discuss these cases and the political conditions that shaped their development and resulted in different outcomes.

The return of democracy in Portugal is distinguished from most other transitions by the strength of the "popular upsurge" (O'Donnell and Schmitter 1986, 54). Following the overthrow of Salazár by the Armed Forces Movement,[13] wide-scale protest and mobilization blossomed into socialist revolution, continuing for over a year and a half, even after the return of democracy (Bermeo 1986; Hammond 1988; Downs 1989).

That the Portuguese movements did not decline and become institutionalized after the restoration of democracy can be explained by factors related to the structure of political opportunities. The most important of these were the government's radical, leftist agenda, its support for grassroots political mobilization, and the lack of continuity from the old and new regimes.

In Portugal institutional changes were rapid and the rupture in patterns of political authority complete, allowing the old regime no opportunity to reverse democratization. Immediately following the coup, the soldiers involved in the takeover dissolved the political apparatus of the dictatorship—the National Assembly, the Corporative Chamber, the various paramilitary organizations, such as the Portuguese Legion, the Naval Brigade, and the Portuguese Youth. The new government also dismissed the President of the Republic and the civil governors of the administrative districts in Portugal and in the overseas colonies (Opello 1985). Once the new government began to settle in, it actively promoted radical sectors of the population and encouraged grassroots activity, so as to further the revolution. It did so by creating linkages with the movements through political education programs and community development and by passing pro-popular pieces of legislation.[14]

A Latin American movement that has caused some social scientists to call into question the political process approach is the Brazilian environmental movement.[15] The Brazilian environmental movement emerged in the context of a democratic transition, but it has not demobilized to the same degree as movements in other democratizing countries. However, if analyzed using the approach put forth here, the lack of demobilization on the part of the Brazilian environmental movement is not surprising.

Brazil is a country of weak political parties with few ties to civil society and, then, only clientelistic ones. The exception to this, the Workers' Party, was an outsider to the negotiations for limited democracy. Thus, it would be difficult for parties to dominate movements or dictate their strategies in the same way as in Chile or Spain. Additionally, unlike the popular movements of Chile and Spain, the environmental movement poses no threat to democratic stability; it tends not to use contentious forms of collective action, does not pose a direct challenge to the state, and has no previous history of "threatening" levels of mobilization that led to the breakdown of democracy. Thus, we should not expect the state or political parties to try to control the movement in an effort to preserve stable, limited democracy.

Conclusion

The issues raised in this essay are important for understanding not only the factors underlying movement outcomes but also the content and quality of democracy that is emerging in the new democracies of southern Europe, Latin America and eastern Europe. In recent years, Chile has become regarded by many policy makers and scholars as the liberal democratic image on which eastern Europe and South Africa should model themselves (Christian 1994; Cash 1993).[16] This positive assessment is based in part on the presumption that in a nascent democracy the absence of open conflict, even where important social problems remain unresolved, is preferable to collective action that may "produce a disorderly spiral of movement-countermovement violence" (Tarrow 1991, 30). In fact, though, by demobilizing movements and attempting to control popular organizations, leaders of these new democracies and of popular movements may be alienating large sectors of society and ultimately be undermining the development of a healthy democratic polity.

The verdict is not yet in on the role that social movements will play in pacted democracies or how successful they will be in "deepening" democratization. However, the research has implications for other transitional countries, such as South Africa, where Nelson Mandela and the African National Congress have been vigilant in keeping labor demands and shantytown protest to a minimum. Popular movement demobilization may help elites navigate smoother transitions; however, if democracy is to survive in the long term, power relations must be restructured in a more democratic way, such that social movements can have a greater voice.

Notes

I wish to thank David Blatt, Ann-Marie Szymanski, Judith Adler Hellman, Doug McAdam, and Tom Rochon for helpful comments on an earlier draft.

1. Social movement theorists have conceived of political opportunity structure in two contrasting ways: first, as relatively stable variations in the formal institutional structures of political systems (state institutions, economic systems) and, second, as more volatile, situational variations in the informal structures of power (degree of political stability, presence or absence of alliances, elite fragmentation) (McAdam 1996). This research views political opportunity structure as the more volatile, situational aspects of power relations.

2. An obvious exception to this trend is China, where soft-liners in the regime allowed the government to massacre prodemocracy demonstrators in Tiananmen Square rather than press for greater democratization. Chile is an unclear case, as social movements did encourage soft-liners to initiate a political opening in 1983; however, in 1984, hard-liners retook the political initiative and reinstated the state of siege.

3. The author recognizes that political party activity is not always safe or free from violence. Likewise, she recognizes that social movements may exercise sufficient discipline when demonstrating so as to make nonconventional forms of participation relatively peaceful. As a general rule, however, political party activity is safer and more peaceful than movement activity, especially that of poor people's movements. This is because poor people's movements lack access to indigenous resources and must make noise to gain the attention of elites.

4. From 1967 to 1970, shantytown dwellers staged over 312 successful land seizures involving 54,710 families, nearly a quarter of a million people (Duque and Pastrana 1972, 265).

5. Cathy Schneider (1995) presents an excellent description of the repression and political violence that occurred in Chile, particularly among shantytown dwellers, in the aftermath of the coup.

6. The AD was a moderate opposition coalition of six political parties: The Republic Party, Radical Party, Social Democratic Party, Christian Democratic Party, Socialist Party, and Popular Socialist Union. The MDP was an opposition coalition of various left-wing parties, including the Communist Party, the Christian Left, AD-MAPU, and MIR. The AC was an opposition coalition of various associations and interest groups, including the truckers' federation, retailers, and professional associations.

7. The *Concertación* (Coalition of Parties for Democracy) is a coalition of seventeen centrist parties that won the presidency in 1989 and 1993. Included are the Christian Democrats, the Socialists, the Party for Democracy, Radicals, Social Democrats, and the Humanist/Green alliance.

8. Hugo Flores, interview, 16 February 1991.

9. Oscar Peña, interview, 20 December 1990.

10. José Nancucheo, interview, 8 March 1991.

11. Sonia Marin, interview, 30 August 1991.

12. The "rupture" strategy called for a freely elected constituent assembly, which would be presided over by a provisional government composed of all democratic parties and would guarantee a place for pro-regime forces. This strategy was favored by the PCE, the Spanish Socialist Workers' Party (PSOE), the Christian Democrats, Social Democrats, Liberals, and several small regional parties until 1977.

13. The Armed Forces Movement (MFA) was composed primarily of junior officers in the Portuguese army, many of whom had fought in the Algerian war of independence and were disillusioned by the Salazár government.

14. For instance, the government passed a decree in September 1974, which required that all habitable vacant housing be rented within 120 days. If not rented, the housing could be legally seized by squatters or the government for low-income housing.

15. See, for instance, Kathryn Hochstetler's (1993) research on the Venezuelan and Brazilian environmental movements.

16. Kathryn Sikkink (1992) discussed changes in regional economic policy and ideology in Latin America, emphasizing the increasingly free-market philosophy of the ECLA. In so doing, she mentioned that Chile has been placed on a pedestal as Latin America's great economic success story.

8

Social Movements and Democratization
The Case of Brazil and the Latin Countries

Salvador A. M. Sandoval

The general question posed in this study is, "To what extent and in which ways do social movements promote democracy in periods of political structural transformation?" There are reasons to believe that there is an important correlation between the outcomes of democratization and the role of social movement intervention, as suggested in the cases of the Latin American countries, Spain, and Portugal. This correlation, however, does not imply that social movements directly and singlehandedly cause specific forms of democratization since regime transformations, government reform, and even policy changes are the result of the complex interaction among multiple political forces including powerholders, polity elites, challengers, and their elite allies. Thus we can expect that any response to this question will be less clear-cut and most likely neither unidirectional nor unidimensional since often setbacks for the social movement at one point in time can become an advantage in future contention, while at other times gains by the social movement actors at one conjuncture can result in disadvantages.

If one understands social movements as forms of participation through collective political action undertaken by segments of disadvantaged populations to attain political change by challenging powerholders, the results of the interaction between challengers-powerholders-allies make searching for specific direct causal effects of social movements on democratization an illusive task, for causal links are usually blurred and possibly lagged by the dynamics of the process of political contention. Nevertheless, it is possible to examine the impact of social movements on the democratization process by analyzing: first, the variation in the collective action patterns during the protest cycle of the democratization period as reflecting different conjunctural factors and outcomes; second, the changes in the framing of claims and forms of movement participation as related to changes in social movement and opposition elites' strategies and goals, and authoritarian elites' responses; and third, the extent to which powerholders tolerate challenges in general and how power elites respond to social movement contention at different conjunctures.

Although the idea of establishing clear and distinct causality between aspects of regime transformation and the influence of the social movements seems unattainable,[1] analyses of cases such as Brazil serve to better understand the complexity of the political process of contention and the extent to which democratization is affected by the interventions of social movements. The relationship between popular contention and democracy is dialectical in as much as popular social movements and labor unrest impact the democratization process through their proliferation and mobilization strategies, forcing powerholders and opposition elites to respond to popular claims through a variety of political strategies aimed at attaining some degree of control of popular protest.[2]

This study examines, for the Brazilian case, the role of popular contention in the transition from a military dictatorship to civilian democracy. We focus on two broad types of collective action as indicators of protest activities: collective mobilizations of popular urban movements and strike activities of the labor movement. Both types of collective mobilizations can be considered protest activity since under military rule all collective action was regarded by the government and military elites as threats to national security and regime stability. Our analysis is structured around the variation in the timing of working-class strikes and of urban social movement collective action as two facets of the protest cycle that characterized the transition period. This period dates from 1977, in which the first collective protest against military rule reappeared after ten years of severe repression, to 1989, which marked the end of the first civilian presidency and the enactment of the Constitution of 1988, which eliminated the vestiges of authoritarian rule in Brazil.

Urban popular contention has taken on diverse forms in Brazil depending on the degree of powerholder patronage of popular organizations, the degree of resistance by elites, and the locus of contention. Thus contentious actions appear in various forms: labor unrest manifested in local workers' strikes and general strikes; mobilizations of popular social movements advocating a large array of political and social changes; and finally spontaneous riots and sackings of food markets, buses and commuter trains. These forms of grassroots protest resemble each other in as much as they use collective action to challenge powerholders and are based on the mobilization of substantial popular resources to press for specific interests.

In conceptually distinguishing forms of popular contention, Charles Tilly (1981, 1982) has classified them, on the one hand, according to the extent to which they are autonomous or patronized by powerholders, and on the other, according to the locus (whether in the local or national political arena) of the targets of mobilization.[3] In this conceptualization, each form of popular contention can be classified according to the intersection of these two variables. This classification scheme is illustrated, in an adaptation for the Brazilian case, in figure 8.1, in which different types of popular collective action are located. Popular contention changes as social movement actors become more autonomous of powerholders and when they become, as movements, more enduring and organizationally complex enough to advance from local political arenas to the national ones. In general, these all can be considered contentious collective actions varying in form, organization, and dynamics depending on their relation to powerholders and the relevant political arena. Given the diversity of forms of popular protest in the Brazilian case, we have opted for the purposes of this study to center our analysis around labor strike activity and urban popular organizations' collective action in the temporal trajectory of contention and its impact on the democratization process.

In its most general form the social movement consists of a sustained

FIGURE 8.1
Types of Collective Action by Levels of Power Orientations and Scope of the Collective Action, Brazil

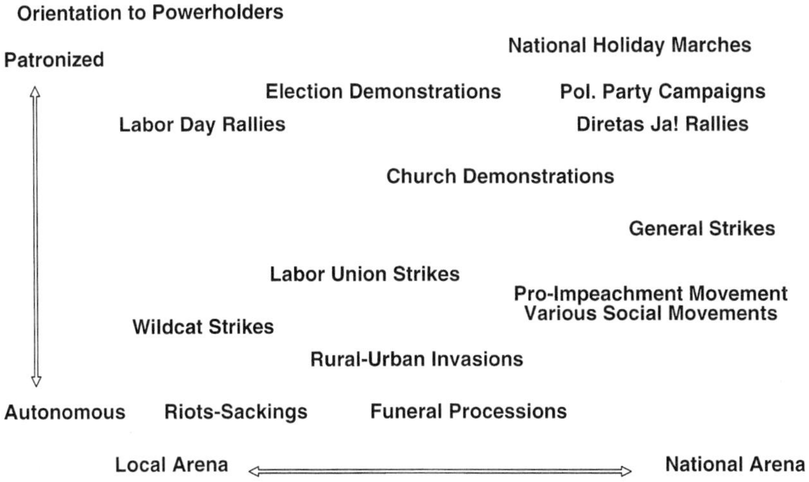

Orientation to Powerholders

Patronized

National Holiday Marches

Election Demonstrations   Pol. Party Campaigns

Labor Day Rallies   Diretas Ja! Rallies

Church Demonstrations

General Strikes

Labor Union Strikes

Pro-Impeachment Movement
Various Social Movements

Wildcat Strikes

Rural-Urban Invasions

Autonomous   Riots-Sackings   Funeral Processions

Local Arena ⟵⟶ **National Arena**

public challenge to powerholders (Tilly 1994). Social movements and the labor movement (as a specific form of a social movement) are standard vehicles for political action, but in times of structural political transformations such as changes in regimes, the incidence of different forms of popular contention must be analyzed diachronically in relation to each other and to changes in elite behavior if one is to assess how social movements influence the process of regime transformation.

The political process approach adopted here posits that protest and outcomes are part of a broader process of political bargaining (Burstein, Einwohner, and Hollander 1995), and not simply the result of elements of the political structure or of characteristics of elite actors. Outcomes are the consequence of the process of contention and bargaining, and as such are a function of each actor's capacity to mobilize resources relative to other actors, within the historical parameters set by political structures as concretized in specific political conjunctures. Thus, analyses of movements' success or failure in achieving their demands should first focus on the broader outcomes of interactions that play out in contention arenas where the social movement encounter adversaries and allies.

Outcomes are closely related to social movement goals. All social movements pursue their goals, some explicitly stated and others more implicit. Yet ascertaining the content of these goals is problematic because social movements have many participants, with different levels of commitment (militants, activists, and followers), and each participant has specific views of what are the movement's goals. In addition, movements often involve several social movement organizations, which may also have their own versions of goals. Finally, since contention is dynamic, social movements' goals change over the course of the movements' political engagement, a result of confrontations and bargains with adversaries and allies. Thus, a working definition of social movement goals should not only include claims and demands articulated by social movement organizations, but also the changes in the content of these claims and demands as an outcome of the political process.

While many of the studies of social movement outcomes have focused on whether or not social movements attain their stated goals, this approach ignores the array of outcomes that are fundamental in any understanding of the role of social movements in the political process and ascertaining their historical significance. By defining outcomes only in terms of policy reforms congruent with demands, other outcomes are overlooked that point to structural transformations and changes in the capacity of social movements to remain key political actors after initial policy gains are achieved. A broader conception of outcomes is necessary in order to enable the analyst to examine the consequences of contention over a protracted period in which there are gains and setbacks, and stated demands are only achieved after years of struggle.

For analytical purposes, outcomes have been classified into three broad categories that guided us in examining the impact of popular contention over the thirteen years of the re-democratization process in Brazil. This typology consists of three categories: (1) *social movement outcomes* are those that impact the internal dynamics of the social movements; (2) *policy legislation outcomes* are those related to policy or legislative changes,[4] and (3) *structural outcomes* are related to changes in the political structure. In all contentious actions, the assumption is that there will always be impacts on the social movement since contention implies not only social movement extrainstitutional activities to achieve their claims but also responses from adversaries and allies to social movement mobilizations. Less certain are impacts on matters related to policy, legislation, or implementation, on the one hand, or impacts on the political structure, on the other. Impacts on implementation, policy, or legislation seem to require less force on the part of social movements than outcomes related to changes in political structure. It is for this reason that our scaled typology of outcomes takes into account the notion that outcomes vary according to the strength of social movement intervention. The outcomes typology permits us to summarize data based on the consequences of contention at different phases of protest activity.

The study focuses on three ways in which social movements influence democratization. First, when social movements defending citizenship rights explicitly demand and gain the extension of one or more of the four elements of democracy (rights and obligations accorded to a large part of the population; their distribution with relative equity among citizens; binding consultation of citizens for public policies and government personnel; protection from arbitrary action by state agents [Tilly 1994]); second, when the movements cause an increase in participation in contentious politics; and third, when social movements introduce into the political arena proactive demands challenging the prerogatives of powerholders and their sustaining elites through direct confrontation of a sort seldom advocated by the more institutionalized opposition elites.

As the case of the democratization in Brazil shows, elite competition in struggles for regime change is a central facet of the political process and, consequently, the relations of the social movements to both authoritarian and traditional opposition elites are important aspects in understanding the fluctuations in popular mobilization. Therefore, these relations have been defined in a manner that allows for comparative analysis of political conjunctures. The behavior of adversary elites can be categorized in three types: confrontational, co-optational, or negotiational. The posture of allied elites can likewise be classified in three types of behavior: cooperative, assimilative, or competitive (della Porta and Rucht 1995). The intersection of these two typological scales is illustrated in table 8.1, which depicts the variability of elite postures faced by social movements in different political conjunctures. This graphic depiction permits us to map the shifts in elite-social movement relations over the period of democratic transition with the purpose of understanding, in part, the variations in collective actions.

Brazil 1977–1989
Democratic Transition and Consolidation

The process of redemocratization in Brazil displayed different patterns of social movement contention that allow us to analyze the role that these

TABLE 8.1
Types of Behaviors of Governmental Elites and Elite Allies' Behavior toward
Social Movements

GOVERNMENTAL ELITES	OPPOSITION	ELITE ALLIES	
	Cooperative	Assimilationist	Competitive
Confrontational	Phase 1: 1977–1980 Sectoral Contention for Democratization	Coalition and Sectoral Contention for Democratization	
Cooptive		Phase 3: 1985–1987 Sectoral Contention and Demobilization in Transitional Politics	
Negotiatory			Phase 4: 1988–1989 Sectoral Contention and State Reforms

played in the process and consequently their impact on the political outcomes. We find, in reviewing the distribution of contention data, depicted in figure 8.2, important variations in the fluctuations of labor and social movement collective action, which reflect the complexity of regime transformation politics. During the period between 1977 and 1989, we find not only phases in which labor and urban social movements simultaneously mobilized in collective protest, but also phases in which only one or the other mobilized in public demonstrations, and years in which there was a decline in both types of movements. The diversity of these fluctuations makes it impossible to find an explanation based on solely structural opportunity factors in as much as periods of regime transformation from authoritarian governments do not generally facilitate either labor or urban social movement contention in such a way as to result in the cycles of protest present in the Brazilian case.

Looking at the years between 1977 and 1989 from the perspective of popular sector collective action, this period of redemocratization can be subdivided into phases according to the distinctive timing of collective mobilizations of the labor movement and the urban popular movements.

FIGURE 8.2
Phases of Popular Contention in Strike Strength and Social Movement
Participation, 1977–1990

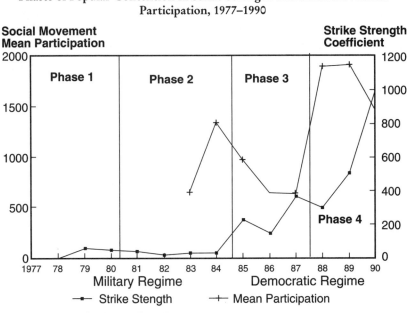

COEF = Duration × Size/1000 × Strike Rate

As shown in figure 8.2, the differences in the fluctuations in the mobilizations of labor and popular social movements produce protest cycles that distinguish four phases of popular protest in the democratization for each form of popular protest. The first protest phase is between 1977 and 1980; the second, between 1981 and 1984; the third, between 1985 and 1987; and the fourth phase, between 1988 and 1989. Each phase displays different dynamics of the political process as authoritarian elites, opposition elites and the popular social actors interacted in different political conjunctures.

Phase 1: 1977 to 1980
Sectoral Contention against Authoritarian Rule

The revival of collective protest action against the continuation of the military regime began in 1977. The early part of the year was characterized by signs of "political decompression" under the more moderate military presidency of Ernesto Giesel, although the forces of repression continued to play a major role in political affairs.

Under the close scrutiny of the armed forces, organized and collective opposition first appeared in the relatively guarded environments of meetings of professional associations or religious ceremonies under the auspices of the church. At its annual congress, for example, the national press association protested the Herzog killing and continued severe press censorship, and issued a call for the end of press censorship and political safeguards for journalists. In a similar manner, on the occasion of the one hundred fiftieth anniversary celebrations of the founding of the first law faculty in the city of São Paulo, two hundred of the most prominent Brazilian jurists issued a manifesto calling for the end of arbitrary authoritarian rule, a return to constitutional democracy and immediate reinstatement of habeas corpus. Likewise, the Brazilian Society for the Progress of Science, the country's oldest scientific association, faced government obstruction of its thirty-seventh annual meeting as the government sought to avoid anti-government criticism by the university community.

In 1977 a resurgence of a few public demonstrations occurred, as university students in the major state capitals and the federal district took to the streets to demand educational reforms, more funding for education, university autonomy, an end to government intervention in the universities, and the direct election of all university officials. Since the students dared to leave the confines of the university auditoriums to mobilize in street demonstrations, the government was swift to repress these actions through police force and subsequent summary expulsions of several university student leaders under the Law 477, which allowed the minister of education to banish—not just expel—students from higher education for political reasons. In addition, some faculty members were dismissed or forced to retire because of their support of student protest.

A second round of mass protest followed from an unexpected quarter, the metal, automotive, and chemical workers of the industrial belt of São Paulo. They were organized in huge unions of hundreds of thousands of members, which were hindered by draconian legislation that obstructed the possibility of legal strikes. All labor disputes were adjudicated by labor courts presided over by government appointed judges, whenever the union leaders threatened to strike.

The cracks in the authoritarian rule and widespread doubts over the veracity of government inflation statistics upon which wage increases depended gave labor militants an opportunity to confront employers and the state within the rules of the autocratic regulatory apparatus. Concerned that the legality of a strike would be challenged by the regime, and aware of the strong possibility of government repression of strikers, union leaders acted as "mediators" as shop-floor activists closed down the largest industrial enterprises of the country. These strikers demanded immediate restitution of their lost wages resulting from the inflation rate falsification by the finance ministry. The government response was to send police into the factories to arrest strikers and break the will of the workers. Within thirty days the first strike in ten years was over, as strik-ers returned to work without having achieved their demands. The following year, other regional unions in the region also struck, following the example of the ABC metal workers of the metropolitan area of São Paulo and making similar demands.[5] The main outcome of these strikes was to thrust progressive labor leaders from São Paulo, Rio de Janeiro, and Minas Gerais into the national political arena, and force opposition elites—who were already attempting to gain democratizing concessions from the military government—to consider the labor movement as a potential ally.

In 1979 labor succeeded in bringing to the foreground not only the organized working-class but also the popular sectors as key actors in the redemocratization process. After the experience of the 1978 strikes, union leaders began to prepare for the coming confrontation with the state at the time of wage readjustments in early 1979. Certain that further strike actions would bring government intervention, the possible arrests of union leaders and repression of strikers, unions, in collaboration with Catholic community leaders, began to prepare their respective organizations carefully to resist the regime.

The unions were able to resist initial repressive measures, as church-based neighborhood organizations mobilized their members to collect food and strike funds, obstruct police patrols by women and children at union headquarters, and open churches and parish halls to workers for union and strike meetings. In response to this popular sector and church support, the government ordered the army into all the affected cities. Soldiers were posted in front of churches to prevent workers from meeting, and working-class neighborhoods and factory districts were patrolled by military forces on the ground and in the air. Union leaders were indicted under the National Security Law for subversion, arrested and held incommunicado for interrogation. By May, other workers had replaced the imprisoned leaders as strike leaders, and together with other sectors opposing the regime organized mass demonstrations of workers, students, university professors, clergy, jurists, and journalists to demand an end to the repression and a negotiated contract. After sixty days, industrialists began to pressure the government authorities to allow for a harmonious return to work since they were fearful that worker discontent could endanger factory installations after the strike. In response, union leaders were released from prison on the condition that workers return peacefully to work.

Workers returned to their jobs, their union still vulnerable and their leaders threatened with convictions under the subversion laws; none of their demands had been met except the expected wage increase provided by law to compensate for the inflation of the previous year. Yet the strikes and the events that accompanied them achieved several outcomes: they forced upon the traditional opposition elites (politicians, church hierarchy, intellectuals, and entrepreneurs) new political actors (labor and social movements) who henceforth would have to be consulted in the negotiations for redemocratization; they altered the political agenda under negotiation to include demands to shorten the timetable for the return to democratic rule and to put an end to the authoritarian provisions in the labor legislation; and they brought about reluctant acceptance by traditional opposition elites of the use of direct collective actions by labor and social movement organizations as a major tactic for pressing for change.

The year-to-year variation in the national patterns of strikes clearly reflects these political factors that characterized the transition from dictatorship to civilian rule.[6] Here we will be observing strikes along three dimensions that vary independently of one another: total strikes per year (strike rates), average strike size, and duration of strikes. The coefficient of overall strike strength is the product of strike rates times duration times size.

Over these three years, the annual pattern of strikes did not alter their basic form but gradually decreased in volume. This decreased volume represents a decline in the strength of the strike actions under the last military government as repression persisted, and workers' organizations shifted strategies toward support of concerted action within the broader democratic coalition. Other indicators of this shift were (1) the sharp decline in the number of workers striking each year (the average number of strikers per strike in 1981 was 6,107, but by 1984 this rate had fallen to 2,946) and (2) the significant yearly decrease of the average strike duration from 8.8 days in 1981 to 3.9 days in 1984.

At first glance the decrease in the average size of the strike could be attributed, in part, to the technical fact of an increased number of strikes in 1983 and 1984, coupled with increased governmental repression of strike activity. A more detailed look at the interactions with the opposition as they responded to military intervention, however, reveals shifts in activities aimed at strengthening mobilization structures and broadening their following within the working class. The decline in labor protest was not only a consequence of the conditions in the political environment, but also the result of the labor movement's own choices in strategy as they joined the broader opposition coalition.

Urban popular movement protest was much less frequent, as labor unrest dominated the latter part of the 1977 to 1981 phase. Since strike activity galvanized resistance to the regime at this time and the urban social movements participated actively in strike support activities, there was little collective action by the social movements, numbering on average less than ten events per year, focused primarily on specific demands of direct benefit to their constituencies. But the lack of any significant popular mobilization in this period did not mean that the urban social movements were unimportant actors on the political scene. Their logistical support and collective action in support of the 1970 and 1980 strikes proved their capacity to mobilize large contingents of the population in confrontational activities, while demonstrating their willingness to join coalition protest against the regime. Thus the period between 1977 and 1980 was a precursor of later, more intense engagement of the labor and urban popular movements in the struggle for democratization.

Phase 2: 1981 to 1984
Coalition and Sectoral Contention for Democratization

After the experiences of the strikes of 1977 to 1981, labor and social movement leaders decided that to achieve a return to democratic rule, while at the same time consolidating the position of the labor and urban popular movements, required the creation of national political organizations capable of adequately representing their interests. Labor leaders undertook discussions among themselves leading to the creation of a national labor central. The formation of a coalition of labor union leaders with a broad ideological outlook made strike actions by more militant unions an issue of much debate in the national labor arena since these actions alienated moderate union leaders and more liberal entrepreneurs who might be won over to the struggle for democracy. In addition, continued strikes threatened the consolidation of a national labor movement with government intervention, since national labor organizations were banned under the military regime. As a result, more progressive labor leaders began to set aside sectoral forms of opposition politics and move toward coalition collective action.

During the years since 1960, there had been a significant expansion of working-class union organizations, many of which increased in militancy in the early 1980s and contributed to the emergence of a genuinely national labor movement.[7] This evolution in working-class organization is further demonstrated by the rise in 1981 to 1983 of the first national labor organizations with broad bases in the unions.[8] These were founded in the wake of a much contested general strike calling for democratization, labor law reform, union autonomy, and consultation over government economic policy with the International Monetary Fund.[9] Although the general strike, the first since 1963, brought out approximately two million workers, thus demonstrating progressive labor organizations' strength, its organizational outcome was to deepen the split between progressives and moderates within the labor movement. Despite the ideological cleavage within the labor movement, however, a consensus persisted that the struggle for democratization should make common cause uniting the various sectors of opposition.

Around this time, labor and popular movement leaders, along with groups of the progressive clergy, intellectuals, and opposition politicians, began laying the foundations for the creation of a working-class-based political party, taking advantage of a government attempt to dismember the only opposition party, the Movimento Democràtic Brasileiro, by dissolving the two legalized parties, thus permitting the formation of other parties. While opposition politicians protested the party reform bill, realizing that it was aimed at disrupting a unified political opposition, labor and popular movement leaders saw the government measure as an opportunity to form a more ideologically committed workers' party. The formation of a working-class-based opposition political party in 1982 required systematic coordination between labor and popular organizations, while avoiding a major fissure in the broader opposition alliance. Henceforward, collective action would have to be calculated within the broader strategy of achieving redemocratization—and contingent upon the commitment from traditional opposition elites that they would abide by demands for far-reaching change in the political structure, not merely a return to electoral politics. Consequently, the second phase of contention was characterized by increased mobilization, not only of labor organizations advocating sectoral interests, but of other social movements, as opposition elites were obliged to tolerated direct action from the more proactive labor and popular organizations.

In spite of the failure to sustain a unified national labor organization, by 1983 labor unrest resumed its upward climb, as strikes almost tripled in number in comparison to the previous five years. The 1983 annual strike rate rose to 1.86 from 0.74 the previous year, and the number of strikes yearly increased for the rest of the decade.[10] Strike demands were directed not only toward work place issues, especially wages and inflation, but, more important, around demands for union autonomy, redemocratization, and consultation.

1983 marked the beginning of an important change in the trajectory of strike activity that continued through the decade. Even though the overall strength of strikes continued to decline (reflecting the smaller size and shorter duration of strikes), there was a three- to fourfold increase in the frequency of strikes over that of the 1980 to 1982 period.

These changes in the strike dimensions represent a second type of strike pattern, characterized by small, frequent strikes in contrast to the larger and longer ones common in more autocratic periods. The change reflects as well a geographic and sectoral expansion of strike activity, as newly involved segments of the working class joined those already active in previous years. These tendencies were repeated in 1984, when there was a continuing decline in overall strike strength but an increase of smaller and shorter strikes.

The trajectory of popular protest in this second phase followed an opposite tendency from that of strikes, with a very significant increase in the mobilizations and collective action of urban social movements as they contributed their resources to the democratic coalition. In 1983 a resurgence of social movement militancy with an important rise in both average numbers participating and number of collective action events occurred. This contrasted with the period 1977 to 1981 when such events were very few in number. In the previous 1977 to 1981 phase, social movement protests could be counted in the tens, but by 1983 these had risen to 305, with an average participation of 654 persons. Unlike the previous period, when there were more generalized sectoral demands for democratization, the mobilization of this second phase (1983–1984) made specific sectoral demands (food prices, housing, transportation, education, and health) but—more important—framed these demands around democratization as a means to achieve them and claimed these interests as part of a struggle in defense of human rights. Thus, we find social movement organizations, like their labor counterparts, adopting a coalition strategy of opposition to the military regime.

In 1984, the process of negotiation with the military was marked by the call for the continuing mass mobilization by progressive segments of the opposition alliance in favor of the ratification of the Oliveira constitutional amendment, which would restore direct elections for president in the fall's election. The nationwide campaign, called the Diretas Já, consisted of mass demonstrations held in the major urban centers coordinated by the coalition of opposition parties, labor unions, and social movement organizations advocating the end of military rule. The opposition coalition had launched the Diretas Já campaign in June 1983, with a street demonstration in Goiania, and these continued until April 1984, when the congress rejected the amendment.[11] The importance of the social movements is evident in the unexpected size of the turnout at each demonstration: for example, Goiania, two hundred thousand; Rio de Janeiro, five hundred thousand; Belo Horizonte, three hundred thousand; Porto Alegre, two hundred thousand; and São Paulo, one million people attending.[12]

The magnitude of the Diretas Já demonstrations contributed to the reduction of other collective action events. Organizations shifted collective action from individual sectoral actions to participation in the broader demonstrations in support of the Oliveira amendment. Even though the opposition coalition failed to bring about passage of the constitutional amendment, it succeeded in consolidating massive mobilizations against the resistance of the regime.

After this failure to achieve redemocratization through constitutional reform, the united opposition faced a presidential election at year's end under the rules of the military regime. The democratic coalition succeeded in hammering out a consensus around the opposition candidacy of Tancredo Neves, a traditional opposition congressman with a progressive past, and a running mate who had bolted from the faction supporting the military to run against the official candidate. With the support of popular social movements, labor organizations, the Church, and professional associations, along with the reluctant support of the more moderate opposition politicians, the Tancredo ticket embarked on a campaign mocking the indirect presidential election process. This campaign repeated the mass mobilization tactics of the Diretas Já campaign, staging rallies in the state capitals that in turnout approximated the previous demonstrations.

On the eve of the convening of the electoral college, rumors spread that hard-line military factions would stage another coup if the opposition won, leading Tancredo Neves and his collaborators to make plans to escape from Brasilia to their home states to resist. On January 15, 1985, the day of the presidential election, the federal district was militarized to prevent any demonstrations pressuring the congress, and the armed forces were placed on alert throughout the country. The government's candidate received 180 votes, while the opposition obtained a total of 446—280 from delegates of the opposition parties and 166 votes from defecting government delegates. In light of the overwhelming victory of the opposition, the already evident mobilization capacity of labor and the social movements, and the readiness of Tancredo Neves and his allies to resist any repressive action, the military establishment conceded defeat. Twenty years of military rule came to an end (Skidmore 1988, 250–53).

Phase 3: 1985 to 1987
Sectoral Contention and Demobilization in Transitional Politics

The victory of the opposition alliance in electing Tancredo Neves to the presidency was not long lived. On the eve of his inauguration, Tancredo was suffering from a painful abdominal disorder and was admitted to Brasilia's main public hospital for surgery. As Tancredo Neves's illness dragged on, however, concern for the president-elect's survival and the prospects of democratization seemed uncertain. With the president-elect in intensive care at the University of São Paulo medical center hospital, rumors about a right-wing conspiracy to eliminate the president-elect circulated. The government was paralyzed over the uncertainty of presidential succession throughout the three months that Tancredo's illness lasted. Neither Tancredo nor his vice president, Jose Sarney, had been sworn in. Worse still, over a large part of his career, the vice president-elect had been one of the military regime's loyal supporters. The opposition parties, along with labor and social movement leaders, questioned the legitimacy of Sarney taking Tancredo's place in the presidential palace. Sarney assumed the day-to-day operations of the government, declaring that he would not make use of any of the authoritarian legal provisions remaining from the previous regime, and appointed a temporary cabinet, composed of prominent opposition politicians.

The death of the president-elect on April 27, 1985, was of such national significance that national television networks transmitted the funeral procession and, more important, labor leaders called work stoppages throughout the country to allow workers to take part. In São Paulo, as in other major industrial centers, unions set up television sets in the workplace and production came to a halt.

The public manifestation of grief that the death of Tancredo Neves provoked was not unlike that which occurred ten years earlier with the death in 1975 of another popular civilian president, Jucelino Kubitschek. At that time, Brazil suffered under the yoke of the most repressive period in its history during the government of General Medici. Kubitschek's death in an automobile accident (since he was a leading opposition figure, it was strongly suspected that it had been deliberately staged) stirred public outrage against the regime, manifested in mass participation in the funeral cortege from Rio de Janeiro to Belo Horizonte, his home state. The family rejected all military honors at his funeral and refused to permit the military police to escort the cavalcade, while mourners sang antigovernment songs and carried signs associating Kubitschek with democracy. As in the Kubitschek funeral, the popular outpouring of grief over the death of Tancredo Neves publicly displayed widespread support for a return to democratic rule.[13] The beginning of the new civilian government under Tancredo Neves's vice president-elect made Sarney himself, and the rest of the old regime's elite, aware that redemocratization was inevitable, and that the popular social movements remained key actors at this turning point.

In comparing labor and social movement mobilizations in this period, then, we find two distinct patterns. On the one hand, the popular social movements—less well organized and more dispersed—contracted under the intensification of partisan competition of government and nongovernment elites. As social movement militants sought to achieve sectoral gains through alliances with party leaders and governmental institutions, collective protest declined. On the other hand, the pattern of labor movement activism was characterized by a strong and steady increase in strike activities. Labor movement organizations, stronger than the popular social movements, enjoyed relative autonomy from partisan politics and the capacity for concerted action against government economic policies and in favor of specific workplace demands.

The first years of the civilian presidency saw major explicit and implicit changes in political structures and in the nature of the political opportunities available for social movements. The political agreements made by the various segments of the opposition coalition in their concerted thrust against the authoritarian regime, and the political-institutional crisis provoked by the death of the president-elect shaped the political conjuncture in which a new government would be formed. The most important political agreement was that substantive structural changes would be formalized exclusively through revision of the national constitution, which was promptly scheduled for 1988. In the meantime, reform and the removal of authoritarian practices were accomplished on an *ad hoc* basis, through either legislative action or simply by administrative inaction. For example, the legally prohibited national labor organizations and the National Student Union became institutionalized within the polity without formal alteration of their legal status.

At all levels of government, civilian party interests dominated government actions: politicians from a broad spectrum of ideological tendencies—aware of the potential of the social movement constituencies—initiated practices, policies, and administrative reforms intended to assimilate, negotiate with, or outright co-opt movement leaders and activists through the so-called "participatory governments." These variously constituted popular consultative councils, social action programs, and advisory staffs were committed to assimilating social movement leaders. Consequently, the tendency was for popular social movements' collective action to decline significantly in the years immediately following the return of civilian rule.

These changes in the trajectory of social movement mobilization are reflected by the decrease in the number of 1985 collective action events to thirty-four, as compared to the 305 events registered in 1983. Although the number of events increased in 1987, the average number of participants per event remained far below the levels of 1983 to 1984. Along with the demobilizing effect of political party competition, the resurgence of union autonomy and progressive labor political action had its effects on social movement demobilization as dedicated militants from grassroots organizations turned to union militancy. The national political organizations (such as the Partido dos Trabalhadores and the national labor central) which the social movements had helped to create in the early 1980s likewise recruited many of their militants from among social movement activists (Rodrigues 1990). At the same time, the Catholic Church, which had been a mainstay of popular social movements during the harsh years of military rule, now faced internal conservative opposition to the progressive clergy's support of popular collective actions, forcing these actors to reduce their role in organizing demonstrations. The outcome of changes in the resources of social movements and political opportunities, social movement collective action declined substantially between 1985 and 1987.

In contrast, labor activism took an upward turn with the end of the military government, making impressive gains in mobilization in Phase 3 (1985–1987) and Phase 4 (1988–1989). In 1989, the final year of the Sarney government, there were 3,164 strikes as compared to the 144 strikes in 1980.

During the 1984 transitional phase, the revival of strike activity revealed important changes in the strength and form of working-class protest, often motivated by the effects of the chronic economic instability and the desire for democratization of union life that dominated the concerns of labor leaders at this time. Remember, the number of strikes had remained relatively small during the last years of military government, when the number of strike actions rarely rose above the 1978 to 1979 levels. This is best understood as the result of the mixed effects of government repression and shifts in opposition coalition strategies in which the labor movement was an active participant.

Yet by Phase 3, beginning in 1985, the increased strike activity can be attributed to the process of democratic transition under the Nova República,[14] when there was a greater tolerance toward worker protest. In spite of the low level of unionization—estimated at around 20 percent between 1986 and 1988—strike activity grew steadily, aimed against rising inflation/government economic policies and aided by the unions increased mobilizational capacity.[15]

In fact, the resurgence of labor militancy only occurred in 1985, the first year of the civilian government, when strike activity increased markedly, as seen in figure 8.3. Strikes not only became more frequent, as the strike rate rose from to 2.54 to 3.28 over the period 1984–1985, but strike duration also increased from 3.9 days to 6.3 days, and the average strike size rose to almost four times that of the previous year, from 2,946 to 11,016. The significance of these changes in strike activity can best be visualized by comparing the annual strike strength coefficient—which combines the three dimensions in one measure (see figure 8.3). Strike intensity surpassed all other years since 1978 in 1985; the strike strength coefficient then equaled 227.63, as compared to 49.34 in 1980 and 29.18 in 1984. Thus, 1985 can be defined as a strike wave year.[16]

After the 1985 strike wave, the strength of strike activity in 1986 declined. One factor that likely contributed to the decline in strike activity was the reduction of the inflation rate from 235.11 percent in 1985 to 65.03 percent in 1986 due to the introduction of a new economic program, Plano Cruzado. Although strike strength on average was lower than in 1985, strike activity accelerated through the year as inflation rose. Since the strike strength coefficients are annual averages for the year, changes within the period are not readily apparent. In this respect it is worth noting that the decline in overall strike strength in 1986 was merely a prelude to the greater strike activity in 1987 as the strike rate rose over the year.

The second major strike wave in the decade came in 1987. The annual strike rate more than doubled from the previous year and reached new historic heights. Similarly, strike duration rose again to an average of 8.2 days, reminiscent of the 1978 to 1980 period, as employers became more resistant to negotiation. The average number of participants per strike, however, was slightly lower than that in 1985, suggesting that more workers in smaller establishments were entering the ranks of strikers protesting the then record annual inflation rate of 415.83 percent. This marked increase in strike activity is summed up in the 160 percent rise in the strike strength coefficient over the 1985 strike wave year.

The recurrence of a strike wave two years after the 1985 wave reflects workers' increasing capacity for mobilization. More workers were becoming involved in labor disputes motivated by the uncontrolled inflation spiral; they demonstrated their increased resistance to employers by holding out for longer periods. The 1987 strike wave marked a new trend in strike activity, for there was a significant change in the mix of strike dimensions from the previous years. From this year until the end of the decade, yearly strike activity was characterized by a larger number of

FIGURE 8.3
Strike Strength and Estimated Participation in General Strikes, Brazil
1980–1996

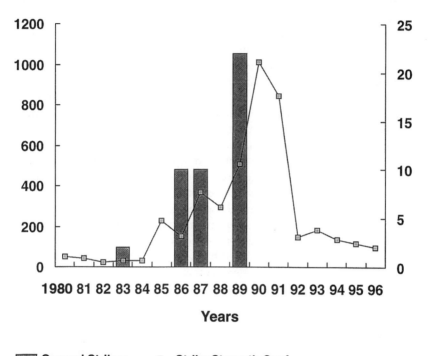

strike events with a lower average number of participants but a longer duration, as opposed to the prior pattern in which there were a larger average number of participants per strike and proportionately fewer work stoppages.

In contrast, 1988 saw less intense strike activity and a reduction in overall strike strength, as generally happens in the years following a strike wave. Nevertheless, the 1988 strike strength coefficient was larger than that in average years, even when compared to the 1985 strike wave. In this respect, we find that each strike wave ushered in successively higher levels of strike activity through the decade, reflecting the increasing capacity of unions to engage workers in collective action.

The democratic transition phase brought a return to sectoral politics by both labor and social movement organizations, with new priority placed on specific sectoral interests as opposed to the coalitional politics of the previous phase. The political conjuncture and the attendant new opportunities were molded by the major structural change begun in the course of democratic transition. This change included, first, the recomposition of the governmental elite, as military and civilian politicians from the dictatorship were eased out of government and replaced by members of the opposition; second, the reformulation of authoritarian laws; third, the placement of both civil and military security and intelligence organs under civilian surveillance, and access to government significantly increased through an intensification of multi-party competition; and fourth, the new openness of government officials to negotiation with the assimilation, or even co-optation, of social movement leaders and activists.

Nevertheless, despite the increased opportunities for mobilization, many popular movement organizations opted for collaboration with governmental and party elites, which resulted in a major demobilization. In contrast, the labor movement chose more confrontational strategies in spite of its greater access to government elites. This difference in the patterns of collective action reflects the specific aspects of the political structure and conjuncture encountered by each type of social movement, and how respective social movement actors evaluated their strengths and weaknesses in relation to the available political opportunities.[17]

Popular movement organizations were more vulnerable to external political party influences, and partisan factionalism resulting from increased inter-elite competition and resulting in reducing their capacity of sustained mobilization. They commanded fewer and less stable resources than did labor, pursued more generic, less sharply focused goals, and faced an often diffuse and ill-defined adversary. Consequently, popular movement leaders saw collaboration with sympathetic politicians as a way to advance their constituents' specific interests. Labor, unlike the popular organizations, was confronted with a more articulated and better organized adversary in the employers' associations and their strong political allies in government. To offset this, labor counted on stronger local, regional, and national organizational structures, a well-defined political agenda of structural reforms, a more stable constituency, and greater mobilization resources capable of pressing their demands at different levels of government. In short, labor had the capacity to act on its interests independently of government or opposition elite patronage. The key segments of the labor movement chose to follow a more confrontational strategy in pursuit of their claims. This resulted not only in increased levels of labor conflict through sectoral strike actions but also in two major general strikes, each of which attracted a national following of approximately 10 million workers (see figure 8.3).

Phase 4: 1988–1989
Sectoral Contention for State Reform

In 1988 and 1989 (Phase 4), social movement protest was primarily characterized by sectoral demand-making conducted as groups struggled to make their impact on the constitutional reform process. During the congressional elections in the second half of 1987, the political environment was excited by prospects of constitutional reform. In 1988 the principal mandate of the congress was the revision and reform of the military dictatorship's federal constitution. Although many of the authoritarian aspects contained in the old constitution had ceased to be observed and less arbitrary practices instituted, the formalization of these democratic measures was postponed until 1988 when the constitutional structure of the state underwent a major overhaul. The revision sought not only to eliminate autocratic features left from previous regimes but also to alter provisions seen by many sectors as obstructions to the development of a modern industrial society. Hence, the political conjuncture that initiated this phase was centered around the activities of the congress as it acted simultaneously as the national constituent assembly.

Conservative and moderate politicians and their supporters had mobilized their energies with the aid of the presidency to avoid the election of a separate constituent assembly, fearing that this would provide progressive political groups, such as the social movements, the socialist and social democratic parties, and the Church an opportunity to dominate the constitutional reform process. After the congressional elections of 1987, when it became clear that these groups had not achieved a majority, the president and the new congress went about preparing the task of constitutional reform.

As a result, the social movement actors were confronted with the task of devising strategies to pressure members of congress in support of their claims. More important, they sought to bring together those with different positions about what the role of these claims ought to be in the consensual formulation of constitutional proposals that would unite diverse movement organizations. Precisely this process had a strong effect on the way contention developed in this period. Certainly, the political conjuncture of democratic reform set the backdrop before which contention was to be acted out. However, the forms, strategies and options of which political opportunities would be taken, and how and when they would be used, were an outcome of the capacities of each type of social movement.

In general, popular social movements returned to the political struggle after a three-year slump in the level of collective activity even more determined to achieve major reforms. From 1987 to 1989, average participation in collective action events tripled from 636 to 1,903. This increase in participation was noteworthy, but even more so because this occurred in a smaller number of collective events, indicating that social movements were staging fewer, but larger and strategically placed demonstrations with a focus on mobilizing larger numbers of supporters. This type of strategy is understandable in the context of a constitutional reform process in which social movement participants lobby members of congress and political parties to support their proposals in the constituent assembly. Because of the strong pressure from the labor and social movements, the constituent assembly devised and instituted mechanisms through which popular sectors could submit their proposals to the various committees.[18]

Further, the significant increase in mobilization reflects a growing disenchantment of social movement militants with elected politicians attention to movement claims in spite of past collaboration. After a few years of close ties with government, social movement organizations were able to reject both the government elites' efforts to co-opt them and opposition elites' assimilative efforts. Social movement discourse became markedly antipartisan, advocating an autonomous role in the political process and a greater predisposition to engage in confrontation politics (Sader 1988). Movements displayed their strength through public demonstrations and their militants once again became active in coalitional action around their specific constituencies' interests, with the goal of presenting unified proposals for constitutional reform and pressuring for their enactment. A variety of forums bringing together professional specialists, politicians and social movement activists emerged to debate, formulate, and propose reforms to the national parliament. Their proposals included housing, health, childcare, education, transportation, human rights, and agrarian reforms, revision of labor relations, and institutional changes.

However, the political conjuncture—pressed by the urgency of political reform—shaped the position of political elites toward the social and labor movements. Conservative government elites took a firmer stand against social movements' demand making as politicians came to perceive the importance of the constituent assembly's proceedings. Furthermore, given that 1989 was a presidential election year, independent social movement activity was seen as threatening, for the Partido dos Trabalhadores had gained support steadily and would be a major opponent in the coming presidential race. Social movements' discontent with government came not only from its incapacity to attend to their demands but also from the ongoing patronage the Sarney administration was extending to the propertied classes, while neglecting programs to improve the social conditions of the lower classes.

Nongovernment elites of the center and center-left also wavered between cooperative and competitive postures toward the social movements. Some of these elites had at times worked with social movements pressing for common demands, but the enhanced conditions for political change present in this period often led these elites to view social movements as competitors over the leadership of a reform-oriented agenda. Consequently, social movement activists found that these elites had become less interested in cooperation, especially in matters of political reform.

Indicative of these changes in the attitudes of political elites are the rates in this period of police repression of collective action—reminiscent of the final years of military rule. While in 1983 and 1984 (Phase 2), on the average 37 percent of protest events prompted police intervention, in 1985 and 1986 (Phase 3) the percentage decreased to 16 percent; in Phase 4, repression once again rose, to 42 percent as shown in figure 8.4. Certainly, as social movements became more intent on having their demands met and as political elites became more adversarial towards contention, police repression once again became highly probable. There was a substantial reduction in the number of incidents of collective action, from 124 in 1987 to 73 in 1988 and 52 in 1989. Nevertheless, urban popular

FIGURE 8.4
Popular Collective Action, Average Participation, and Percent of Events Repressed by Police, 1983–1990

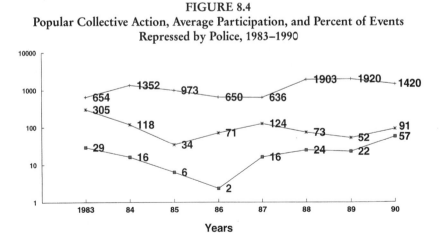

movements were able to mobilize three times as many participants as in previous years, averaging 1,900 people per demonstration in 1988 and 1989 as compared to 600 in 1986–1987 (figure 8.4).

In 1988, in spite of inflation reaching record heights (1037.62 percent for that year), strike rates did not reach the levels of the previous year. In fact, both the strike rate and average number of strikers decreased slightly in 1988 from their 1987 level, while duration increased only slightly. Consequently, the strike strength coefficient was 296.43, a decline from 369.08 in 1987, but certainly higher than any of the other years considered here. This decline can best be understood in the context of the political conjuncture. The previous years' strike wave and general strike and the failure of government to bring spiraling inflation under control led it to implement yet another economic stabilization plan, the Plano de Verão, which postponed discontent as workers waited to see the results. Another political factor that affected the strike rate was that the constitutional reform process redirected the political activities of labor leaders, like their urban popular movement counterparts. They turned away from strikes to the task of forging consensus within the ranks of labor about the needed constitutional reforms that would guarantee workers' jobs and establish a base for future labor relations. The complicated task of arriving at constitutional proposals by an ideologically divided labor movement was time-consuming, as labor organized itself locally, regionally and nationally to reach a common position. At the same time, they devised joint strategies to pressure for its enactment. The decline in strike activity at this time, therefore, was more the outcome of the interaction of the organizational and ideological characteristics of the labor movement and the political conjuncture dominated by the constitutional reform process than the lack of opportunity for contention.

This becomes more clear when one looks at the following year, the last of the Sarney administration (1989), which was marked by yet another strike wave and the largest general strike in the country's history, representing a significant expansion of worker participation in strikes. By any standard, the general strike was successful. It reached a new high in mobilizing approximately twenty-two million workers across the various regions of the country. This third strike wave in the decade was the working-class response to the hyperinflation that continued to grip the country, threatening severe economic consequences for workers. Labor disputes almost doubled from the previous year (1988), a 1.5 increase over the prior strike wave year of 1987. This new upsurge in unrest was largely provoked by the economic instability brought about by hyperinflation, but also influenced by the 1988 gains in changes in the national labor relations system during the constituent assembly.

The intense activities of the labor and urban popular movement organizations attempting to influence the constituent assembly paid off in the inclusion in the 1988 constitution of many of their claims. Labor succeeded, in one fashion or another, in obtaining important changes in labor relations and union autonomy, first advocated in the 1979 strikes. The popular social movements achieved the adoption of many constitutional provisions on social issues which govern the formulation of ordinary legislation and social policy. Special provisions guaranteed political and civil rights, undoing decades of authoritarian rules and practices.

Another legacy of the social movements was the rise of the Workers' Party to national prominence. Founded in the early 1980s under authoritarian rule, by 1989 the Partido dos Trabalhadores had become sufficiently consolidated to run its own presidential candidate, Luiz Ignacio da Silva (Lula), the leader of the 1978–80 metal workers strikes. In the running from the first round of voting to the run-off elections against a center-right candidate, Lula lost to the latter by about 4 percent of the national vote. In spite of his loss, the fact that a leftist working-class candidate was able to rise to such political prominence within such a short time attests to the capacity of the labor and urban popular movements organizations as agents of change in Brazilian society.

In the eleven years considered here as the period of redemocratization, then, indeed, the social movements had a major impact on the democracy which emerged in Brazil. Nevertheless, it is difficult to pinpoint a direct causal relation between mobilization and political transformation because, as this study shows, the causal relation between popular contention and democratization is intertwined with the interaction of other actors and diverse political conjunctures. As the combined effects of social protest, opposition elite pressures, and authoritarian elite maneuvers transformed political circumstances from one phase to another, labor movement and popular social movement actors followed variable and complex trajectories over the period.

In the first phase, both the popular movement and the labor movement were autonomous collective actors with their actions directed to the local political arena, demonstrating proximate ties and collaborative activities. In the second phase, both movements became closely allied in their efforts for redemocratization and creation of new political organizations would better represent their interests in the national political arena. In the phase in which the first civilian government began, the movements moved in different directions; labor continued in a more autonomous and national vector while the popular social movements returned to a local scope of action and closer collaboration with political elites. It is this phase which has concerned most of the studies on social movements and democratization. These works have decried the failure of popular organizations to maintain their independence from established political elites. In the fourth phase, popular collective actors returned to a more autonomous, nationally focused position and renewed collaboration with the labor movement which maintained its autonomous and national level orientation.

The two trajectories demonstrate movement dynamics that are quite distinct from one another. In the case of Brazil, all the democratic demands made by the labor and urban popular movements eventually achieved institutional form in the 1988 constitution, but their concretization was a task which required eleven years of contention, chipping away at resistance, at first from military rulers and later from former civilian allies. The Brazilian case does not point to unidirectional or unidimensional explanations, but demonstrates the complexity of any analysis of social movements and political change. The data may be seen as the component tiles fit into an interpretative mosaic that deciphers the trail of political change.

Social Movements and Democratization: Beyond the Brazilian Case

Generalizing beyond the Brazilian case and considering other countries of Latin America and southern Europe that underwent processes of democratization, two factors appear to be relevant in cross-national comparisons of the impact of social movements on democratization. A first factor is the relative autonomy of social movement organizations and their actions from either regime elites or opposition elite coalitions. In Brazil, as shown, autonomy meant that social movement actors not only possessed the conditions for independent intervention in the political arena but, more important, became effective actors in confronting authoritarian regime elites and in bargaining with traditional opposition elites by pressing to broaden the terms of the transition to democracy and eventually remaining key actors in the post-dictatorship period.

A second factor relevant to understanding the role of social movements in democratization is the capacity for coalition building of established opposition elites. In this case we conclude that the capacity of coalition building encompasses two central features: cohesion among opposition elites within the coalition confronting authoritarian regimes and the incorporation of new actors (especially independent social movements) into the opposition coalition. This capacity of cohesion and incorporation not only contributed, in the Brazilian case, to a clearer agenda for democratic change among the coalition actors, but also permitted the emergence of a consensus about the scope of subsequent political reforms in which popular collective actors' claims would be addressed.

Although extrapolating some conclusions from the Brazilian case to other countries runs the risk of oversimplification, the relationship of these two dimensions is depicted in figure 8-5, on which are situated along two axes the names of several countries that underwent the transition from dictatorship to democracy in the last two decades. As figure 8.5 indicates, we argue that there is a significant correlation between, on the one hand, the degree of democratic regime stability, and on the other, each country's experience with regard to social movement autonomy and cohesion and coalition building of opposition elites. The figure affords a simplified expression of both the currently predominant elite-oriented, top-bottom theories of democratic transition of scholars like Guillermo O'Donnell and Philippe C. Schmitter (1988), Adam Przeworski (1986), and Terry Karl (1990) represented by the cohesion/coalition-building variable; and the collective mobilization, bottom-top theories of Reinhard Bendix (1977), Stein Rokkan (1975), Barrington Moore (1970), and Charles Tilly (1995) represented by the autonomy of social movements variable.

On the left side of the figure we have situated Argentina, Chile, and Peru under the heading of less stable democratic institutions. Countries like Argentina and Chile have endured recurrent confrontations with authoritarian forces since the return to civilian rule. In these countries, social movements have been consistently subordinated to the opposition parties, which were less successful in building a strong opposition coalition. In-

FIGURE 8.5
Democratic Regime Stability by Levels of Social Movement Autonomy and
Elite Coalition and Cohesion Capacity

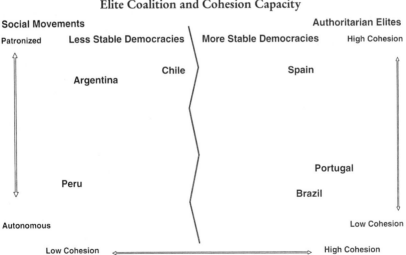

deed, such coalitions were often fragile and on the verge of disarray as their members many times conditioned their opposition actions to maneuvers to obtain partisan advantage in negotiations with the armed forces. In the case of Chile, where repression of the labor movement and popular organizations was more severe, the years of military rule allowed for the emergence of relatively autonomous labor and neighborhood organizations of a moderate tendency. The emergence of elite opposition to the military regime (Barrera and Valenzuela 1986) and the growing momentum to end military rule brought about a renewal of traditional party rivalries as factions of the opposition coalition sought to undermine the political potential of other coalition members (Garretón 1989b). This strong party competition within union ranks and other popular organizations reproduced the factionalism present in the elite coalition (Valenzuela and Valenzuela 1986) compromising the autonomy of popular protest activity as a force in the transition to democracy. The consequences entailed the weakening of the opposition's capacity to negotiate with the military a significant withdrawal of the armed forces from civilian politics in the post-transition regime, thus setting the conditions for recurrent confrontations between civilian authorities and the military.

As a result, redemocratization occurs in Chile with a clear preservation of the military's ascendancy over the civilian government. Among the prerogatives carried over from the dictatorship were: the designation of the dictator Pinochet to the position of head of the armed forces until 1998 when he is to assume a lifelong seat in the senate; the prerequisite that constitutional reforms be approved by military-dominated institutions; and the allocation to the armed forces of the foreign earnings coming from Chile's copper mines, the country's main export industry. Since the return of civilian rule, a number of civilian-military crises have marked post-transition political life as the civilian government faces the military's refusal to abide by institutional norms.

In Argentina, in a somewhat similar fashion, the traditional partisan cleavages between the Peronista and the Civica Radical parties were also reflected in similar divisions within the labor movement and other social movement organizations. As each partisan group attempted to gain advantage at the expense of the other during the transition period, the result was a fragmented opposition coalition whose factionalism permeated labor unions and most social movement organizations (Jelin 1987; Palermo 1987). This simultaneous weakening of opposition elite cohesion and lack of social movement autonomy meant that redemocratization would occur with a strong presence of the armed forces in subsequent civilian politics. Since the return to civilian rule, Argentina has gone through frequent crises of threats to institutional stability from barrack revolts and other forms of military pressure.

Peru exemplifies another variant of transition to unstable democracy, different from the Chilean and Argentinean cases, and it illustrates another facet of our interpretation. The Peruvian opposition elites were severely fragmented, unable to effectively build a viable coalition to negotiate a return to stable civilian rule (Ballón 1986). In addition, unlike the Chilean and Argentinean cases, Peruvian popular social movements were largely autonomous of these opposition elites but lacking any significant access to the polity (Stokes 1995). As social movements in the interior of the country grew, elites were neither able to include these new political actors into the coalition nor were they able to establish any ascendancy over them (Slater 1985). The unstable democracy that Peru experienced culminated in the Fujimoro takeover because civilian elites had traditionally lacked cohesion and failed to form anti-authoritarian coalitions while social movements emerged as strong independent actors in the political arena. The combination of fragmented political elites and autonomous social movements dissociated from the political structures has meant the weakening of democratic institutions and recurrent military interventions.

On the other side of the graph, one finds the countries that have had more success in establishing stable democratic institutions. There is, on the one hand, the case of Spain in which opposition elites were able to create a stable coalition to confront the authoritarian establishment; the social movements were closely tied to these opposition elites, intervening in moments when the coalition elites required that mass pressure be brought to bear on the regime. In the decades of the Francisco Franco dictatorship, political opposition parties were severely curtailed and labor evolved in a more autonomous fashion, serving as the grassroots base for future partisan politics. Less dependent on its links to opposition political elites and parties, the labor movement played an important role in the transition to democracy in terms of offering mass support for opposition elites in pressuring the Franco dictatorship (Gunther, Sani, and Shbad 1988). The relative autonomy of the labor movement is best exemplified in its role in subscribing to the Pacto de Moncloa, a broad political agreement between the several factions within the opposition coalition, aimed at providing the transitional government with the political and economic conditions necessary for establishing a viable democratic government. Under the pact, labor agreed to postpone several economic and political demands until democratic stability could be achieved. In addition to underwriting the opposition coalition's plan for the democratic transition, the labor and social movements had an important role in safeguarding the democratic transition by acting as a dissuading force against attempts of authoritarian entrenchment and coups (Fishman 1990).

Another variation, similar in several respects to the Brazilian case, was the Portuguese experience. Opposition elites demonstrated a significant level of cohesiveness, and effective intent in coalition building and incorporation of emerging new political actors during the transition process. Social movements autonomy was significant and even encouraged by the military faction allied to civilian opposition elites. It laid down the mass-based support for regime change but also guaranteed that previously excluded segments of the population would be empowered and have access to the new civilian government. This provided essential conditions for the formation of stable democratic institutions in as much as political elites accepted social movement actors into the polity and made their interests known without destablizing effects on the nascent democratic institutions.

In summary, figure 8.5 serves two purposes: first, it simplifies a more complex argument about the interrelation of social movement mobilization and elite negotiation of democratic transitions; and second, it portrays the two main theoretical perspectives on the role of social movements in political change. The bimodal distribution of the cases in the figure suggests that social movement involvement in the democratization process, under conditions of cohesive and coalition-building opposition, promotes the formation of stable democracies, as the older school of democratization theory proposed and contrary to more recent interpretations. The figure also suggests interesting hypotheses as a point of departure for further investigation into the role and impact of social movements on democratic transition outcomes in comparative perspective.

Notes

For their helpful comments, I would like to thank Louise Tilly, Charles Tilly, Joel Stillerman, Behrooz Moazami, Themis Chronopoulos, Marco Giugni, Mauricio Font, Alexei Waters, and the participants of the Contentious Politics seminar at Columbia University and the Think, Then Drink seminar at the Center for Studies of Social Change, New School for Social Research.

1. In discussing precisely the question of the relation between social movements and democratization, Charles Tilly (1994, 22) stated:

Let me suggest that at best the proliferation of social movements only promotes democracy under limited conditions: it only occurs when movements organize around a wide variety of claims including explicit demands for democracy and the state gains capacity to realize such claims at least as fast as the claims increase. But the conditions for these conditions are problematic as well. Indeed, democratic theorists have always posed precisely these two questions: under what conditions ordinary people actually demand democracy, under what conditions state capacity grows to meet these demands.

Perhaps we can take some comfort from the observation that the analysis of relationships between social movements and democratization leads us straight to major unresolved problems of democratic theory.

2. The statistical data for this study area are derived from a number of sources: for strike activity I have relied primarily on strike data from my study of forty-five years of strike actions in Brazil, the Brazilian ministry of labor and the Departamento Inter-Sindical de Estatistica e Estudos Socio-Economicos-DIEESE (Sandoval 1994; forthcoming in Brazil, Editora Atica); for the social movement data I have used data collected from newspaper sources compiled by the Instituto Brasileiro de Analise Sociais e Economicos-IBASE and the Centro de Documentação e Pesquisa Vergeiro in a research project under the supervision of Prof. Salvador A. M. Sandoval and with preliminary data analysis reported in Kauchakje (1992).

4. Our classification of policy outcomes is based on the "types of policy responsiveness" discussed in Burstein et al. (1995), 282–84.

5. The strikes took place, not in the city of São Paulo, but rather in the industrial belt composed of the cities of Santo André, São Bernardo, and São Caetano, commonly referred to as the ABC region.

6. Two partial but informative analyses of strike activity for the period between 1982 and 1985 are CEDI-Centro Ecumenico de Documentação e Informação, *Trabalhadores Urbanos no Brazil/82–84* (São Paulo: CEDI, Aconteceu Especial 16, 1986); Marcia de Paula Leite, "Tres Anos de Greves em São Paulo 1983–1985," *Revista São Paulo em Perspectiva* 1 (no. 2; July–September 1987), 50–64. For a brief description of the situational circumstances around which this strike activity occurred for the period 1980 to 1986, see *Brazil 1986: Relatório sobre a Situação Social do Pais* (Campinas: Nucleo de Estudos de Políticas Públicas, Universidade Estadual de Campinas, 1987), 54–86. For 1987, see *Brazil 1987: Relatório sobre a Situação Social do Pais* (Campinas: Nucleo de Estudos de Políticas Públicas, Universidade Estadual de Campinas, 1989), 111–45.

7. Of the nonagricultural workers' unions, 42.7 percent were founded after 1960, raising the number of labor unions from 1,670 before 1960 to 2,916 in 1988. Of these post-1960 unions, 69 percent were created between 1971 and 1988. Similarly, 40.5 percent of industrial workers' unions were founded in the period after 1960, as were 46 percent of bank workers' unions, and 65 percent of teacher, health, and other service workers' unions.

8. The early steps in forming such an organization took place in 1981 in a national conference of the working classes (Conferência Nacional das Classes Trabalhadoras—CONCLAT), which in 1983 split over ideological cleavages to form two major national confederations—the Central Unica dos Trabalhadores (CUT) and the Central Geral dos Trabalhadores (CGT).

9. For a more detailed discussion of the initial rise of the CUT and CGT, see CEDI-Centro Ecumenico de Documentação e Informação, *Trabalhadores Urbanos no Brazil/82–84* (São Paulo: CEDI, Aconteceu Especial 16, 1986), 41–47; Margaret E. Keck, "The 'New Unionism' in the Brazilian Transition," in *Democratizing Brazil,* Alfred Stepan ed. (New York: Columbia University Press, 1990).

10. The *annual strike rate* is the proportion of the number of strikes per

100,000 workers in the nonagricultural work force. For a more detailed analysis of strike activity, see Sandoval 1994.

11. For a discussion of the autonomy-patronage relation to powerholders as a characteristic of social movements and other collective action, see Tilly 1981. See especially diagram on pages 7–8.

12. This political campaign was from the beginning part of the strategy of the opposition parties' coalition to pressure for approval of the constitutional amendment. While the Diretas Já demonstrations resembled those of social movements, the fact remains that the Diretas Já collective action was organized and coordinated by the opposition parties, which in many cases already controlled state and municipal governments. In this respect, we have opted not to include these demonstrations as social movement collective action, even though the massive popular turnout can only be explained by the involvement of a large array of social movement organizations. For a rich, detailed factual account of the Diretas Já mobilizations, see Ricardo Kotscho, *Explode Um Novo Brasil: Diário da Campanha das Diretas* (São Paulo: Editoria Brasiliense, 1984).

13. We are inclined to understand another massive outpouring of grief, in 1994, over the death of Airton Senna, the Brazilian world champion in Formula 1, as demonstrating political frustration over the detours that the democratization process had taken at that time when national political institutions were still plagued with widespread corruption, inefficiency and incompetence.

14. The Nova Republica is the name given to the José Sarney administration 1985–1989, the first civilian government following the military dictatorship.

15. Instituto Brasileiro de Geografia e Estatistica-IBGE, *Pesquisa Nacional por Amostra de Domicilios,* Suplemento no. 1, Associativismo (Rio de Janeiro: Fundação Instituto Brasileiro de Geografia e Estatística, Departamento de Emprego e Rendimento, 1986), Table 3, 46; IBGE, *Participação Político-Social, 1988: Brazil e Grandes Regiões* (Rio de Janeiro: Fundação Instituto Brasileiro de Geografia e Estatística, Departamento de Estatísticas e Indicadores Sociais, 1990), Table 4.1, 8.

16. According to Shorter and Tilly (1974, 106–7), a "strike wave occurs when both the number of strikes and the number of strikers in a given year exceed the means of the previous five years by more than 50 percent." I have defined strike waves by the Shorter and Tilly definition, but included in that definition change in the coefficient of strike strength, which exceeds the mean of the previous five years by 50 percent.

17. This fact has been clearly documented by a wide variety of social movement analysts as a phenomenon occurring in all types of social movements regardless of geographic region. With reference to some studies on the recruitment and co-optation of social movement militants into political party machines or municipal administrations, see Pedro Jacobi, "Movimentos Sociais Urbanos no Brasil: Reflexão sobre a Literatua nos Anos 70 e 80", in *ANPOCS Bib—Boletim Informativo e Bibliográfico de Ciências Sociais* (no. 23, January–June, 1987), 26; Julio Assis Simões, *O Dilema da Participação Popular: A Etnográfia de Um Caso* (São Paulo: Editora Marco Zero/ANPOCS, 1992), see chapters 3 and 5; Renato Raul Boschi, *Arte da Associação: Politica de Base e Democracia no Brasil* (Rio de Janeiro: IUP-

ERJ-Editora Vertice, 1987), 46–58; Maria da Gloria Marcondes Gohn, *A Força da Periferia: A Luta das Mulheres por Creches em São Paulo* (Petropolis: Editora Vozes, 1985), 139–52; Ruth Corrêa Leite Cardoso, "Os Movimentos Populares no Contexto da Conslidação da Democracia" in *A Democracia no Brasil: Dilemas e Perspectivas,* ed. Fábio Wanderley Reis and Guillermo O'Donnell (Rio de Janeiro: Editora Vertice, 1988), 374–77; Maria da Gloria Marcondes Gohn, *Movimentos Sociais e Luta pela Moradia* (São Paulo: Edições Loyaloa), 161–64; Pedro Roberto Jacobi, *Movimentos Sociais e Políticas Públicas* (São Paulo: Cortez Editora, 1989), 157–59; Maria da Mercês Gomes Somarriba and Mariza Rezende Afonso, "Movimentos Urbanos e Estado: Novas Tendências" in *Movimentos Sociais,* ed. Pompermayer, 106–9; Mariza Rezende Afonso and Sergio de Azevedo, "Cidade, Poder Público e Movimento de Favelados" in *Movimentos Sociais,* ed. Pompermayer, 135–38; Sonia E. Alvarez, *Engendering Democracy in Brazil: Women's Movements in Transition Politics* (Princeton, NJ: Princeton University Press, 1990), ch. 6. For references on the recruitment of social movement activists into the labor movement, see Leoncio Martins Rodrigues and Adalberto Moreira Cardosos, *Força Sindical: Uma Análise Sócio-Politica* (Rio de Janeiro: Editoria Paz e Terra, 1993), 70; Michel Marie LeVen, "Movimento Operario e Sindical, 1972–85", in *Movimentos Sociais,* ed. Pompermayer, 38–41; Hamilton José Barreto de Faria, "A Experiência Operária nos Anos de Resistência: A Oposição Sindical Metalurgica de São Paulo e a Dinâmica do Movimento Operário (1964/1978)," master's thesis, Pontificia Universidade Catolica de São Paulo, 1986, ch. 3 and 4; Ivanise Leite de Miranda, "O Individuo Representativo: Considerações Sobre as Relações entre Valores Individuais e Consciência Social," Ph.D. diss., Universidade de São Paulo, 1992) vol. 2.

18. This procedure resulted in a massive formation base, comprising thousands of pages of documents from the initial proposals through the committees' reports and records of its debates to the final versions of proposed amendments submitted by each committee to the plenary of the congress where these proposed amendments underwent further reformulations as a result of the debates and negotiations between the federal deputies.

9

Collective Action, Change, and Democracy

Alberto Melucci and Timo Lyyra

In the complex societies of today, we are witnessing a progressive divarication of social conflicts from political action. It is becoming a commonplace observation that the forms of conflict emerging in the last thirty years do not express themselves through articulation of political claims and grievances in the first place. Rather, in them we have seen stagings of cultural challenge raised to the dominant language, to the codes that organize information and shape social practices. The actors involved in these conflicts have shifted their focus from class, race, and other more traditional political issues toward the cultural ground. The pivotal dimensions of daily life have substituted the totalizing designs of the past movements, and new actors have laid claim to their autonomy in making sense of their lives. Displacing the question of means, these actors introduce issues that recast the question of societal ends: they address the difference between sexes, ages, cultures; they probe into the limits of human intervention in nature; they concern themselves with health and illness, birth and death. The action of movements deliberately differentiates itself from the model of political organizations and assumes increasing autonomy from political systems; it becomes intimately interweaved with everyday life and individual experience.

Collective Action and Social Change

The increasing separation between cultural phenomena that bring an issue to light on the one hand, and the political actors who translate them in the political arena on the other, is bringing us anew to the question of how, if at all, the conflictual component raised by social movements is embodied in political actors. In contemporary forms of collective action, the political dimension often represents nothing more than a residue; it is only in the course of the processes of their visible mobilization that they come to address the political system as such (Laraña, Johnston, and Gusfield 1994; Darnovsky, Epstein, and Flacks 1995; Johnston and Klandermans 1995). To be sure, the idea of a universal struggle connected with the figure of a unified historical subject, handed down to us from the industrial society, has already been undermined by recent research focusing on movement networks, mobilization, and organization (Freidman and McAdam 1992; Klandermans 1989; Zald and McCarthy 1987; Morris and McClurg Mueller 1992). In its place, we have been shown the complex construction of collective action and the crafty negotiations through which the manifold orientations behind the movements' confrontational thrust are mustered for public events (Melucci 1989, 1996a; Klandermans 1992).

Yet, these investigations have only served to underline the theoretical shortages of our understanding when addressing the import of contemporary movements from the standpoint of the broader society. Compared to our increased awareness of the intricate processes of collective action formation, not as much has been made out of this material toward an understanding of the kind of societal effects that today's social movements produce. Nor has the gradually extended framework of these studies helped us to bridge the gap between the constantly arising conflicts that affect today's society, and the ways in which they are processed by the various institutional actors and incorporated into stable social arrangements, habits, and norms.

In the following, we want to examine the potential and the capacity of contemporary social movements to act as agents of social change and political transformation in modern, differentiated societies, defined by systemic complexity and the increasing importance of information as the central resource in their functioning and reproduction. Yet, for this task, it becomes necessary to redefine the analytical space traditionally reserved for the discussion of influence and outcomes in the study of movements. We must allow new questions to engage our concepts and analytical instruments to help the analysis gravitate beyond the confines of the common political interest that nourishes the talk of "social movements." The last vestiges of the historicist paradigm making movements the progressive protagonists of political change persevere today in the union of old Marxists aspirations and scientifically respectable approaches to measurable dimensions of action. These elements combine into a framework limiting itself to clearly definable confrontations between purposive-rational actors and the state. This perspective, however, by default suppresses the evident point pressed by the heterogeneous movements themselves: that the present forms of organized struggle, as social phenomena, are not entirely reducible to political mediation. Their objectives are marked by the characteristic of low negotiability; only a portion of collective demands can be mediated and institutionalized through political representation and decision making. More poignantly still, recent forms of collective action, if they do not reject outright, largely ignore the political system and generally display disinterest toward the idea of gaining access to political power and seizing control over the administrative apparatuses. Today, we can no longer afford to deflect from the significance of such observations: we cannot simply relegate to the analytical margins the fact that these goals have given way to a desire for immediate control over the conditions of existence and to claims to independence from the surrounding system—a feature that is frequently cited as a "political weakness" of contemporary movements, but which in fact should force new ways of posing the questions about the relationship between movements and political systems.

To remain open to the challenge of such seemingly novel dimensions, the analysis must proceed by way of analytical distinctions if it is to grasp the different meanings of an empirical form of collective action, which always combines a plurality of orientation and affects different levels of a social system (Melucci 1989, 1996a). The question of meaning is always involved and implicitly addressed in social movement research, yet seldom translated into a conscious analytical operation organizing the whole undertaking. In this chapter, we want to make the point of explicitly addressing this deficiency, in order to assess the effects of various forms of collective action. But before it becomes possible to evaluate the outcomes of actions, one must understand the action itself—what the actors are struggling for. At the most general analytical level, the study of collective action must, therefore, address what is at stake in societal conflicts. The analyst must account for the systemic field, its logic, the processes that enable it to reproduce and change. It is at this level of generality that the crucial issues and the vital resources that provoke social conflicts may be identified, and the direction of the conflict clarified.

When this order of questioning is not ignored but explicitly involved in the investigation, one can analytically separate forms of action that belong to different levels of a social system (practices in the everyday, symbolic action of movements, pressure directed at institutions of political system, claims for redistribution of costs and benefits, for example) and single out their specific outcomes, including those that are measurable—without forcibly reducing them to the effects on the political system. Here it is the perspective that makes all the difference in the way we can treat the various themes saturating the discourse on social movements (such as, most broadly, "rights," "democracy," "politics"). Only by comprehending this plurality of levels and their mutual relations can we show how, why, and to what extent change takes place; for it is change, after all, that we are still addressing behind the clout of collective action.

But what "change"? In the analysis of movements and their outcomes, it seems that the crux of the problem is attached to this question. To better specify it, we want to first pose the question of the existence of antagonistic conflicts of systemic scope: whether one can conceive of a dominant logic that disperses itself over a variety of areas of the system, producing hereby a great diversity of conflictual sites and actors, and whether there are dimensions of contemporary collective action that express new systemic conflicts and challenge new forms of social domination in complex societies. After that, we can address social change as a differentiated and multidimensional problem, drawing the conceptual consequences deriving from it for the problem of the outcomes of social movements. In this connection, we formulate the question of the autonomy of collective action, and discuss other theoretical approaches regarding their capacity to account for the evident consequences of movements' action. Finally, we extend our analysis of outcomes to embrace their analytical and normative consequences for democratic concerns underlying much of the movement research.

Collective Action in the Information Age

At present, we note, the formative context of all action is changing. With mixed feelings of amazement and fear, we are witnessing the impressive development of communication technologies, the creation of a global media system, the disappearance of historical political cleavages, and the collision of cultural differences within national societies and on a world scale, resulting from their reciprocal exposure. The repercussions of events and issues in one corner of the globe soon are felt in another, amplified and unpredicted; interdependence creates a transnational arena for issues and social agents. Never before have human cultures been exposed to such a momentous reciprocal confrontation, and never has the cultural dimension of human action been as directly addressed as the core resource for production and consumption: the world of which we speak today is a global world of a planetary scale, and this is made possible only by information, or the cultural processes by which we represent our world to ourselves.

More than a political question, however, the emergence of the transnational dimension to issues and agents is in the first place a sign that human action by now is capable of culturally creating its own space. To a far greater degree than any society in the past, the one in which we live has developed the capacity of subjecting its environment to purposeful action, extending its area of operation to its own natural bases in biological substructures with the means of science and technology: it "socializes" its own action at the same rate it brings "natural" constraints under social control.

The arenas of action have immensely broadened, and the reflexive capacity to produce an awareness of action (that is, a symbolic representation of it) above its specific content highlights the vast potentials of formal reflexivity, of pure symbolic capacity, of the acknowledgement of the production of meaning in action within the limits set at any given moment by the environment and the biological structure. Action is no longer appropriated in the form of its results; recognition of the capacity for action grows relatively independent of its products, becoming the ability of the actors to recognize themselves precisely as such—as actors able to recognize their own capacity to produce action (Melucci 1996b).

The depth of these transformations in the logic and the processes that guide complex societies allows us to speak of a qualitative leap in the social conditions of life. Our experience becomes wholly mediated (that is, by the media); reality is to an increasing extent contacted through artificial signs (images, words, sounds) representing it. The cognitive frames and the relations which enable us to make experience out of reality more and more depend on the information available to us. Individuals thus become the loci of social processes, as nodes socially constituted for both receiving and transmitting that information.

This dramatic change in the conditions of social and individual life means that analysis of the ways in which information is used to construct reality becomes of unprecedented importance for all efforts to comprehend action, whether collective or produced by the individual.

Contemporary societies operate on tightly woven networks of high-density information. For their proper functioning, they require the development of a distinct degree of autonomy of their component parts. They must at once presuppose and depend on individuals, groups and subsystems, which act as self-regulating units capable of sending, receiving, and processing information, circulated as the core resource in their operation and maintenance over time. Society acts on the system as a whole, just as it now does on single individuals: on their symbolic capacities, on their personal resources for defining the meaning of their own actions. Development of formal skills of action, decision-making, and continuous learning is encouraged as a disposal of motivational and symbolic resources on the part of the individual elements of which these societies are composed. Yet, every increase in the systemic differentiation simultaneously threatens social life with further fragmentation, lack of communication between its constituent elements, and atomized individualism, thus calling for deeper integration of individual and collective practices. While on the one hand, then, complex societies distribute resources with which individuals can identify themselves as autonomous subjects of action, they, on the other hand, at the same time expect the same individuals to "identify-with"—to function as dependable and effective terminals in complex information circuits.

To guarantee their internal integration, it becomes, therefore, necessary for highly differentiated systems to extend the system's control over the symbolic levels of action, so as to include in its scope the precarious spheres where the meanings and motives of behavior are constituted. Control can no longer restrict itself to the external regulation of the production and appropriation of resources; it must increasingly intervene in the internal processes of the formation of attitudes as well. Its key focus shifts from the manifest forms of behavior to motives and the meaning of action, to operate through those hidden codes that organize all information and knowledge used in the construction of meaning. To render individuals and groups predictable and dependable social actors, increasing control is applied to people's routine existence by the apparatuses of regulation, which exact identification and consensus. Social intervention shifts to the domain of individual motivation and, further, to the subtle foundations of action in biological structure.

When complex societies are driven by the need to mobilize individual resources and activate high-density, highly differentiated networks of organization, information, and decision making, in the process individual action comes to acquire an elective function as individuals are granted increasing opportunities to control and define the conditions of their own lives. Thereby, a complex system becomes the culprit in the creation of its own dilemmas: the consequences of its own operation today produce the countertendencies that come to fruition in the formation of oppositional forces arising against it. In the contradictory fact that the same resources must be distributed and withdrawn, entrusted and then placed under control, the systemic demands behind these processes themselves provide room for ambivalence, a terrain of new cultural possibilities and conflicts. A society of apparatuses imposes identity by defining the sense and direction of individual action through the tightly woven networks that transmit its symbolic models. Conflicts thus shift toward the new goals of reappropriation and reversal of the meaning produced by distant and impersonal apparatuses. These large organizations operating across the borders of economic, political, and cultural spheres adopt instrumental rationality as their "rationale" and tend to impose on individuals an identification based on these instrumental criteria. Social conflicts emerge in those fields of social life that are directly exposed to the most powerful and intense flow of information, where resources are invested the most and where individuals and groups at the same time are subject to the greatest pressure to incorporate in their everyday behavior the requirements and the standards of systemic normality.

Multidimensionality of Change

This more complicated picture of the conflict scenario helps us to move away from the infrasocial conception of change (forces of change below the visible dimension of social relationships: Nature, History, Natural Law, Progress, Revolution) that in turn had first followed its metasocial conception (eternal and cyclical return of the same; Will of Gods), and to start thinking of change in social terms. We must turn from a naive idea of change as a natural flow manifest in all things to a definition of change as an analytical concept. Change cannot be addressed as a homogeneous social phenomenon, but only as a variation in social relations which should be differentiated according to the systemic point of reference: elements or levels of the system involved. Within this general definition, moreover, we must distinguish between, first, the synchronic point of view (definition of the system and its structure) and the diachronic point of view (analysis of the processes through which a system changes), i.e. between structural and conjunctural factors; and, second, adaptive changes (range of variations which does not affect the structure) and changes of structure (variations that entail a redefinition of the elements of a system and their mutual relationships).

Starting from these analytical distinctions, two important theoretical points must be added that address the social dimension of conflict and change. On the one hand, change internal to a system should not be seen only as the process of adaptation required to cope with the "natural" variability of elements and their relations, and with alterations in the environment. It also results from the exigencies of maintaining the system within the compatibility limits of its dominant social relationships. On the other, forms of antagonist action contend the specific way in which resources are produced, and challenge the goals of social production and the direction of change as such. They make manifest a clash over the control and allocation of crucial resources; they assert and defend new definitions of the objectives, relations, and means of social production.

In the synchronic reality of complex systems erected on the pervasive role of information and its global scope, change is always specific and cannot be directly transferred from one level or subsystem to another. To imagine a structural change that at once involves all the levels of the actual society is to entirely misconstrue the workings of such societies; excluding the (nonetheless real) possibility of catastrophic events, it is unlikely that a social system can be affected by change in all its elements and relationships simultaneously: structural changes are effected as the work of combined processes taking place at different levels and different times. The social field in complex societies is never organized into the simple geometry of good and evil we can detect in the popular structure of political parlance. It is, instead, a system of interweaving opposites, of ambivalences, of multiple meanings, which actors seek to bend to their goals so as to lend meaning to their action. In complex systems, change is a field of tensions and balances to be managed, not a process towards ultimate emancipation. Every variation in the structure does have effects on the whole, but always in a mediated fashion. And this, as we point out below, becomes a point of importance for the discussion of the movements' influence in contemporary complex society.

A concrete social movement is always a complex and heterogeneous process that unfolds within a field of opportunities and constraints and contains a magma of empirical components. A movement operates within various organizational systems at once; it lies within one or more political systems; it acts within a society comprising various coexisting modes of production. Its action thus involves a whole range of issues, actors, forms of action, modes of organization, and objectives; it weaves together its different roots in multiple meanings, legacies from the past, the effects of modernization and rationalization, resistances to change. Movements are constructed, multipolar action systems. Therefore, in each particular case such "magma" must first be disassembled by analysis and then reconstructed into a system of meaningful relations if the movement's meaning and direction are to be understood.

It is thus not always easy to identify the elements that allow us to speak of an antagonistic orientation of collective action. A movement can fall under a variety of other fields of action: in some cases, we might better speak of conflictual networking, a claimant movement, or a political movement (see Melucci 1996a). Furthermore, where forms of control propagate themselves and permeate daily life and existential choices, they render the empirical distinction between protest and marginality, normality and pathology, and social movements and deviance more difficult to draw. In each case at hand, it is only by looking at how movements can be located according to their orientations of action and the system of social relationships affected by the action that we can with analytical categories identify their different outcomes.

However, where we analytically can detect the presence of such an antagonistic dimension, collective action, by the sheer fact of its existence, represents in its very form and models of organization a message broadcast to the rest of society. It makes manifest the existence of a conflict concerning some basic orientations of society: it serves to reveal to and caution the society of the crucial problems it faces, to announce the critical divisions that have opened up within it. It claims for real the bogus priority that the day-to-day experience, affective relations, and the deep motivations of individual behavior have received in a society that intervenes in the very roots of individual life. These areas of human experience become the terrain in which crucial social conflicts are bred, in which new powers and new forms of resistance and opposition confront each other. The great stages of the private life cycle—birth, adolescence, adulthood, love, old age, death—become crucial nodes of sensibility for collective action; they enter the public domain and become fields of human experience to be reappropriated. Educational and training processes, interference in the biopsychic structure, the regulation of interpersonal behavior, and the creation and transmission of information are some of the areas where the "normalizing" rationality of the apparatuses clashes with the collective demands for the right to autonomous definition of identity. Normality and pathology, health and sickness, have become issues that now transcend the traditional confines of medical or psychiatric knowledge to affect the meaning of action itself.

In the first place, antagonist action raises issues that are not addressed by the framework of systems rationality, dedicated to the effective implementation of whatever has been decided by anonymous and impersonal powers operating through the apparent neutrality of technical expertise. Conflicts involve the definition of the self in its biological, affective, and symbolic dimensions, in its relations with time, space, and "the other." It is the individual and collective reappropriation of the meaning of action that has been put at stake in the forms of collective involvement making the experience of change in the present a condition for creating a different future. Conceived most broadly, the challenge embodied in the otherwise heterogeneous movements action keeps raising questions about meaning, beyond the technical neutrality of procedures that tends to install itself in institutions and governs their role in society. Instrumental objectives nevertheless continue being pursued, though they become more precise and particular in their scope, affecting institutions in different ways we shall analyze in the last part of this chapter.

Antagonism and Autonomy

In view of the above, we may be led to ask whether social movements might not become the mode of operation of information society. In a complex society, conflicts constantly renew themselves and are spread to all levels of society; in it, the capacity for autonomous social action, as already noted, is allowed, in fact promoted, for systemic reasons. Could we then not speculate about the extent to which the increasing autonomization of collective action might today be reaching a point where collective action constitutes itself as a specific level of the system? Increasing real interdependence and autonomy on a global level have brought us to draw more and more on a common field: behind the facade of their manifest variations emerging with differences and similarities, it is the same problems and possibilities that circulate around the world. A "movement society," picked up as a possibility by Tarrow (1994a), would then indicate more than a mere proliferation of movements, arising more easily and more continuously and spreading more rapidly than they used to do, all as a result of increasing opportunities and resources that facilitate their formation. Rather, what we are witnessing is a change that has to do with something qualitatively different in the character of social life, something else than just a numerical multiplication of means and opportunities accounting for action formation and the increased access availed to them. As a result of the increasing differentiation of societies and the greater autonomy of the various systems that constitute them, it has today become more possible to pursue antagonist action without the mediation of organizations or institutions. But indeed, we might as well proceed so far as to ask whether the notion of a movement itself, which originally stood for an entity acting against the political and governmental system, has now been rendered inadequate as a description of the autonomous social space emerging for collective action: in it, we find temporary and fragmented actors forming from reticular networks. In this space, collective actors act more and more as pure media, broadcasting to the rest of society the message of the mere existence of a dilemma, of the presence of a conflict over meaning. Should we still call them "movements"? Whatever the case, the space of these movements has become a distinct and independent area of the system that no longer coincides with either the past forms of organization of solidarity or the conventional channels of political representation (Melucci 1984; on the role of civil society in the same direction, see also Cohen and Arato 1992).

These two—organization of preexisting reserves of solidarity and participatory action that arises in direct response to the political opportunities and exigencies—are descriptions of movement activity that we can detect in the past forms of collective action, even if there is no need to assign to them the status of stages in a historical progression of movement forms; a concrete movement, as said, always combines a variety of coexisting, even conflicting, orientations, objectives, and forms of action. Yet, at the same time, they do in a certain sense reflect dimensions of different historical conditions and situations faced by the movements in societies preceding the present one; on such action orientations were based the achievements of collective phenomena arising in the era of national consolidation and industrial conflict, in a modernizing context thrusting communal entities, occupational groups, class movements, the underprivileged and the disenfranchised against the state in defense of their interests and goods. While such orientations obviously have not disappeared into the dustbin of history, our question, nevertheless, is this: How do the analytical framework we have outlined above and the general theoretical approach we have so far pursued affect our perspective when it comes to assessing the outcomes of social movements in the information age? What, in other words, can be said of the effects of the movements' action in a highly complex society where an autonomous space of collective action has been produced in the operation of the global system itself, in an interdependent world more and more distinguished by the differentiation of its levels and the formalization of its principles? Is there something that such a perspective allows us to see that is not readily visible from perspectives analyzing the consequences of the action of contemporary movements through more conventional lenses?

At the moment, we are still struggling to free ourselves from the legacies of the industrial society. In the present situation where our preparedness to conceptually comprehend the nature of the societal transformations affecting our lives inevitably trails behind the pace of those changes, we remain dependent on the already available vocabulary in addressing what is now qualitatively different. Thus, the study of social movements, too, displays the dilemmas of having to discuss the emergent phenomena with the analytical instruments belonging to a period of the past. In particular, when turning to the questions of the movements' influence on the overall society, we can see the affinity in the literature on collective action and social movements to a conceptual universe born to a world where the forces of both domination and opposition were drawn along the relations of a hierarchically organized society with its boundaries still unsettled. The analytical instruments informing the discussion of the outcomes of the movements are those of the Enlightenment and emancipation: identity vs. interest; state vs. society; public vs. private; inside vs. outside. In a planetary society without a center, however, they leave us trapped in a precarious position where our language to address contemporary movements no longer corresponds to the coordinates of collective action.

Today, we must differentiate between the levels of outcomes and distinguish their dimensions the same way we differentiate the levels and dimensions of society opened up for the influence of action, and then ask whether the perspective allows us to bring into focus outcomes that are usually not considered as such. We must be analytically and theoretically prepared to consider all the consequences of contemporary movements' action, whether they are to be detected at the level of the everyday life of the individuals, in aspects of the political system, or at the symbolic level of the global system. Today still, most of the energy of the students of collective action is expended in attempts to delineate, with maximum clarity and purpose, its effects as they become manifest in the form of reform, or modernization of the functioning of systems and organizations. In fact, such a focus on the state in all its articulations still constitutes the *raison d'être* of the whole enterprise of the study of social movements, explaining the tendency to persistently hold on to the substantive terminology of "movements" that itself, like the paradigm of "revolution" looming in its background, entirely belongs to the language of mechanics long since purged even from our descriptions of physical reality. In the framework that privileges the political dimension in the production of movements' action, we are probably witnessing the final efforts to keep intact the legacy of the critical social theory of the last century. Today, however, it is no longer possible to let pass unnoticed the very visible consequences that follow from contemporary collective phenomena for forms of life at the level of personal existence and everyday practices. Such repercussions in individual ways of life, biographies, day-to-day attitudes, and action orientations are beginning to be documented with greater precision and focus. Yet, what remains to be addressed after exhausting the range of consequences at these two levels is the possibility of movements to produce outcomes that are not solely related to changing contents and variations in the existing pattern of the social order. We must be able to ask questions that allow outcomes of qualitatively different type to be specified, and for this purpose we need an analytical perspective that accommodates the issue of the existence of dilemmas of systemic scope, of structural effects of antagonist action in a complex society based on information. Such a perspective, we claim, is provided by an approach that is able to comprehend the autonomization of collective action for systemic reasons, portray its constitution as a separate sphere of action where individual and society, contradiction and conflict, structure and change intersect, and where the symbolic function of movements is not restrained to mere protest or expressive affirmations but carries along with it effects that are structural in nature, relating to the system as a whole.

The current approaches to the study of social movements, we maintain, do not articulate a sufficiently differentiated framework to accommodate such a perspective. They display an affiliation to the structure of a dualistic language that today stands in the way of a full understanding of the impact and potential of the movements' action in contemporary society. Behind the sophisticated tools and concepts developed for their purposes, what we are offered in them is still a choice between two standpoints: The State or Society? Institutions or people? Domination or emancipation? In essence, this vocabulary is relayed to us through what we could, for linguistic convenience, consider as two opposing paradigms in social movement theory: the paradigm of politics and the paradigm of society. It is sustained today in the representative analysis of, respectively, the rational choice and resource mobilization theories and the European tradition of social criticism and critical theory. On the one side, we find a well-established research tradition which grants primacy to politics and organizations as the model of collective action, and, on the other, a broader social theory has developed that, in its action perspective, posits the ideal of the social as the counterparty in the struggle of domination headed by the systemic structures of the modern society. Taken as a whole, to be sure, the two models of politics and society have provided us with corrective tools that have done much to advance our overall understanding of the social function and place of movements from where it was left with the theories of mass society and collective behavior. They each yield a coherent framework grounding a particular analytical space through which it has been possible to clarify the operation, forms of organization, aims, and effects of the movements as a social phenomena, normal in the trajectory of social life. Yet they both depend on assumptions that prevent the formulation of the problem of the movement outcomes along the lines of the questions we have posed above. As a result, either their focus on the outcomes is too restricted, concentrating on specific dimensions of the system only, or they fail to provide an adequate conceptualization of the autonomy of collective action and the role of its antagonist dimension. In the first case, we do not capture the antagonistic charge of movements that relates to the structural dimensions of the system as a whole; in the latter, such an antagonistic capacity can hardly be portrayed as realistic at all, or it takes up all of the space reserved for the movements' action, with movements conceptualized as quasi-ontologically performing their "progressive" role in society. Either way, the prospects for autonomous collective action in a planetary information society emerge distorted and detached from the concrete conditions of life where movements operate.

The most complete and developed example of a theory that takes its starting point in the institutional effects produced through mobilized movement actions is given in the work of Charles Tilly. This very influential perspective can be taken as a representative general theory under which other current approaches, such as the resource mobilization and rational choice theories, can be seen to come together and combine, even if distinct in their particular aspects (Tilly 1978, 1986; Tarrow 1989a, 1994a; see also Morris and McClurg Mueller 1992; Zald and McCarthy 1979, 1987; Jenkins and Klandermans 1995; Dalton and Küchler 1990). In assessing the movements' outcomes, this approach exhibits clear features of what could be called political reductionism. By limiting the analysis to disruptive public confrontations with authorities of a national state, its practitioners are led to examine the effects of such action on the same level: their interest is directed at political reform carried out through processes of modernization confining themselves within an organizational and a political system. For Tilly and Tarrow, for example, what is at stake is the issue of membership in a polity and (re)distribution of membership privileges among social actors. In the strategic game of maneuvering for institutional effect to alter the rules governing access, participation, or decisions that define the political system, significant social dimensions of action are eclipsed by readily measurable, high-visibility features of organized actors mobilized for efficacious production of tangible advantages through temporary events. We are given a highly complex scenario of how, in pursuit of their goals, collective actors resourcefully evolve and acquire the capacity to act as unified political subjects and skillfully interact with political opponents within a field of opportunities and constraints, but the goals that in this perspective are posited for such action through its causal criteria of success hardly exhaust the range of attainable outcomes deriving from the operation of social movements in a contemporary society. In an interdependent global system relying on high-density information, to begin with, it is not possible to know a priori whether or not a specific form of action will impact the political system; and even when it may do so, the fact itself does not attribute any special value to that level of action. More important, however, while Tilly himself has provided an account of the historical developments answering for the emergence of an autonomous (what he calls "proactive") character of movement action, and others have pointed out the formation of a "social movement sector" in modern societies (Zald and McCarthy 1979, 1987), in the absence of a more diversified understanding of the scope of this action and its achievements it becomes impossible to conceptualize just such a space it occupies in a differentiated information society. Without means to start discussing the nature of the contemporary movements' challenges, grounded in the interpretation and elaboration of needs of the autonomous space of collective action, their antagonist charge goes unobserved and indistinguishable from other dimensions of action. In the strict sense, then, no *social* collective action even exists; we are, instead, confronted with strategically oriented reform actors analytically indistinct from political pressure groups, even when they do not act within the formal frame of a political system. Yet, it is precisely this political focus that has come to dominate the discussion of the outcomes of social movements in the still small number of studies that have recently set about to address the issue (Rucht 1990, 1996a; Giugni 1995a; Rohrschneider 1993; Rüdig 1991; Gamson 1990; Huberts 1989; Kitschelt 1986).

What is left out of the resource mobilization and rational choice framework, the sphere of social relations anchored in the everyday interaction and experience of individuals, is all the more powerfully introduced through the dualistic social theory developed by Habermas (1984, 1987, but also 1996). Where rational choice and resource mobilization theories are drawn to the domain of political participation due to the privilege given to the strategic dimensions of action, in this instance we are presented with a preponderant image of the social sphere resting on the idea of a lifeworld as the space of communication logically distinct from, and prior to, the level of the institutional domain of economy and politics. The objective of the society is to gain control over, and democratically organize, the institutional order, including the political and economic systems, but when such a goal is no longer attainable through a direct conveyance of practices, procedures, and values to govern the operation of such systems, a capacity is expected of the social to at least recognize and bulwark its extant democratic substance (solidarity, freedom, equality) against the extraneous forces of power and money constantly hovering over and against it. As social life is threatened by deformations in the form of instrumentalization or commercialization of its constitutive relations, the space of the social thus becomes a space of resistance to the intrusive logic of domination by power or money, responding to its own, immanent capacity to pose a pure alternative to the model of administrative apparatuses and the market.

Thus, in this case, we see the antagonist dimension of conflicts but not the autonomy of collective action. Such an autonomy of action, which is the prerequisite for the development of its antagonist thrust, is not captured to the extent that movements emerge only by way of "reaction," in the extraordinary situations of crises and dysfunctions: they respond to disturbations in the (at least normatively) normal process of social and everyday life. Collective action becomes protection of identities, reinforcement of cultures; in its most "proactive" or offensive dimension, it has the limited capacity to lend itself to politics of identity, or to the creation of a revitalized public culture better activating the existing institutions.

On the other hand, both the antagonistic and autonomous dimensions of collective action are stressed by Alain Touraine, working from a perspective containing largely similar basic assumptions (1977, 1995). For him, antagonism of action is the fundamental component of what can be called a social movement, struggling for influence on the basic directions of social change in a permanent contestation over the society's historicity, its dominant orientations. Yet, in the scenario he lays out, a society where collective action for change has become a stable and decisive component of its basic functioning, this one particular dimension of collective action alone matters as its relevant feature. Indeed, it becomes its exclusive defining characteristic; all other levels of the social structure besides its overall orientation become less important, or even irrelevant, and correspondingly have no role in the analysis of movements' impact. While the autonomy of antagonist collective action is maintained as an essential part of Touraine's "sociological" society, he remains constrained to the analysis of The Social Movement of postindustrial society and fails to take account of outcomes related to other levels of collective action, as produced by the diversification and complexification of the context of action in contemporary society.

Consequences of Social Movements in Complex Society

The different general paradigms behind the approaches to the study of collective action, then, can each bring up dimensions and aspects of influence that social movements exert, or can potentially exert, on the different levels of the system. However, none of the standpoints they express provides for a perspective that could take into account both the emergence of autonomous space for collective action and the differentiation of a global social structure. But how would such a perspective, again, affect and enable our assessment of the outcomes?

One reason for the relative incapacity to conceptualize the production of movement outcomes and their specific character, we have claimed, is a permanent bias lingering in the study of collective action: the tendency to consider social movements as protagonists producing "positive," "progressive" outcomes. Characteristically, students of social movements share in common an underlying normative assumption: the interest in social movements is an interest in the democratization of society. We, to be sure, by conviction participate in the same attitude; yet, it is this bias we wish to raise to awareness and explicitly address. Movements do not necessarily produce results that fall in line with our wishes regarding their direction; there is nothing that assures us of the suppression of the scenario of opposite outcomes, of the elimination, or at least marginalization, of the omnipresent possibility of the dark side to the movements' action. Today, moreover, the relational context of all action in the multipolar fields of complex systems renders it increasingly more difficult to situate a movement simply at the Right or the Left, along the safe coordinates of the industrial society. Finally, we are faced with a situation where movements and countermovements with increasing frequency appear together, jointly defining the field of societal dilemmas.

As a discursive artifice, however, we will nevertheless proceed, as we have done so far, in compliance with the field rule of "positive" outcomes; yet, what remains implicitly present is always also the opposite side. The differentiation of levels to which we have referred above cannot be elaborated here in any greater detail (see, instead, Melucci 1996a), but from the perspective it afford us we can separate out different types of outcome from an analytical, not descriptive, point of view. Let us now suggest a provisional list of possible outcomes of collective action that corresponds to the overall theoretical and analytical framework we have elaborated in the foregoing, without still necessarily exhausting the whole potential of this framework; our purpose is simply to illustrate the significance of the point of view emerging with it.

(1) In its antagonistic dimension, collective action makes visible the form of power typifying contemporary society, revealing its operation behind the neutrality of procedures and languages. Such symbolic challenges are cultural tools; nevertheless, their effects in information systems are structural in nature: they regard the system as a whole and affect the structural constitution of power. The forms of the challenge operate through a transformational reversal, or upsetting, of information-organizing codes, bringing out in the open the hidden and unbalanced capacity of defining and naming social practices and realities. In this, movements are "offering," not just "asking," with what they offer constituted in their action itself, by its forms and processes which introduce an alternative to the dominant codes. This power cannot be identified as a matter of culture alone; where information becomes the core resource of the system, it is a structural and structured power. Operating at this level, collective action produces "symbolic waste": part of its impact always remains beyond the possibility of becoming fully institutionalized, due to the nature of the dilemmas addressed through the conflictual issues. This "waste," however, is such only from a strictly "economistic" point of view, from a narrowly defined notion of rationality; rather, in a global system, this capacity of collective action to address planetary dilemmas beyond their institutional dimensions permeates social life, fueling effects at other levels and preparing conditions for the reemergence of the issues elsewhere, in other forms.

(2) A side effect (but a very important one in our kind of societies) of the aspect of symbolic waste is the contribution to the setting of public discourse and public agenda that movements make. The recent work on framing processes in social movements (e.g., Snow and Benford 1992) and on the interaction of movements and public discourse (Gamson and Modigliani 1989; Gamson 1992b) addresses precisely this level of influence. From our perspective, however, what is important here is that this constitutes the first level of the institutionalization of the outcomes of movements' action, particularly through the workings of the mass media. More important still, it is a measure of the capacity of a given society to process its own conflicts in a more or less "democratic" fashion, according to the degree to which the controversial nature of the issue can be addressed, the different voices concerned in it heard, etc.

(3) At the political level, collective action carries an impact on two main features of the political system. The capacity of the society to represent interests and make decisions within a set of consensual rules implies a double limitation: On the one hand, the space for inclusion is constitutionally limited by the structure of interests and positions in society; on the other, the functioning of the machinery through which the political system operates is devised to preserve that same structure. Collective action can open up these structural boundaries of the political system at its three principal levels: criteria of access, channels of representation, processes of decision making. On these three levels, collective action can both redefine the constitutive boundaries or change the internal rules of the game (it is usually these three effects that are referred to by the parlance of "reform" or "democratization").

(4) Collective action is the main channel in the selection of new elites for institutional life. Participation in collective action is a learning process, and through it are acquired the know-how and the skills for the new forms of power continuously needed in the management of uncertainty characteristic of a complex society. When movements are institutionalized, they provide the supply of personnel renovating power positions and bringing in new cultures, languages, competencies, and expertise. Such "New Rulers," through this very function, introduce in the political system issues that are raised by movements, thereby transforming them into new rules and new power. Areas where movements provide new elites and cultures responding to the needs that arise from the emergence of new uncertainties include today the media system, the educational system, corporate life (e.g., business ethics, environmental concerns), academic life (e.g., environmental studies, gender studies, international funding of research on a world scale through foundations), and nongovernmental organizations (NGOs). These areas, again, are easily connected to the political system, or may themselves become a breeding ground for the formation of cosmopolitan elites, creating patterns of circulation on a national and global level. From the point of view of movements' influence, such connections and interrelations would present a promising new ground for empirical research.

Next to the emergence of new rulers, we can see the formation of counterelites, of "Transmitters" conveying to the subsequent waves of collective action the skills and knowledge acquired in the course of their previous experiences of involvement and participation. Ideological learning, organizational abilities, tactical wisdom, and accumulated information on relevant areas are made available to the next generation of collective action (or across different sectors of movement activity) through those making a personal career out of participation, moving along from one movement to another and carrying along with them the historical memory and accrued experience deriving from previous action or membership in other movements (as seen, for example, in the biographical continuum that can often be detected stretching from working-class movements, union activism, and the organizations of the New Left to contemporary feminist, environmental, and antinuclear or peace movements).

(5) Connected to this level, but analytically distinct from it, is the impact of movements in modernizing organizations. What is in question here is the organizational improvement at a functional level, or substitution of technologies. A recent example is the "green" culture providing business organizations and urban administration with sets of environmental regulations and technical innovations aimed at ecologically sound performance.

(6) At the most reticular and diffused level of social life, movements contribute to innovation in everyday life. New customs, languages, relationship patterns, and lifestyles are indications of such effects. Here, too, phenomenology of everyday life becomes increasingly important as a research tool in connecting the macro level of collective action to the individual experience in the minute textures of day-to-day practices (cf. Melucci 1996b). Diffusion of feminist attitudes and the "greening" of our common culture are probably the most impressive manifestations of such near-pervasive transformations of attitudes taking place through the incorporation of themes originating in recent collective action; their statistical distribution across the social spectrum testifies to the relative independence that such diffusion enjoys with respect to the more fundamental social values and political preferences held by individuals.

(7) In a mass consumption society, restructuring of the market through the redefinition of the actors and the goods circulating in it is another consequence of collective action. New producers are introduced to the market and old sectors become marginalized, new commodities are demanded and offered in response to the needs expressed through movement action; overall consumption patterns undergo redefinitions. The labor market itself may become transformed according to the emerging preferences.

What is always present as a possibility, though, is the reversal of effect on any or all of the analytical levels just indicated. Such countereffects are largely intuitive, and their presence must be left for empirical inquiry to clarify in each particular case. Camouflaging of power, ritualization of public discourse, closure of the political system, decay of institutions, crisis at the functional level, fundamentalism in customs and culture, and restrictions of the market, are all possible obverse outcomes to be investigated according to the nature of the collective action in consideration and the specific context of the arena where action is observed. There has certainly been no dearth of new social actors gaining prominence today who could be considered as both a cause and an effect, both instigators and products, in conjunction with these phenomena. Among them are the fundamentalists, the ideologists who, after the movement has exhausted its possibilities and decayed, continue cultivating the original myth of the movement and its purity in small circles of "Theologians," engaged in exegetic activity on its canonical texts and excommunicating unorthodox currents. Every generation of collective action produces its own "theological," fundamentalist sects of this breed which, passing through their life cycle, die out peacefully, perhaps having even experienced periods of growth simply by exalting their doctrinaire nature. Yet there are also those drawing from the same sources of origin that are propelled forward along the violent dimension inherent in the determination to protect the purity of the original gospel: they are the "Grand Inquisitors" of small sects, turned to a pure affirmation of their own existence, to an expressive search for their own identity no longer tied to any instrumental objectives, who in the desire to at least save their own souls dispatch their desperate message in the purifying acts in which the heretics and the unfaithful are sent to the stake and the fire by the infallible judgment of the righteous and the rare. This, of course, is the road's end of the terrorist or often the guerrilla. Though usually no more than a sect, in a situation of crisis or deep deprivation, however, these preachers of salvation-by-any-means may find a mass audience prepared to heed their integralist call (typically, in peasant revolts led by urban intellectuals nurtured in small sectarian circles of this type).

Many of these latter phenomena can be traced back to the interplay between movements and the political system, reflecting the extent to which an autonomous space for collective action to form and exist in society according to its character has become established, stabilized, and protected. In these cases, we are dealing with outcomes of collective action that could not grow into, and traverse its career as, a social force conducive to the creation of new institutional arrangements. Such a distorted trajectory of social movements whose processes of formation or conflictual thrust have become curbed or deflected—and these we must distinguish from the countermovements serving as genuine representatives of a dilemmatic message noted above—is a relational product, commonly of the incapacity of the political actors to comprehend and represent the emerging conflicts, or of the unresponsiveness of institutions to the impulses carried by the movements (see Melucci 1981; Wellmer 1984). Where the possibility of movements to express themselves on their own terrain is obstructed, where their initiatives find no inlet into the political system or are met only with the latter's repressive response, the margins of action of movements are progressively narrowed and their conflictual impulses frustrated. In the blockades thwarting their formation, whether at the level of their sources in individual experience or affecting the coagulation of their message in the communicative and interactive accomplishments of networks and associations, the broadcasting of that message to the broader society, or its gradual embodiment in political actors, lie the roots of many of those outcomes we associate with the regressive manifestations of movements of our time. The short-circuited flow of communication among social actors themselves, and between them and the instances of the political system, has as its results the formation of sclerotic or retrogressive identities confronting the intolerant shell of institutional apparatuses insulated from the ambit of the social dynamics manifested in movements. In the escalating process, a vicious circle of repression and reaction in which we witness a mutual reinforcement of the tendency to entrench positions locked in opposition and close the ranks, both the degree of openness or resistance of the political system to the existence and impulses of an autonomous social space, and the level of reflexivity attained in the latter by the movements regarding their own role in the production of the means and ends of their action, are factors that should be carefully examined when separating the outcomes from their origins.

Social Movements and Democracy

It is now that the question must be posed: Can one, then, specify conditions under which the "democratizing effects" of collective action would be more likely to materialize and can be promoted? Obviously, the line of questioning we are following here is both analytical and one that brings us to a normative and prescriptive conclusion: any interest in it, including ours, derives from a commitment to the ideal of democracy and democratic rights. To tie it more sharply with the terms of our discussion so far, we might specify the problem as follows: How can collective action emerge and bring issues to the political systems as agendas for decision making, as creation of new rules for institutional life, as new guarantees protecting and fortifying the domain for movements to autonomously form, gather momentum, and exert their influence along the lines of the analytical schema just laid out? In other words, what kind of political conditions can create a space for the pluralist game of meaning implied by the emergence of the information society, a space in which the seeds of ambivalence produced in the operation of the contemporary systems can be openly manifested and developed in new forms of action?

Our answer, in fact, has already been indicated in its elements along the analytical steps we have taken towards the formulation of the question itself. In the contemporary complex societies, neither the causes nor the effects of the processes implied in the project of democracy can be unproblematically referred to the operations of the political system. The conditions for democratic outcomes of social movements today rest on the autonomy of the social space of collective action, and on its capacity to yield an activated public space through a permanent transformation of issues into sets of new rights. These two conditions, moreover, stand in a mutually reinforcing relation. In the processes referred to by the latter, the former is at the same time expressed and constituted: by naming their rights, social actors name themselves. For it is in the language of rights that society has come to utter its own recognition of itself as an emergent terrain invested with the potential to constitute itself as sphere of autonomy outside the order of the political system and its institutions. By the same token, it is on this very apprehension by social actors of the right to name themselves, on the claims advanced to express and realize their principled "right to have rights" (as formulated by Hannah Arendt; see Lefort 1986), that also the political affirmation of democracy relies in a differentiated society with a widening gap between the seedbed of its conflictual stimuli and the identity of its political actors. That is, in so asserting themselves, collective actors affirm and substantiate precisely this autonomy that is the key condition for such processes to emerge in which they themselves can become activated and fulfill their function in society. But to become effective, again, the awareness of right itself requires the consolidation of a social space for collective deliberation, experience, and action in which it can be articulated and asserted. In the course of the organization of actions into goal-oriented movements occupying that space, it can assume a form of address that, through the language of rights claims, can be dealt with in the political system. Making possible the public treatment of issues for which they serve as a forum, such social spaces thus provide access to the problems that touch the whole society; furthermore, through the content of those claims, they offer a channel for further extending and expanding the existing possibilities that allow for the flow of experience from the critical areas of society where that experience is constituted to the mechanisms of collective problem solution. And today, as we have noted, the preconditions of precisely this kind of a space are already prepared by the system itself.

The prospects for the promotion of these existing possibilities, therefore, hinge on the reality of two complementary and mutually dependent accomplishments: On the one hand, there is the necessity of circumscribing, safeguarding, and reinforcing the autonomy of the societal public sphere for collective action, and of guaranteeing it through institutional rules. On the other hand, it becomes equally necessary to continuously expand and redefine such a space as a specific symbolic space through the naming of new needs and identities and the institutionalization of their message as new rights; only in this way can the new dilemmas calling for collective solutions be brought out in the open and the malleability of such solutions for societal self-organization, called for by the very nature of those dilemmas, be guarded. What we must concern ourselves with, therefore, are the possible conditions of "cultural freedom" as social spaces for self-construction, self-determination, and self-reflection that allow the movements to live their double existence within the invisible networks of society and in the temporary mobilizations through which they become publicly manifest, facilitating the conflictual recognition of new needs and the articulation of their dilemmatic message.

With this understanding, the question of rights is posed in a new light: it can no longer be presented as a matter of access to political participation and distribution of benefits in the first place, or at least directly. Instead, it addresses, on the one hand, the conditions of individual and group experience and, on the other hand, the mediation between the arenas in which such experience becomes crystallized in issues and the political system into which it must flow for processing by the institutional actors if it is to exert influence on the organization of social life. The condition for the symbolic function of movements in revealing the loci and stakes involved in the constantly arising conflicts that affect today's society is their elemental rootedness in the domains of experience in which these conditions become first manifested. Within the sphere of everyday life, brought under intense focus in the wake of the information society, take place the fragile processes of identity formation. What we today still delineate as the sphere of "privacy" is increasingly conditioned by conflictual experiences of the presence of a dilemma, and in it is maintained the sense of selfhood grounding the action capacity and the social competencies required for the formation of networks of human relations underpinning the structures of public life (Melucci 1996b; see also Cohen 1996). Yet, without their crystallization in publicly recognizable claims addressed to the political system by collective actors, the emerging needs and identities fostered in these conditions will remain inconsequential beyond their pure self-affirmation and short of institutional results through which the conditions for their own formation can again be guaranteed. Where change has become a permanent feature of society, the sites where the conflictual impulses coalesce around the new claims must be kept open and constantly created anew through the action of movements themselves. The need for the free formation and maintenance of identities at the everyday personal-interpersonal level must thus be complemented by its translation at the collective level, in terms of the construction of collective identities; only then can movements form and carry the impulses detected in the "private" experience to their fruition in messages broadcast to the broader society.

And discussion of rights in the context of movements and democracy must therefore regard the protection of the critical social areas in which the autonomy of movements' action is constituted: the everyday conditions ensuring the inviolability and autonomy of the person in her private existence, and the institutional arrangements guaranteeing a framework for free communication and association in public life. The detection and recognition of the contemporary conflicts and the promotion of the possibilities for processing these conflicts, as should be clear by now, are linked in the work of movements pushing for their expression precisely to this very effect. The defense and establishment of such rights through whose operation the intermediate areas presupposed for this function can be guaranteed, would then represent, perhaps, the primary democratic accomplishment of social movements, to the extent we are in a position to identify one at all in the overall situation of ambiguity, complexity, and mediatedness of all effects characterizing the information society. With this statement, we then arrive in what looks like a circular conclusion: in a way, rights themselves appear now to represent both the form and the content of democratic efforts, both their means and their ends.

This view of democratic possibilities no doubt represents a modest position, compared to the past aspirations attached to the idea of a transparent society freed of power. Quite rightly, it could be claimed that its ambitions are limited to clarifying no more than the mere minimum of preconditions necessary for those open-ended processes to emerge in which the boundaries of the political can be constantly challenged and redrawn. Indeed, in them we are only provided with formal frames to be filled with content in the particular conditions and circumstances, in the course of that constant feeding and formulation of issues vitalizing the public space. Such a view, however, is adopted with an awareness of the limits and possibilities of human action in a differentiated society of our time; today, any view of democracy must incorporate the facticity of an irreducible quota of conflicts, which only through a constant management of unresolvable tensions may be rendered into a creative force, into a reservoir of transformative energies; the alternative outcome is the risk of their becoming dissipated in destructive violence otherwise taking their place.

Confronted with the implications of this scenario, we face the task of incorporating the issues, of engaging the need interpretations, redefinitions of norms, identities, roles, and discourses pushed to the forefront by collective actors, while at the same time attempting to reduce the margins of silence and shadow constantly fed by the processes of exclusion arising from the system's own operational requirements (made visible in those individuals unable to fulfill the tasks of a competitive society, cultures destroyed by a standardized media market, groups labeled by their inadequacy to fit the social standards of efficacy). Here all depends, on the one hand, on the consolidation and expansion of autonomous public spaces for the expression of the conflicts and demands that develop in the everyday life, and, on the other hand, on the openness of the components of the political system that can allow the questions raised by collective action to become the subject of policy-making negotiations by political actors. The increasing distance we see extending between the two, however, need not necessarily be so great in the end: interdependence and the role of information allow a margin of ambiguity that renders seemingly weak and local forms of action potentially able to exert an enormous influence far beyond their actual size and immediate effect. This, to repeat, may nevertheless take place only to the extent that a space can be kept open for listening to just such voices and translating their message into new rules and institutions.

Conclusion

The Future of Social Movements

Doug McAdam

Over the past quarter century or so, the study of social movements has developed into something of a minor "growth industry" in the social sciences. The trend has been most pronounced in sociology, but is clearly evident in political science, history, and geography among other social science disciplines. What accounts for this trend? Nothing so much as real world events. The rise of the Left protest cycle of the 1960s and 1970s served to reintroduce and relegitimate the movement form in the industrial West, where it has since become established as a quasi-institutionalized feature of the political landscape. In the meantime, western-style social movements have proliferated throughout the world over the past two decades. The Chinese student movement that captured worldwide attention in the spring of 1989; the anti-apartheid movement that ended white rule in South Africa in the early 1990s; contemporary environmental activism in Ecuador, Brazil, and a host of other developing countries; the rise of national women's movements around the globe; all of these instances attest to the spread of the modern social movement form over the past twenty or so years.

So does the global proliferation of western-style social movements tell us all we need to know about the future of the social movement form? Reflecting the trend in the West, should we simply expect social movements to become more commonplace everywhere? Well, yes and no. We certainly expect organized protest activity to remain a ubiquitous feature of political life as we enter the new millennium, but, if the recent renaissance in movement scholarship has taught us anything, it is that the modern social movement, like all forms of popular politics, is itself a fluid social phenomenon subject to change through institutional pressures, popular innovation, and a host of other evolutionary pressures. Given this, it makes sense, as we bring this volume to a close, to speculate a bit about the future of the social movement. What changes do we envision as we embrace the new millennium? Four trends seem well worth watching in this regard.

Institutionalization and the Rise of a "Movement Society"

In a recent volume, David Meyer and Sidney Tarrow (1998) coined the term "movement society" to characterize what they see as the increasing incidence and institutional form of social movements in western democratic polities. The Meyer-Tarrow argument is entirely consistent with McCarthy and Zald's early (1973) formulation of the resource mobilization perspective in which they argued that the trend of social movements in America was toward increasing professionalization and formal organization. While perhaps not acknowledging the diversity of social movement activity in the United States, McCarthy and Zald nonetheless captured a discernible shift in the dominant form of that activity. We see nothing in the events of the past quarter century to contradict either the McCarthy-Zald assessment or the Meyer-Tarrow claim that the western democracies are becoming "movement societies." Nor do we envision a reversal of these trends anytime soon. As with other once "radical" political forms (e.g., political parties, unions, etc.), the social movement is well on its way to being institutionalized as a feature of western democratic politics.

What is our evidence for this conclusion? Direct observation would seem to lend a certain face validity to the claim, but we can marshal more systematic data as well. Recent years have seen a rash of large-scale research projects aimed at mapping the temporal incidence of "protest events" in a number of western democracies.[1] The first of these efforts was Sidney Tarrow's study of the Italian "protest cycle" of the 1960s and 1970s (Tarrow 1989). Tarrow used newspaper accounts of protest events to create time-series data on movement activity in Italy from 1965 to 1975. Temporally, the next of the protest events studies was the ambitious project mounted by Hanspeter Kriesi and a number of his students. Comparative in nature, the project sought to compare the ebb and flow (and character) of protest activity in France, Germany, Switzerland, and the Netherlands over the period from 1975 to 1989. Again relying on newspaper data, the project has thus far produced a book summarizing the main comparative findings (Kriesi, Koopmans, Duyvendak, and Giugni 1995) as well as specific monographs on each of the four countries studied (Duyvendak 1995; Duyvendak, van der Heijden, Koopmans, and Wijmans 1992; Giugni 1995b; Koopmans 1995). Inspired by both the promise and limitations of the Kriesi project, researchers at the Wissenschaftszentrum Berlin für Sozialforschung launched a massive project of their own, designed to map the patterning of West German protest activity in the post–World War II period. Under the direction of Freidhelm Neidhardt and Dieter Rucht, the so-called PRODAT project was expanded, following reunification, to include an analysis of protest activity in the former East Germany as well. Though ongoing, PRODAT has yielded preliminary time-series estimates of West German protest activity from 1950 to 1995, as well as a more limited portrait of movement activity in the former East Germany covering the years from 1991 to 1995. In turn, these efforts have spawned a host of others, whose results will only add to the cumulative portrait of trends in protest activity within the democratic West that is emerging from this collaborative research program.

What does this emerging portrait tell us? Net of idiosyncratic peaks of protest activity in each of the five countries for which we now have data, the general trend seems clear. Movement activity has risen steadily in the postwar period throughout the western democracies (Kriesi et al. 1995; Rucht 1996b). If Debra Minkoff's data on the rate of founding of U.S. social movement organizations (SMOs) can be shown to generalize across the democratic West, then the same is true of movement-related organizational activity (Minkoff 1997). That is, the trends in protest activity and SMO founding parallel each other, with the two exercising interesting and temporally specific reciprocal effects on each other.

What are we to make of this general trend? Since the bulk of the data discussed above concerns liberal-left movements, we might be tempted to surmise that the fortunes of the constituencies represented by these movements have improved as a result of the expansion in liberal-left movement activity. But impressionistically such a conclusion would be hard to reconcile with trends in institutionalized politics over the 1970s and 1980s. Admitting of considerable national variation in these trends, one would still seem to discern a general shift to the right in the western democracies during this general period. Such a characterization would certainly seem to apply to the United States and Britain in the 1980s and France more recently. But such global characterizations of national politics are always suspect, missing, as they inevitably do, the contextual details that may contradict the more general trend.

If we move, however, from the level of general system characterizations to a focus on more specific policy domains, we again seem to confirm the general drift to the right among the western democracies. Take welfare policy: what once seemed like a relatively secure set of social provisions throughout the West has been compromised in country after country. The idea of the "welfare state" is even under attack in the very Scandinavian countries that most fully embraced the vision as recently as a decade ago. Fueling the assault on the social compact have been supply-side economics and other conservative fiscal policies. Restrictive immigration legislation has been enacted in a host of western European countries as well, with France and Germany leading the way.

At the very least, it would be hard to read the evidence as a suggestion that the apparent increase in liberal-left movement activity in the western democracies has been accompanied by a consequent leftward shift in institutionalized politics. The opposite, in fact, might be closer to the truth. So what was wrong in our original surmise? Why has the general rise in liberal-left movement activity not resulted in policies more in keeping with the interests of those initiating the action? Two possibilities come to mind. First, the increase in liberal-left movement activity has been offset and perhaps exceeded by a simultaneous rise in right-wing mobilization. Unfortunately, we are not yet in a position to evaluate this claim. It is a regrettable feature of social movement scholarship that, reflecting the values of most practitioners, leftist movements far outnumber right-wing efforts as the empirical foci of study. Thus, we lack systematic time-series data on right-wing movements within the western democracies. The Kriesi project gathered such data but, to this point, has devoted almost all of its attention to mapping the temporal patterning of the leftist "new social movements" that arose in western Europe in the late 1960s and 1970s. The PRODAT project will allow for this kind of comparative time-series census of right- and left-wing protest activity for Germany, but has yet to be deployed in this way. So, for now, we are left to adjudicate this first hypothesis impressionistically. And our impression is that, with the possible exception of the United States, right-wing protest activity has generally lagged behind liberal-left activity in the western democracies during this period. If this impression is ultimately born out by data on right-wing movements comparable to that gathered by Kriesi, Tarrow, Minkoff and others for the left, then the puzzle will remain: why the disjuncture between the incidence and character of movement and institutionalized politics?

The second possible answer to the question is that the western democracies have gone a long way toward institutionalizing the organization forms and repertoires characteristic of the protest movement as it developed in the West in the post–World War II era. And through institutionalization, they have effectively robbed the movement of the disruptive potential from which it drew most of its effectiveness. The result has been a general spread and acceptance of the form coupled with a sharp decline in its effectiveness as a means of mobilizing political leverage. And here, unlike the first hypothesis, there would seem to be growing evidence that not only bears upon, but tends to support, the argument being advanced.

Having traditionally eschewed systematic research on agents and systems of social control, a number of social movement analysts have recently turned their attention to this general topic.[2] Chief among these pioneers has been Donatella della Porta (1992, 1995) whose 1995 book, *Social Movements, Political Violence, and the State,* represents a landmark publication in this developing subfield. The book summarizes della Porta's comparative research on the evolution of political violence and "the policing of protest" in Germany and Italy from 1960 to 1990. Among the central findings she reported in the book are: (1) a marked tendency toward less political violence, and (2) convergence and increased professionalization of protest policing in both countries. The two trends are related. If political violence was more common in Germany and Italy in the late 1960s and early to mid-1970s, it is, at least in part, because the actions of police (and other agents of social control) encouraged violence. The increased professionalization and routinization of protest policing have served, in turn, to tame and civilize movement activity.

The work of John McCarthy, Clark McPhail, and various colleagues (McCarthy and McPhail 1998; McCarthy, McPhail, and Crist 1995; Mc-Phail, Schweingruber, and McCarthy 1998) on the development by the National Park Service police of a registration system to routinize political demonstrations on the Mall in Washington, D.C., is entirely consistent with della Porta's findings. Like their counterparts in Germany and Italy, the Park Service police have endeavored to institutionalize protest, in large part, to reduce the likelihood of disruption and violence. Nor, according to the authors, is this trend confined to these three countries alone. Just as movement researchers have come to recognize the ubiquity of inter- and intramovement diffusion processes (McAdam and Rucht 1993; Soule 1995), McCarthy, McPhail, and colleagues report proactive efforts by the Park Service to make their policing repertoires available to law enforcement personnel in countless other localities, both in the United States and abroad.

There is reason to both applaud and lament this general trend toward institutionalization. Any move toward more professional, less arbitrary, police practices is, of course, desirable. Laudatory too is the genuine impulse by many enlightened social control officials to facilitate the peaceful expression of dissent. There is, however, a disquieting irony in this trend. It may well be that, by thoroughly legitimating and institutionalizing protest, the western democracies will render it increasingly ineffective as a social-change vehicle. This fear stems from the conviction that social movements have traditionally derived much of their effectiveness from their ability to disrupt public order as a means of inducing good faith bargaining by their opponents.

Consider the telling comparison between two campaigns in the U.S. civil rights movement: the Freedom Rides and the 1961–62 desegregation campaign in Albany, Georgia:

Supremacists responded to the threat posed by the [freedom] rides with a series of violent and highly publicized acts of resistance such as the bus-burning at Anniston, Alabama, on May 14 [1961] and the mob attack on the Freedom Riders six days later in Montgomery. In turn, these flagrant disruptions of public order forced a reluctant administration to intervene in support of [civil rights] interests. . . . That these favorable federal actions were in some sense coerced is suggested by former CORE director James Farmer in his account of the strategy underlying the rides: "our intention was to provoke the Southern authorities into arresting us and thereby prod the Justice Department into enforcing the law of the land." (Farmer 1965, 69)

The next major campaign provides an interesting contrast . . . not so much for what transpired as for what did not. The campaign took place in Albany, Georgia, during the final two months of 1961 and throughout the summer of the following year. [The data show an increase in movement activity but no] corresponding increases in white supremacist and government activity. This is consistent with accounts of the campaign. Those accounts stress the firm control exercised by police chief Laurie Pritchett over events in Albany. While systematically denying demonstrators their rights, Pritchett nonetheless did so in such a way as to prevent the type of major disruption that would have prompted federal involvement. (McAdam 1982, 176–77)

What Chief Pritchett did was routinize the mass arrest of civil rights demonstrators as a way of neutralizing the movement's disruptive potential. His motives were clearly to stifle, rather than ensure, dissent, but the impact of the current trend toward the institutionalization of protest may almost surely have the same effect. Regardless of intent, the routinization of movement activity robs challengers of their ability to disrupt—or threaten to disrupt—public order as a means of creating negative inducements to bargaining on the part of their opponents. There are two potential long-term effects of this strategic paralysis. Either challengers fail to devise innovative new tactics that restore to movements their disruptive potential—or they do so. In the first scenario, the effectiveness of movements as change vehicles is drastically limited. In the second scenario, movements are forced to adopt increasingly radical forms of disruption—including violence—as a way of reinvigorating the movement as a form of coercive politics. Neither of these outcomes would be terribly salutary, but they are worth considering as we ponder the future of social movements.

The Global Spread of the Social Movement Form

If the trend toward increased institutionalization of movements in the democratic West is disquieting, it would seem to be accompanied by a parallel development that is more salutary. We refer to the spread and increasing incidence of the modern social movement form in nondemocratic, nonwestern settings. The dramatic examples at this essay's start (e.g., the 1989 Chinese Student movement, the anti-apartheid struggle in South Africa) would appear to be just the tip of a very large iceberg. The list is seemingly endless; take the "revolutions" that toppled the various Soviet satellites in the late 1980s and early 1990s. Though these popular revolts are typically referred to as "revolutions," they looked nothing like the "typical" revolution, in either its French (1789), American (1775), Russian (1917), or Chinese (1949) variants. Instead, what happened throughout the Soviet system resembled nothing so much as western-style mass movements. The resemblance was perhaps closest in Poland, Czechoslovakia, the Baltic Republics, and the former Soviet Union itself, but even in East Germany where no western-style movement organization (à la Solidarity in Poland or Civic Forum in Czechoslovakia) emerged, the "revolution's" reliance on mass demonstrations, reform appeals, and traditional institutions (e.g., the Church) as mobilizing structures marked the struggle as far closer to the western movement form than to its revolutionary counterpart. Indeed, in retrospect, it is hard to say what was more surprising about the "revolutions" in eastern Europe—the fact that they took place or the form they took.

The list of surprising examples grows larger. It would be hard to think of many contemporary regimes that are more repressive than the current socialist-military government in Burma. Given the oppressive context, what would a political analyst predict about the possibilities for collective action and the form that any such action would take? Conventional wisdom would hold that the chances of organized action in opposition to such a brutal regime would be minimal. And that, if such action were to develop, it would almost certainly take a covert, revolutionary form. And yet, what should arise in this unpromising setting but the "Four Eights Democracy Movement," so-named for the date—August 8, 1988—of a key nationwide demonstration that helped set the movement in motion. Like its contemporaries in eastern Europe, the Burmese movement featured most of the earmarks of a western-style social movement. These included: peaceful mass demonstrations, a clear reform frame—"To achieve democracy, our cause" emerged as the movement's main slogan—and the creation of western-style movement organizations to coordinate protest activity (Hlaing 1996).

We could multiply our list of examples indefinitely—the anti-Marcos movement that brought Aquino to power in the Philippines (Boudreau 1997); the "mothers movement" that developed in Chile in the mid- to late 1970s in opposition to the Pinochet regime (Noonan 1995)—without increasing our understanding of the phenomenon. Having illustrated the general trend, we turn to the question of mechanisms to try to understand why the modern western movement form is being adopted by so many disparate challengers around the globe.

One obvious possibility is the global revolution in communication associated with such technological innovations as fax, e-mail, and instantaneous television transmission via satellite. This revolution is implicated in the spread of the western movement form in at least two ways. First, these innovations—especially the spread of television—has made the western movement "package," with its characteristic organizational forms and action repertoires, more generally familiar, and thus culturally "available," to nonwestern peoples.

The second way in which these technological advances have facilitated the spread of the form speaks to the two-way nature of communication. That is, these innovations have not simply been a conduit through which new cultural materials have been made available to far-flung populations, but they have also served as the vehicles by which these populations have sought—in unprecedented fashion—to mobilize "world opinion" (or specific regimes) on their behalf. Nowhere was this phenomenon more in evidence than in the case of the Chinese student movement in the spring of 1989. The conscious courting and use of the foreign media by the students during the Tiananmen Square occupation is one of the consistent empirical observations that runs through the literature on the movement (Calhoun 1994; Esherick and Wasserstrom 1990; Guthrie 1995; Smith and Pagnucco 1992; Walder 1995). Indeed, Esherick and Wasserstrom (1990) characterize the movement as a sustained exercise in "political theater." But theaters require audiences. And what the Chinese students understood was that, given the historically unresponsive nature of the communist regime, their best hope might lie in playing to a broader global audience. Hence, the importance of the western media and other new ancillary forms of communication (i.e., the fax).

But for any communicative performance to be effective, the medium through which the message is delivered has to be reasonably familiar to the intended audience. This principle creates a certain pressure toward cultural convergence on the part of otherwise culturally disparate claimants. So, while much about the Tiananmen Square demonstrations remained culturally distant and fairly opaque to a western audience, the self-conscious adoption by student leaders of certain kinds of western movement conventions made much of it familiar (or apparently so—think only of the western tendency to confuse the Goddess of Democracy with the Statue of Liberty) as well. Brandishing signs and banners written in English may be an obvious example of this, but it is hardly a trivial one. Absent the presence of the western media and the audience it implied, earlier cohorts of Chinese student activists relied almost exclusively on more traditional means of dissent—namely, wall posters written in native characters. The shift to English-language placards and banners (augmented, of course, by wall posters) speaks to the more general tendency toward cultural convergence that one sees occurring, not just in China, but everywhere the western media has penetrated.

There is at least one other mechanism, independent of the global information revolution, that has helped to spread the western movement form. But this additional mechanism has so many implications for the future of social movements that we want to take it up separately.

The Rise of Transnational Advocacy Networks and the Exportation of the Movement Form

Exposure to the western movement form can come from sources other than the new media discussed in the previous section. The various cultural conventions that define the modern movement template are being "exported" on what would seem to be an unprecedented scale by a growing and diverse pool of nongovernmental organizations (NGOs). These NGOs include transnational movement organizations, Protestant and Catholic religious institutions, and even multinational corporations. Increasingly, subsets of these NGOs comprise what Keck and Sikkink (1998, 2) refer to as "transnational advocacy networks." In their words, "a transnational advocacy network includes those relevant actors working internationally on an issue, who are bound together by shared values, a common discourse, and dense exchanges of information and services." Such networks tend, in their view, to form around issues of broad value salience, such as women's rights, human rights, and the environment.

Though these networks have often been loosely characterized as transnational social movements, the designation would seem to be misplaced. We agree with Tarrow (1998, chap. 11) when he says that "advocacy networks seem to lack the categorical basis, sustained interpersonal relations, and the exposure to similar opportunities and constraints" that typically characterize domestic social movements. The organizations that comprise an advocacy network also rarely engage in the kinds of action that we tend to associate with social movements. Instead, their role is typically limited to publicizing conditions in other countries and to providing resources and information to fledgling movement groups elsewhere. Pamela Burke's (1997) work on the growth of environmental activism by the indigenous peoples of Ecuador provides a fascinating example of the latter kind of activity. Though still at a fairly early stage, Burke's research has focused on the active involvement of two very different kinds of NGOs—transnational social movement organizations (TSMOs) and multinational corporations—in the growth of an environmental movement among native Ecuadorans. The TSMOs—including the National Resources Defense Council, Friends of the Earth, and the Rainforest Action Network—have served as the key allies in this case. Indeed, so proactive were they that one wonders whether the movement would have developed in their absence. And the form the movement has taken bears the clear imprint of the institutional reform tradition to which the TSMOs are themselves committed. Even the movement's framing of the issues is a western democratic export. Clearly "environmental justice" for "indigenous peoples" owes more to contemporary western conceptions of these issues than to traditional Ecuadoran understandings.

For their part, the multinationals have played a lesser, more reactive, role in the movement. But in responding positively to some of the demands of the native movement, they too, in Burke's view, have emerged as significant, if somewhat unlikely, allies in the struggle for environmental justice in Ecuador.

In designating the rise of these networks as one of the significant contemporary trends shaping the future of social movements at least two cautions are in order. We are first of all mindful that the transnational facilitation of domestic protest is not a new phenomenon. Even ignoring the venerable tradition of nations fomenting or supporting disorder within rival states—think only of the role of the French in the American Revolution—it is easy to identify many instances of the transnational sponsorship of domestic movements. Examples would include the role of the British Anti-Slavery Society in establishing similar organizations elsewhere, and the efforts of itinerant communist organizers throughout the industrial West in the years prior to 1917. If not unprecedented, however, we do think the scale on which this transnational advocacy is occurring is unprecedented. We think it is taking on a more routine, quasi-institutionalized character, as well.

But, in arguing for the increased significance of transnational advocacy, we also want to distance ourselves from what we see as the exaggerated claims for the rise of a "global civil society" (Wapner 1995) or a "world society" (Meyer, Boli, Thomas, and Ramirez 1997). While we may well be entering an era in which nation-states will increasingly share sovereignty with various kinds of transnational (and even subnational) institutions—more on this below—at present we do not see any convincing evidence that the fundamental prerogatives of states have been ceded to geographically broader jurisdictions. Only if and when this happens can one plausibly invoke the image of a global—or at least, transnational—civil society.

Notwithstanding this second caution, the increasing incidence and institutionalized form of transnational advocacy have significant implications for the future of social movements. For what such advocacy makes possible is the same kind of elite facilitation of protest at the transnational level that McCarthy and Zald (1973) first described at the national level. So just as McCarthy and Zald saw a host of national organizations—principally foundations, religious institutions, and governmental agencies—supporting the growth of an increasingly large "social movement sector" in the United States, scholars such as Keck and Sikkink, Wapner, and others would appear to be documenting the exportation of the same professionalized social movement form from the democratic West to the developing world.

Some recent work by Cress and Snow (1996) helps explain the tendency toward organizational isomorphism evident in the exportation process. In a detailed case study of homeless mobilization in Denver, Colorado, the authors show that elite facilitation of movement activity turns on what might be termed a process of "organizational matching." That is, resource providers and incipient movement groups seek to find partners whose framing of the issue and organizational routines are broadly compatible with their own. Where such compatibilities can be established, sustained movement activity is likely to occur.

All well and good. But the stark resource imbalance between the parties to the exchange leads us to suspect that the outcome of this matching process is typically going to turn on just how successfully the incipient movement group can adjust to or adopt the cultural and organizational conventions of the potential sponsor (Pfeffer and Salancik 1978). When viewed in transnational relief, this tendency merely reinforces the general trend toward the spread of the western social movement form to other regions of the world.

Movements as Multilevel Games: The Rebirth of "Composite" States

Living, as we are, in an era dominated by nation-states, there is a tendency on the part of analyst and citizen alike to view all of human history, or at least that part of it that followed the agricultural revolution, through a nation-centric lens. There are many manifestations of this, but the one we are concerned with here is the tendency to imagine people as embedded in and subject to one principal sovereign authority. So even when one recognizes that older governing authorities, such as far-flung empires, or tiny city-states, did not resemble the modern nation-state, there is a tendency to conceive of them as exercising more or less exclusive sovereignty over a territory and people in much the same way that nation-states have done for the past two hundred years or so. But this is clearly a distortion of history. What te Brake (1997, 13) says about sixteenth- and seventeenth-century Europe could well be generalized to most of settled human existence. Most of the time, ordinary people have "acted in the context of overlapping, intersecting, and changing political spaces defined by the often competitive claimants to sovereign authority over them." Te Brake terms these kinds of overlapping, intersecting jurisdictions as "composite states." Tarrow (1997) prefers the term "composite polity." Marks and McAdam (1996) call them "multi-level polities." Notwithstanding these terminological differences, all of the authors are referring to the same phenomenon—political contexts in which ordinary people confront, not a single sovereign authority, but multiple jurisdictions with variable, but still clear, authority over their lives.

We reference this phenomenon because we think that we may be entering a period in which the more or less exclusive sovereignty enjoyed by the nation-state over the past two centuries may well be reverting to the more historically typical situation described above. So instead of exercising a near authoritative monopoly over its citizenry, states may increasingly share sovereignty with a host of other transnational and even subnational jurisdictions. The clearest case of this happening to date concerns the impact of European integration on the formal political authority exercised by the member nations of the European Union (EU). In exchange for the anticipated benefits—especially economic benefits—of union, these nations have agreed to cede some of their governing authority to an elaborate set of EU institutions and policy-making bodies.

It is still too early to tell just how far integration will go and how stable the institutional arrangements it produces will prove to be, but you can bet that if the arrangement comes to be seen as successful in delivering to the member countries the hoped-for benefits, the experiment could well set in motion other efforts at transnational confederation. Indeed, the impetus behind the implementation of the North American Free Trade Alliance (NAFTA) probably reflects this process in miniature. And while NAFTA more closely resembles a traditional trade agreement between nations than any kind of serious experiment in shared sovereignty, in the creation of such transnational institutions as the Border Environmental Cooperation Commission, it has at least set a minimal precedent in the latter direction. One could even imagine, on some distant temporal horizon, the current set of true transnational institutions (e.g., the United Nations, the World Court, the International Monetary Fund, etc.) being augmented by others, and their authority broadened and formalized so as to embed all nations in a set of binding transnational jurisdictions.

None of these trends suggests to us the specter of "disenfranchising societies" (Castells 1997). We suspect, instead, that nation-states will remain the principal locus of governmental authority, but with some of their jurisdictional autonomy ceded to other decision-making bodies. If current trends prove us right, the real question becomes, what would the rise of these multilevel polities mean for the future of the social movement form? We see two important implications of the trend.

Mobilizing at Multiple Levels

First, to the extent that nations come to share sovereignty with other jurisdictions, you can expect social movement dynamics to more closely resemble the two- or multilevel games that game theorists are so fond of analyzing. In one sense, this would not really represent a qualitative departure from the present situation. That is, even though it has generally escaped the attention of social movement analysts, movements in particular kinds of states (e.g., federated systems) have long operated in the context of multiple jurisdictions. The United States is an obvious case in point. There exist four primary levels of institutional power in the United States. These four are the institutions of municipal, county, state, and federal government. Predictably movements in the United States have long displayed a certain relentless opportunism when it comes to these institutional jurisdictions. That is, movement groups have sought to mobilize at whatever level(s) they interpret as most vulnerable or receptive to challenge.

As a practical matter, this means that the foreclosure of opportunities at the federal level need not spell decline for movements willing to operate at other levels of the system. The 1970s, for example, have generally been regarded as a time of decline for left movements in the United States. With conservative Republicans in the White House for most of the decade and Democratic margins in both houses of Congress shrinking, the national-level political opportunity structure may, indeed, have been a good bit less facilitative of left movements during the period than was true for most of the 1960s. But anyone who was attuned to left movement activity during this period would have reason to quarrel with this simple account of movement decline. It is hard to reconcile the image of decline with the growing strength and activity levels of various left movements during the decade of the 1970s. Among the most vital of these movements were the women's, environmental, and antinuclear struggles. But what all these movements shared in common was a decided preference for mobilization and action at the state and local levels. The organizational forms and general ideology of the New Left no doubt encouraged local forms of action as well. But, in the absence of other institutional levels, these internal movement factors would have mattered little. That is, had these movements only had recourse to a national political opportunity structure, they would have foundered badly. The multiple state, and especially local, institutional sites available to these movements meshed well with their forms of organizations and ideological distrust of big, bureaucratic movements and allowed these various struggles to thrive during a period of contraction in national-level opportunities.

The general point is that, while not entirely absent from movement dynamics in the era of national sovereignty, this recourse to multiple institutional levels will only increase if the trend toward shared sovereignty continues. As the clear exemplar of this trend, the EU already affords ample evidence for the increasing salience of these kind of two-level games in the structuring of movement dynamics in Europe. Regional nationalist movements, such as those in the Basque Country and Catalonia in Spain or Wales in England, have established substantial lobbying operations in Brussels, both as a hedge against EU-level moves by their respective national governments that might disadvantage them and as a proactive attempt to take advantage of the various programs and funds that the EU has established to safeguard the autonomy and advance the development of Europe's regions (Marks 1992, 1993; Marks and McAdam 1996). All of this EU level activity has occurred even as the nationalists have grown ever more active at the national and grassroots level in pressing their claims (Johnston 1991).

Many other movements in Europe have adopted this same kind of two-level approach to mobilization. Reflecting their transnational understanding of the issue, environmentalists were perhaps the quickest to mobilize in this fashion, establishing an impressive institutional presence in Brussels, pursuing litigation before the European Court of Justice, and successfully competing for seats in the European parliament, while simultaneously expanding their operations at local and national levels (Marks and McAdam 1996). Indeed, in some cases the national movements were galvanized into action by their countries' entrance into the EU. This was clearly the case for countries such as Portugal, Greece, and Spain, which had been slow to implement strong environmental policies on their own. Entrance into the union afforded the national movements EU-level resources and allies with which to better pass their claims.

This latter case makes it clear that shared sovereignty does not simply mean mobilizing at multiple levels, but, where applicable, playing these levels off against each other. As noted elsewhere (McAdam 1982, 1983), the U.S. civil rights struggle affords a wonderful example of the kind of multilevel game that successful movements are often able to orchestrate. While it generally mobilized at the local level in the South, the movement's real target during the civil rights phase of the struggle was the federal government. But movement strategists understood that their best chances of forcing a reluctant *federal* government to act was by exploiting the tendency of *state and local* law enforcement personnel to respond violently to civil rights demonstrations. Public support for the movement grew apace of these incidents and pushed federal officials into embracing broader and more favorable changes in civil rights policy.

It should be noted that state authorities, nonstate elites, and countermovement groups have recourse to these multiple levels as well, and are just as intent in seeking to adjudicate issues at whichever levels they feel are most favorable to their interests. So while most national environmental movements have benefited by recourse to EU-level resources and policies on the issue, one could argue that the opposite has been true with respect to most European labor movements. The removal of various restrictions on economic activity spanning national borders has had the effect of liberating capital from the constraints of national-level bargains forged over the past century with unions, while depriving those unions of the safeguards and guarantees contained in those agreements (Tilly 1995c).

The bottom line is, the multiplication of jurisdictional authority does not confer some sort of natural advantage on challenging groups. Indeed, it obliges them to mobilize at various levels, thereby stretching their already thin resources all the more. And while it offers them multiple sites for contestation, their opponents are afforded the expanded strategic options inherent in these various sites, as well. Finally, there is a third way in which the trend toward shared sovereignty, as exemplified by developments in the EU, may, in the short run, disadvantage movement groups.

Brussels, "the Democratic Deficit," and the Institutionalization of Movement Activity

Obsevers of group mobilizations in the EU find that there is relatively little social movement activity there. If one is looking for the forms of activity—marches, mass meetings, public protests—we have come to associate with the modern social movement form, one sees little evidence of mobilization (Imig and Tarrow 1995).

This is not to say, however, that social movements are absent from the EU. Alongside the many thousands of interest groups organized there, one finds a significant number of social movement actors, including environmental organizations, farmers' groups, and labor union federations. But, by and large, these groups do not act in Brussels as they do in their national contexts. Instead of demonstrating their grievances before the mass media, they lobby European Commission officials, hire consultants to write impact reports, coordinate policy papers among themselves, hire lawyers to pursue cases before the European Court of Justice, and, only on occasion, organize public protests outside the European Parliament building in Strasbourg.

There are several obvious reasons why the traditional repertoire of the modern social movement form is so little in evidence at the EU level. First, it is time consuming and expensive to transport activists to the relevant sites of EU decision making. This is not so much a problem for those living in the vicinity of, say, Brussels or Strasbourg, nor is it a problem for movement actions that involve just a few professional activists (as is often the case with Greenpeace). But geography is a formidable barrier to labor-intensive forms of public protest for those living in the outer territories of the EU where the costs of travel to the center remain prohibitively high.

Second, public discourse is deeper at the national level, in individual member countries, than it is in Europe as a whole. Individual attachment and identification remains considerably stronger to territorial communities at the local, regional, and national levels than at the level of the Union (Marks and Haesly 1996). The relative weakness of attachment at the EU level is matched by the relative absence of news media spanning Europe. With the exception of sports and cable music television, mass media in Europe are still mostly pitched to distinct national audiences rather than to an overarching European audience. The absence of a single shared language is obviously a key factor in this. Even movement groups with a clear EU-level focus are apt, when seeking to mobilize public support, to operate at the national level within a clearly defined cultural and linguistic discourse, than in the European "Tower of Babel."

Finally, and most important, the structure of political opportunity in the EU is decidedly more open to narrowly institutionalized forms of action than to the conventionally unconventional tactics we have come to associate with the modern movement form. There are four key policy-making institutions in the EU—the Commission, Council, Court and Parliament—and only the latter occasionally provides a compelling target for conventional movement activity.

This last observation underscores a more general point that is often lost in discussions of political opportunity structure. The basic structure and temporal shifts in institutionalized power affect not only the timing and locus of movement activity, but the form it takes as well. In the case of the European Union, the almost total absence of democratic decision-making bodies—the so-called "democratic deficit"—serves to discourage the forms of popular politics that grew up around democratic institutions in the national context. Or to put the matter differently, the preponderance of narrow, consultative bodies in the EU has put a premium on the kinds of legalistic, lobbying activities one sees dominating the scene in Brussels.

In one sense, we have come full circle. We began our impressionistic sketch of trends by noting that the forms of action we have come to associate with the modern social movement were in danger of losing their disruptive force in the western democracies as a result of a clear process of routinization. The absence of democratic institutions in the EU compounds this problem for European movements, by discouraging the use of the standard kit-bag of disruptive tactics at the level of the Union.

All we have tried to do in this conclusion is to stimulate thought on the future of the modern social movement form. Our conjectures are merely that. But even if our speculation proves wildly inaccurate, we think the exercise is an interesting and important one; interesting because it reminds us that the social movement, like all forms of politics, is being constantly modified through use, and, therefore, is worthy of study as a dynamic phenomenon in its own right. The importance of the exercise derives from the belief that movements, thanks to their impact on processes of incorporation, transformation, and democratization, have functioned as a critically important vehicle of social change since the inception of the form in the early nineteenth century. If one values the availability of such vehicles, speculating a bit about the future of the form takes on a certain urgency. This is especially true if one shares our sense that the modern movement form may be losing its potency in the democratic West, even as it diffuses rapidly elsewhere in the world.

Notes

This chapter was prepared while the author was a Fellow at the Center for Advanced Study in the Behavioral Sciences. I am grateful for financial support provided by a grant from the National Science Foundation (#SBR-9601236) that helped defray some of the costs of my Center Fellowship.
1. The recent popularity of "protest event" research represents a return to a methodology that enjoyed considerable currency in the 1970s and early 1980s. Pioneered by Charles Tilly and some of his colleagues (Tilly, Tilly, and Tilly 1975; Shorter and Tilly 1974), the technique was adapted by Charles Perrow to the study of the U.S. protest cycle of the 1960s and 1970s. Several groundbreaking publications came out of the latter project (Jenkins and Perrow 1977; Jenkins 1985; McAdam 1982, 1983).
2. For an exception, see Marx 1974, 1979.

References

Abrahamian, Ervand. 1982. *Iran between Two Revolutions*. Princeton, NJ: Princeton University Press.

Aguilar Fernandez, Paloma. 1995. "Amnesty, Amnesia and Memory: The Pro-Amnesty Mobilizations in the Transition to Democracy in Spain (1975–1978)." Paper presented at the annual meeting of the American Political Science Association, 30 August–1 September, Chicago.

Alberoni, Francesco. 1984. *Movement and Institution*. Translated by Patricia C. Arden Delmoro. New York: Columbia University Press.

Alvarez, Sonia, and Arturo Escobar. 1992. "Conclusion: Theoretical and Political Horizons of Change in Contemporary Latin American Social Movements." In *The Making of Social Movements in Latin America*, edited by Sonia Alvarez and Arturo Escobar, 317–30. Boulder, CO: Westview Press.

Amenta, Edwin, Bruce G. Carruthers, and Yvonne Zylan. 1992. "A Hero for the Aged? The Townsend Movement, the Political Meditation Model, and U.S. Old-Age Policy, 1934–1950." *American Journal of Sociology*, 98: 308–39.

Amy, Douglas J. 1990. "Environmental Dispute Resolution: The Promise and the Pitfalls." In *Environmental Policy in the1990s: Toward a New Agenda*, edited by Norman J. Vig and Michael E. Kraft, 211–34. Washington, DC: Congressional Quarterly Press.

Anderson, Benedict. 1991. *Imagined Communities*. New York: Verso.

Astin, A. W., H. Astin, A. Bayer, and A. Bisconti. 1975. *The Power of Protest*. San Francisco: Jossey-Bass.

Atkinson, Michael, and William D. Coleman. 1989. "Strong States and Weak States." *British Journal of Political Science* 19: 47–67.

Aubert, V., A. Bergounioux, J-P. Martin, and R. Mouriaux. 1985. *La forteresse enseignante: la fedération de l'education nationale*. Paris: Fayard.

Babb, Sarah. 1996. " 'A True American System of Finance': Frame Resonance in the U.S. Labor Movement, 1866 to 1886." *American Sociological Review* 61: 1033–52.

Baker, Keith M. 1990. *Inventing the French Revolution*. Cambridge: Cambridge University Press.

Ballón, Eduardo. 1986. "Los movimientos sociales en la crisis: El Caso Peruano."

In *Movimientos sociales y crisis: El Caso Peruano,* edited by Eduardo Ballón. Lima: DESCO—Centro de Estudio y Promoción del Desarrollo. 13–42.

Banaszak, Lee Ann. 1996. *Why Movements Succeed or Fail: Opportunity, Culture, and the Struggle for Woman Suffrage.* Princeton, NJ: Princeton University Press.

Barber, Benjamin. 1984. *Strong Democracy.* Berkeley: University of California Press.

Barbet, D. 1988. "La FEN en Mai–Juin 1968." Paper presented to the Colloque sur acteurs et terrains du mouvement social de 1968, Paris, November, CRSMSS.

Barkan, Steven E. 1984. "Legal Control of the Civil Rights Movement." *American Sociological Review* 49: 552–65.

Barnes, Samuel, and Max Kaase. 1979. *Political Action: Mass Participation in Five Western Democracies.* Beverly Hills, CA: Sage.

Barrera, Manuel, and J. Samuel Valenzuela. 1986. "The Development of Labor Movement Opposition to the Military Regime." In *Military Rule in Chile: Dictatorship and Opposition,* edited by J. Samuel Valenzuela and Arturo Valenzuela. Baltimore, MD: The Johns Hopkins University Press, 230–69.

Beckwith, Karen. 1985. "Feminism and Leftist Politics in Italy: The Case of UDI-PCI Relations." In *Women and Politics in Western Europe,* edited by Sylvia Bashevkin, 19–37. London: Frank Cass.

Bendix, Reinhard. 1977. *Nation-building and Citizenship.* Berkeley: University of California Press.

Berger, Peter L., and Thomas Luckmann. 1966. *The Social Construction of Reality: A Treatise in the Sociology of Knowledge.* Garden City, NY: Anchor.

Berkowitz, William R. 1974. "Socioeconomic Indicator Changes in Ghetto Riot Tracts." *Urban Affairs Quarterly* 10: 69–94.

Bermeo, Nancy. 1986. *Revolution within the Revolution.* Princeton, NJ: Princeton University Press.

Bier, Alice Gail. 1979. "Urban Growth and Urban Politics: A Study of Neighborhood Associations in Two Cities in Spain." Ph.D. diss., Cornell University.

Bilis, Michel. 1979. *Socialistes et pacifistes: l'intenable dilemme de françaises socialistes franç;alises, 1933–1939.* Paris: Editions Syros.

Birnbaum, Pierre. 1988. *States and Collective Action: The European Experience.* Cambridge: Cambridge University Press.

Bogan, Ruth, and Jean Fagan Yellin. 1994. "Introduction." In *The Abolitionist Sisterhood: Women's Political Culture in Antebellum America,* edited by Jean Fagan Yellin and John C. Van Horne, 1–19. Ithaca, NY: Cornell University Press.

Boudreau, Vincent. 1997. "At the Margins of the Movement: Grassroots and Cadre in Philippine Protest." Ph.D. diss., Department of Political Science, City College of New York.

Bourricaud, F. 1982. "France: The Prelude to the *Loi d'Orientation* of 1968." In *Universities, Politicians and Bureaucrats,* edited by H. Daalder and E. Shils, 31–61. Cambridge: Cambridge University Press.

Breuilly, John. 1992. "Liberalism or Social Democracy? Britain and Germany,

1850–1875." In *Labour and Liberalism in Nineteenth-Century Europe: Essays in Comparative History*, edited by John Breuilly, 115–59. Manchester, UK: Manchester University Press.

Bridgford, J. 1989. "The Events of May: Consequences for Industrial Relations in France." In *May '68: Coming of Age*, edited by D. L. Hanley and A. P. Kerr, 100–16. London: Macmillan.

Browning, R. P., D. R. Marshall, and D. H. Tabb. 1984. *Protest Is Not Enough: The Struggle of Blacks and Hispanics for Equality in Urban Politics*. Berkeley: University of California Press.

Bunce, Valerie. 1981. *Do New Leaders Make a Difference? Executive Succession and Public Policy under Capitalism and Socialism*. Princeton, NJ: Princeton University Press.

Burke, Pamela. 1997. "The Globalization of Contentious Politics: The Case of the Amazonian Indigenous Rights Movement in Ecuador." Paper presented at the annual meeting of the American Political Science Association, August 30. Washington, DC.

Burstein, Paul. 1979. "Public Opinion, Demonstrations and the Passage of Antidiscrimination Legislation." *Public Opinion Quarterly* 43: 157–72.

———. 1985. *Discrimination, Jobs, and Politics*. Chicago: University of Chicago Press.

Burstein, Paul, Rachel L. Einwohner, and Jocelyn A. Hollander. 1995. "The Success of Political Movements: The Bargaining Perspective." In *The Politics of Social Protest*, edited by J. Craig Jenkins and Bert Klandermans, 279–81. Minneapolis: University of Minnesota Press.

Burstein, Paul, and William Freudenburg. 1978. "Changing Public Policy: The Impact of Public Opinion, Anti-War Demonstrations and War Costs on Senate Voting on Vietnam War Motions." *American Journal of Sociology* 84: 99–122.

Burton, Michael, Richard Gunther, and Jon Higley. 1992. "Introduction: Elite Transformations and Democratic Regimes." In *Elites and Democratic Consolidation in Latin America and Southern Europe*, edited by John Higley and Richard Gunther, 17–37. Cambridge: Cambridge University Press.

Bütschi, Danielle, and Sandro Cattacin. 1994. *Le modèle suisse du bien-être*. Lausanne, Switzerland: Réalités sociales.

Button, J. W. 1978. *Black Violence: Political Impact of the 1960s Riots*. Princeton, NJ: Princeton University Press.

Calhoun, Craig. 1994. *Neither Gods nor Emperors*. Berkeley: University of California Press.

Campero, Guillermo. 1987. *Entre la sobrevivencia y la acción política: Las organizaciones de pobladores en Santiago*. Santiago: ILET.

Canel, Eduardo. 1992. "Democratization and the Decline of Urban Social Movements in Uruguay: A Political-Institutional Account." In *The Making of Social Movements in Latin America*, edited by Sonia Alvarez and Arturo Escobar, 276–90. Boulder, CO: Westview Press.

Capdevielle, J., and R. Mouriaux. 1988. *Mai 68: l'entre-deux de la modernité: Histoire de trente ans*. Paris: Presses de la Fondation Nationale des Sciences Politiques.

Cardoso, Fernando Henrique. 1986. "Entrepreneurs and the Transition Process: The Brazilian Case." In *Transitions from Authoritarian Rule: Latin America*, edited by Guillermo O'Donnell, Philippe Schmitter, and Laurence Whitehead. Baltimore, MD: The Johns Hopkins University Press.

Carnes, Mark C. 1989. *Secret Ritual and Manhood in Victorian America*. New Haven, CT: Yale University Press.

Carter, April. 1992. *Peace Movement: International Protest and World Politics since 1945*. London: Longmans.

Cash, Nathaniel. 1993. "A New Rush into Latin America." *New York Times*, 11 April, C1.

Castells, Manuel. 1983. *The City and the Grassroots*. Berkeley: University of California Press.

———. 1997. *The Information Age: Economy, Society, and Culture II*. Oxford: Blackwell's.

Cattacin, Sandro, Marco Giugni, and Florence Passy. 1997. *Mouvements sociaux et Etat: Mobilisations sociales et transformations de la société en Europe*. Arles, France: Actes Sud.

Cawson, Alan. 1986. *Corporatism and Political Theory*. Oxford: Basil Blackwell.

Ceadal, Martin. 1980. *Pacifism in Great Britain, 1914–1945: The Defining of a Faith*. Oxford: Clarendon Press.

Chalendar, J. de. 1970. *Une loi pour l'université*. Paris: de Brouwer.

Charlot, J. 1989. "The Aftermath of May 1968 for Gaullism, the Right and the Center." In *May '68: Coming of Age*, edited by D. L. Hanley and A. P. Kerr, 62–81. London, Macmillan.

Chickering, Roger. 1975. *Imperial Germany and a World without War: The Peace Movement in German Society, 1892–1914*. Princeton, NJ: Princeton University Press.

Christian, Shirley. 1994. "Free Market Lessons of Chile's 'Chicago Boys.' " *New York Times*, 8 October, D4.

Clawson, Mary Ann. 1989. *Constructing Brotherhood: Class, Gender, and Fraternalism*. Princeton, NJ: Princeton University Press.

Clemens, Elisabeth S. 1993. "Organizational Repertoires and Institutional Change: Women's Groups and the Transformation of U.S. Politics, 1890–1920." *American Journal of Sociology* 98: 755–98.

———. 1997. *The People's Lobby: Organizational Innovation and the Rise of Interest Group Politics*. Chicago: University of Chicago Press.

Cobb, Roger W., and Charles D. Elder. 1983. *Participation in American Politics. The Dynamics of Agenda Building*. Baltimore, MD: Johns Hopkins University Press.

Cohen, Jean L. 1996. "Democracy, Difference, and the Right of Privacy." In *Democracy and Difference: Contesting the Boundaries of the Political*, edited by Seyla Benhabib, 187–217. Princeton, NJ: Princeton University Press.

Cohen, Jean L., and Andrew Arato. 1992. *Civil Society and Political Theory*. Cambridge: MIT Press.

Cohen, Miriam, and Michael Hanagan. 1995. "Politics, Industralization and Citizenship: Unemployment Policy in England, France, and the United States, 1890–1950." *International Review of Social History* 40: 51–90.

Collette, Christine. 1989. *For Labour and for Women: The Women's Labour League, 1906–1918*. Manchester, UK: Manchester University Press.

Constable, Pamela, and Arturo Valenzuela. 1991. *A Nation of Enemies*. New York: W. W. Norton.

Converse, P. E., and R. Pierce. 1989. "Attitudinal Roots of Popular Protest: The French Upheaval of May 1968." *International Journal of Public Opinion* 1: 221–41.

Cooper, Sandi. 1991. *Patriotic Pacifism: Waging War on War in Europe, 1815–1914*. New York: Oxford.

Costain, Anne N., and Steven Majstorovic. 1994. "Congress, Social Movements and Public Opinion: Multiple Origins of Women's Rights Legislation." *Political Research Quarterly* 47: 111–35.

Crawford, Sue E. S., and Elinor Ostrom. 1995. "A Grammar of Institutions." *American Political Science Review* 89: 582–611.

Cress, Daniel M., and David A. Snow. 1996. "Mobilization at the Margins: Resources, Benefactors, and the Viability of Homeless Social Movement Organizations." *American Sociological Review* 61: 1089–1109.

Croteau, David, and William Hoynes. 1994. *By Invitation Only: How the Media Limit Political Debate*. Monroe, ME: Common Courage Press.

Crozier, Michel, Samuel Huntington, and Joji Watanaki. 1975. *The Crisis of Democracy: Report on the Governability of Democracies to the Trilateral Commission*. New York: New York University Press.

Dahl, Robert. 1971. *Polyarchy*. New Haven, CT: Yale University Press.

Dahlgren, Peter, and Colin Sparks, eds. 1991. *Communication and Citizenship: Journalism and the Public Sphere*. London: Routledge.

Dalton, Russell, and Manfred Küchler, eds. 1990. *Challenging the Political Order: New Social and Political Movements in Western Democracies*. New York: Oxford University Press.

d'Anjou, Leo. 1996. *Social Movements and Cultural Change: The First Abolition Campaign Revisited*. New York: Aldine de Gruyter.

Darnovsky, Marcy, Barbara Epstein, and Richard Flacks, eds. 1995. *Cultural Politics and Social Movements*. Philadelphia: Temple University Press.

David, Paul. 1985. "Clio and the Economics of QWERTY." *American Economic Review* 75: 332–37.

Della Porta, Donatella. 1992. "Social Movements and the State: First Thoughts from a Research on the Policing of Protest." Paper presented to the Conference on European/American Perspectives on the Dynamics of Social Movements, August, Catholic University of America, Washington, DC.

———. 1995. *Social Movements, Political Violence, and the State: A Comparative Analysis of Italy and Germany*. Cambridge: Cambridge University Press.

———. 1996. *Movimenti collettivi e sistema politico in Italia, 1960–1995*. Bari, Italy: Laterza.

———. 1999. "Protest, Protesters and Protest Policing: Public Discourses in Italy and Germany from the 1960s to the 1980s." In *How Social Movements Matter*, edited by Marco Giugni, Doug McAdam, and Charles Tilly. Minneapolis: University of Minnesota Press.

Della Porta, Donatella, and Dieter Rucht. 1995. "Left-Libertarian Movements in Context: A Comparison of Italy and West Germany, 1965–1990." In *The Politics of Social Protest: Comparative Perspectives on States and Social Movements*, edited by J. Craig Jenkins and Bert Klandermans, 229–72. Minneapolis: University of Minnesota Press.

DeNardo, James. 1985. *Power in Numbers*. Princeton, NJ: Princeton University Press.

DiMaggio, Paul J., and Walter W. Powell. 1983. "The Iron Cage Revisited: Institutional Isomorphism and Collective Rationality in Organizational Fields." *American Sociological Review* 48: 147–60.

Downs, Charles. 1989. *Revolution at the Grassroots: Community Organizations in the Portuguese Revolution*. Albany: State University of New York Press.

Duff, Peggy. 1971. *Left, Left, Left: A Personal Account of Six Protest Campaigns, 1945–64*. London: Alison and Busby.

Duque, Joaquin, and Ernesto Pastrana. 1972. "La mobilización reivindicative urbana de los sectores populares en Chile, 1964–1972." *Revista Latinoamericana de Ciencias Sociales* 4: 259–94.

Duyvendak, Jan Willem. 1995. *The Power of Politics: New Social Movements in France*. Boulder, CO: Westview Press.

Duyvendak, Jan Willem, Hein-Anton van der Heijden, Ruud Koopmans, and Luuk Wijmans, eds. 1992. *Tussen verbeelding en macht: 25 jaar nieuwe sociale bewegingen in Nederland*. Amsterdam: SUA.

Echols, Alice. 1989. *Daring to Be Bad: Radical Feminism in America, 1967–1975*. Minneapolis: University of Minnesota Press.

Eckstein, Susan. 1989. "Power and Popular Protest in Latin America." In *Power and Popular Protest*, edited by Susan Eckstein. Berkeley: University of California Press.

Ehrmann, H. 1983. *Politics in France*. 4th ed. Boston: Little, Brown.

Eisinger, Peter K. 1973. "The Conditions of Protest Behavior in American Cities." *American Political Science Review* 67: 11–28.

Ellingson, Stephen. 1995. "Understanding the Dialectic of Discourse and Collective Action: Public Debate and Rioting in Antebellum Cincinnati." *American Journal of Sociology* 101: 100–44.

Emirbayer, Mustafa, and Jeff Goodwin. 1996. "Symbols, Positions, Objects: Toward a New Theory of Revolutions and Collective Action." *History and Theory* 35: 358–74.

Entman, Robert. 1989. *Democracy without Citizens*. New York: Oxford University Press.

Esherick, Joseph W., and Jeffrey N. Wasserstrom. 1990. "Acting Out Democracy: Political Theater in Modern China." *The Journal of Asian Studies* 49: 835–65.

Espeland, Wendy N. 1996. "Death Becomes Them: Commemoration, Biography, and the Ritual Reconstruction of Professional Identity among Chicago Lawyers in the late 19th century." Unpublished manuscript.

Esping-Andersen, Gosta. 1985. *Politics against Markets: The Social Democratic Road to Power*. Princeton, NJ: Princeton University Press.

Evans, E. 1983. *The Forging of the Modern State: Early Industrial Britain, 1783–1870*. London: Longman.

Evans, Richard J. 1987. *Comrades and Sisters: Feminism, Socialism, and Pacifism in Europe, 1870–1945.* New York: St. Martin's Press.

Evers, Adalbert. 1990. "Shift in the Welfare Mix: Introducing a New Approach for the Study of Transformations in Welfare and Social Policy." In *Shifts in the Welfare Mix,* edited by Adalbert Evers and Helmut Wintersberger, 7–29. Boulder, CO: Westview Press.

———. 1993. "The Welfare Mix Approach: Understanding the Pluralism of Welfare System." In *Balancing Pluralism,* edited by Adalbert Evers and Ivan Svetlik, 3–31. Aldershot, UK: Avebury.

Farmer, James. 1965. *Freedom—When?* New York: Random House.

Fédération de l'Education Nationale (FEN). 1969. "Les Etats généraux de l'université nouvelle. "*Enseignement public* 5 bis.

Ferree, Myra Marx, and Patricia Yancey Martin, eds. 1995. *Feminist Organizations: Harvest of the New Women's Movement.* Philadelphia: Temple University Press.

Fine, Sidney. 1969. *Sit-Down: The General Motors Strike of 1936–37.* Ann Arbor: University of Michigan Press.

Fishman, Robert M. 1990. *Working-Class Organizations and the Return to Democracy in Spain.* Ithaca, NY: Cornell University Press.

Fomerand, J. 1974. "Policy Formulation and Change in Gaullist France: The 1968 Orientation Act of Higher Education." Ph.D. diss., City University of New York.

———. 1975. "Policy Formulation and Change in Gaullist France: The 1968 Orientation Act of Higher Education." *Comparative Politics* 7: 59–89.

Fortín Mapocho. 1990. "Tomas Desestabilizan", 7 August.

Frank, Dana. 1994. *Purchasing Power: Consumer Organizing, Gender, and the Seattle Labor Movement, 1919–1929.* New York: Cambridge University Press.

Fraser, Nancy. 1995. "What's Critical about Critical Theory." In *Feminists Read Habermas,* edited by J. Meehan, 21–55. London: Routledge.

Friedman, Debra, and Doug McAdam. 1992. "Collective Identity and Activism: Networks, Choices, and the Life of a Social Movement." In *Frontiers in Social Movement Theory,* edited by Aldon Morris and Carol McClurg Mueller, 156–73. New Haven and London: Yale University Press.

Gallino, Luciano, ed. 1993. *Dizionario di sociologia.* Torino, Italy: UTET.

Gamson, Josh. 1989. "Silence, Death, and the Invisible Enemy." *Social Problems* 36: 351–67.

Gamson, William A. 1975. *The Strategy of Social Protest.* Homewood, IL: Dorsey Press.

———. 1988. "Political Discourse and Collective Action." In *From Structure to Action: Social Movement Participation across Cultures,* edited by Bert Klandermans, Hanspeter Kriesi, and Sidney Tarrow, 229–44. Greenwich, CT: JAI Press.

———. 1990. *The Strategy of Social Protest.* 2d ed. Belmont, CA: Wadsworth Publishing.

———. 1992a. *Talking Politics.* Cambridge and New York: Cambridge University Press.

————. 1992b. "The Social Psychology of Collective Action." In *Frontiers in Social Movement Theory*, edited by Aldon D. Morris and Carol McClurg Mueller, 53–76. New Haven, CT: Yale University Press.

Gamson, William A., and David S. Meyer. 1996. "Framing Political Opportunity." In *Comparative Perspectives on Social Movements: Political Opportunities, Mobilizing Structures, and Cultural Framings*, edited by Doug McAdam, John D. McCarthy, and Mayer N. Zald, 275–90. New York: Cambridge University Press.

Gamson, William A., and Andre Modigliani. 1989. "Media Discourse and Public Opinion on Nuclear Power." *American Journal of Sociology* 95: 1–37.

Gamson, William A., and Gadi Wolfsfeld. 1993. "Movements and Media as Interacting Systems." *Annals of the American Academy of Political and Social Science* 528: 114–25.

Gamson, William A., Bruce Fireman, and Steven Rytina. 1982. *Encounters with Unjust Authority*. Homewood, IL: Dorsey Press.

Gans, Herbert. 1979. *Deciding What's News*. New York: Vintage.

Garnham, Nicholas. 1986. "The Media and the Public Sphere." In *Communicating Politics*, edited by Peter Golding, Graham Murdock, and Philip Schlesinger. New York: Holmes and Meier.

Garretón, Manual Antonio. 1989a. *The Chilean Political Process*. Boston: Unwin Hyman.

————. 1989b. "Popular Mobilization and the Military Regime in Chile: The Complexities of the Invisible Transition." In *Power and Popular Protest*, edited by Susan Eckstein. Berkeley: University of California Press.

Gash, N. 1979. *Aristocracy and People: Britain, 1815–1865*. London: Edward Arnold.

Gaussen, F. 1990. "Universités 68–90: Même causes, mêmes effets?" *Le Monde* (Jan. 19): 1, 10.

Gelb, Joyce, and Marian Lief Palley. 1987. *Women and Public Policy*. Princeton, NJ: Princeton University Press.

————. 1996. *Women and Public Policies: Reassessing Gender Politics*. Charlottesville: University Press of Virginia.

Gerhards, Jürgen. 1996. "Discursive and Liberal Publics." Working paper. Berlin: WZB.

Gerlach, Luther P., and Virginia P. Hine. 1970. *People, Power, and Change: Movements of Social Transformation*. Indianapolis: Bobbs-Merrill.

Gianni, Matteo. 1994. "Les liens entre citoyenneté et démocratie sur la base du débat Libéraux-Communautariens." *Etudes et recherches* 26. Département de science politique, Université de Genève.

Gitlin, Todd. 1980. *The Whole World Is Watching: The Media in the Making and Unmaking of the New Left*. Berkeley: University of California Press.

Giugni, Marco. 1994. "The Outcomes of Social Movements: A Review of the Literature." Working paper 197. New York: Center for Studies of Social Change, New School for Social Research.

————. 1995a. "Outcomes of New Social Movements." In *New Social Movements in Western Europe*, by Hanspeter Kriesi, Ruud Koopmans, Jan Willem Duyvendak, and Marco G. Giugni, 207–37. Minneapolis: University of Minnesota Press.

———. 1995b. *Entre stratégie et opportunité: Les nouveaux mouvements sociaux en Suisse.* Zurich: Seismo.

Giugni, Marco, and Florence Passy. 1997. *Histoires de mobilisation politique en Suisse: De la contestation à l'intégration.* Paris: L'Harmattan.

Goldstone, Jack A. 1991. *Revolution and Rebellion in the Early Modern World.* Berkeley: University of California Press.

———. 1994. "Is Revolution Individually Rational?" *Rationality and Society* 6: 139–66.

———, ed. Forthcoming [a]. *The Encyclopedia of Political Revolutions.* Washington DC: Congressional Quarterly Press.

———. Forthcoming [b]. "Elite Crisis, Regime Transformation and the Collapse of the U.S.S.R." In *Elite Crises and Regime Change,* edited by John Higley and Mattei Dogan.

Goodman, Nelson. 1978. *Ways of Worldmaking.* Indianapolis: Hackett.

Goodwin, Jeff. 1993. "Why Guerrilla Insurgencies Persist, or the Perversity of Indiscriminate Violence by Weak States." Paper presented at the annual meeting of the American Sociological Association, August, Miami, Florida.

———. 1994. "Toward a New Sociology of Revolutions." *Theory and Society* 23: 731–66.

Gottdiener, M. 1985. "Hegemony and Mass Culture: A Semiotic Approach." *American Journal of Sociology* 90: 979–1001.

Gould, Carole. 1988. *Rethinking Democracy.* Cambridge: Cambridge University Press.

Gourevitch, Peter A. 1978. "Reforming the Napoleonic State." In *Territorial Politics in Industrial Nations,* edited by L. Graziano, P. J. Katzenstein, and S. Tarrow, 28–63. New York: Praeger.

———. 1986. *Politics in Hard Times: Comparative Responses to International Economic Crises.* Ithaca, NY: Cornell University Press.

Grignon, C., and J.-C. Passeron. 1970. *Innovation in Higher Education: French Experience before 1968.* Paris: OECD Case Studies in Higher Education.

Groux, G. 1988. "Les cadres et le mouvement de mai: un moment, une rupture." Paper presented to the Colloque sur acteurs et terrains du mouvement social de 1968, November. Paris, CRSMSS.

Gunther, Richard, Giacomo Sani, and Goldie Shbad. 1988. *Spain after Franco: The Making of Competitive Party System.* Berkeley: University of California Press.

Gurr, Ted Robert. 1969. *Why Men Rebel.* Princeton, NJ: Princeton University Press.

———. 1980a. "On the Outcomes of Violent Conflict." In *Handbook of Political Conflict,* edited by Ted Robert Gurr, 238–94. New York: Free Press.

———, ed. 1980b. *Handbook of Political Conflict: Theory and Research.* New York: Free Press.

Guthrie, Douglas J. 1995. "Political Theater and Student Organizations in the 1989 Chinese Movement: A Multivariate Analysis of Tiananmen." *Sociological Forum* 10: 419–55.

Haas, Peter M. 1989. "Do Regimes Matters? Epistemic Communities and Mediterranean Pollution Control." *International Organization* 43: 377–403.

Haavio-Mannila, Elina. 1981. "The Position of Women." In *Nordic Democracy: Ideas, Issues, and Institutions in Politics, Economy, Education, Social and Cultural Affairs of Denmark, Finland, Iceland, Norway, and Sweden,* edited by Erik Allardt et al. 555–88. Copenhagen: Det Danske Selskabl.

Habermas, Jürgen. 1984. *The Theory of Communicative Action.* Volume 1, *Reason and the Rationalization of Society.* Translated by Thomas McCarthy. Boston: Beacon Press.

———. 1987. *The Theory of Communicative Action.* Volume 2, *Lifeworld and System: A Critique of Functionalist Reason.* Translated by Thomas McCarthy. Boston: Beacon Press.

———. 1989 (1962). *The Structural Transformation of the Public Sphere.* Cambridge: MIT Press.

———. 1996. *Between Facts and Norms: Contributions to a Discourse Theory of Law and Democracy.* Translated by William Rehg. Cambridge: MIT Press.

Hallin, Daniel, and Paolo Mancini. 1984. "Speaking of the President: Political Structure and Representational Form in U.S. and Italian Television News." *Theory and Society* 13: 829–50.

Hammond, John. 1988. *Building Popular Protest.* New York: Monthly Review Press.

Hardy, Clarisa. 1986. *Hambre + dignidad = Ollas Comunes.* Santiago: PET.

———. 1988. *Organizarse para vivir.* Santiago: PET.

Haupt, Georges. 1972. *Socialism and the Great War: The Collapse of the Second International.* Oxford: Clarendon Press.

Hause, Steven C., with Anne R. Kenney. 1984. *Women's Suffrage and Social Politics in the French Third Republic.* Princeton, NJ: Princeton University Press.

Hebdige, Dick. 1979. *Subculture: The Meaning of Style.* London: Methuen.

Heclo, H. 1974. *Modern Social Policies in Britain and Sweden: From Relief to Income Maintenance.* New Haven, CT: Yale University Press.

Hervieu-Léger, D. 1988. "Mai 1968 et les Catholiques: Les cas de la Mission Etudiante." Paper presented to the Colloque sur acteurs et terrains du mouvement social de 1968, November, Paris, CRSMSS.

Hipsher, Patricia. 1994. "Political Processes and the Demobilization of the Shantytown Dwellers' Movement in Redemocraticizing Chile." Ph.D. diss., Cornell University.

Hirschman, Albert O. 1970. *Exit, Voice, and Loyalty: Responses to Decline in Firms, Organizations, and States.* Cambridge: Harvard University Press.

Hlaing, Kyaw Yin. 1996. "The Mobilization Process in the Four Eights Democratic Movement in Burma." Paper presented at the annual meeting of the Asian Studies Association, April, Honolulu, Hawaii.

Hobsbawm, Eric. 1974. "Peasant Land Occupations." *Past and Present* 62: 120–52.

Hobson, Barbara, and Marika Lindholm. Forthcoming. "Collective Identities, Women's Power Resources, and the Construction of Citizenship Rights in Welfare States." *Theory and Society.*

Hochstetler, Kathryn. 1993. "Non-Institutional Actors in Institutional Politics: Organizing about the Environment in Brazil and Venezuela." Ph.D. diss., University of Minnesota.

Holworth, Jolyon. 1984. *France: The Politics of Peace.* London: Merlin Press.

Holzner, Burkart, and John Marx. 1979. *Knowledge Application: The Knowledge System in Society.* Boston: Allyn and Bacon.

Huberts, Leo. 1989. "The Influence of Social Movements on Government Policy." In *Organizing for Change: Social Movement Organizations in Europe and the United States,* edited by Bert Klandermans, 395–426. Greenwich, CT: JAI Press.

Hunt, Lynn. 1984. *Politics, Culture, and Class in the French Revolution.* Berkeley and Los Angeles: University of California Press.

Hunt, William. 1983. *The Puritan Moment.* Cambridge: Harvard University Press.

Imig, Doug, and Sidney Tarrow. 1995. "The Europeanization of Social Movements? First Results from a Time-Series Analysis of European Collective Action, 1985–1993." Paper presented at the Conference on Cross-National Influences and Social Movement Research, 15–18 June, Mt. Pèlerin, Switzerland.

Ingram, Norman. 1991. *The Politics of Dissent: Pacifism in France, 1919–1939.* Oxford: Clarendon Press.

Jelin, Elizabeth. 1987. "Movimientos sociales y consolidación democratica en la Argentina actual." In *Movimientos sociales y democracia emergente 1,* edited by Elizabeth Jelin, 7–33. Buenos Aires: Centro Editor de América Latina.

Jenkins, J. Craig. 1985. *The Politics of Insurgency: The Farm Worker Movement in the 1960s.* New York: Columbia University Press.

Jenkins, J. Craig, and Bert Klandermans, eds. 1995. *The Politics of Social Protest: Comparative Perspectives on States and Social Movements.* Minneapolis: University of Minnesota Press.

Jenkins, J. Craig, and Charles Perrow. 1977. "The Insurgency of the Powerless: Farm Workers' Movements (1946–1972)." *American Sociological Review* 42: 249–68.

Johnston, Hank. 1991. *Tales of Nationalism: Catalonia, 1939–1979.* New Brunswick, NJ: Rutgers University Press.

Johnston, Hank, and Bert Klandermans, eds. 1995. *Social Movements and Culture.* Minneapolis: University of Minnesota Press.

Kaelber, Lutz F. 1995. "Other- and Inner-Worldly Asceticism in Medieval Waldensianism: A Weberian Analysis." *Sociology of Religion* 56: 91–109.

Kanter, Rosabeth Moss. 1972. *Commitment and Community: Communes and Utopias in Sociological Perspective.* Cambridge: Harvard University Press.

Karapin, Roger S. 1993. "New Social Movements and Democracy in West Germany." Ph.D. diss., Center for International Affairs, Harvard University.

Karl, Terry. 1986. "Petroleum and Political Pacts: The Transition to Democracy in Venezuela." In *Transitions from Authoritarian Rule: Latin America,* edited by Guillermo O'Donnell, Philippe Schmitter, and Laurence Whitehead, 196–220. Baltimore, MD: Johns Hopkins University Press.

———. 1990. "Dilemmas of Democratization in Latin America." *Comparative Politics* 23: 1–21.

Karstedt-Henke, Sabine. 1980. "Theorien zur Erklärung terroristischer Bewegungen" [Theories for the Explanation of Terrorist Movements]. In *Politik der inneren Sicherheit* [The Politics of Internal Security], edited by E. Blankenberg, 198–234. Frankfurt: Suhrkamp.

Katzenstein, M., and C. M. Mueller, eds. 1987. *The Women's Movements of the United States and Western Europe: Consciousness, Political Opportunity and Public Policy.* Philadelphia, PA: Temple University Press.

Kauchakje, Samira. 1992. "Movimentos Sociais Populares Urbanos no Brasil de 1983 a 1990." Master's thesis, Universidade Estadual de Campinas.

Kaufman, Robert. 1986. "Liberalization and Democratization in South America: Perspectives from the 1970s." In *Transitions from Authoritarian Rule: Comparative Perspectives*, edited by Guillermo O'Donnell, Philippe Schmitter, and Laurence Whitehead, 85–107. Baltimore, MD: The Johns Hopkins University Press.

Keane, John. 1991. *The Median and Democracy.* London: Polity Press.

Keck, Margaret, and Katherine Sikkink. 1998. *Activists beyond Borders: Transnational Advocacy Networks in International Politics.* Ithaca, NY: Cornell University Press.

Keeler, J. T. S. 1993. "Opening the Window for Reform: Mandates, Crises, and Extraordinary Policy-Making." *Comparative Political Studies* 25: 433–86.

Kitschelt, Herbert. 1986. "Political Opportunity Structures and Political Protest: Anti-Nuclear Movements in Four Democracies." *British Journal of Political Science* 16: 57–85.

———. 1993. "Social Movements, Political Parties, and Democratic Theory." *Annals of the American Academy of Political and Social Sciences* 528: 13–29.

Klaarhamer, Roel. 1986. "Nuestra lucha es más grande que la casa." Master's thesis, Catholic University, Nijmegen, Netherlands.

Klandermans, Bert. 1992. "The Social Construction of Protest and Multiorganizational Fields." In *Frontiers in Social Movement Theory*, edited by Aldon Morris and Carol McClurg Mueller, 77–103. New Haven and London: Yale University Press.

———, ed. 1989. *Organizing for Change: Social Movement Organizations in Europe and the United States.* Greenwich, CT: JAI Press.

Koblik, Steven. 1988. "Sweden, 1917: Between Reform and Revolution." In *Neutral Europe between War and Revolution*, edited by Hans A. Schmitt, 111–32. Charlottesville: University Press of Virginia.

Koelble, Thomas A. 1991. *The Left Unraveled: Social Democracy and the New Left Challenge in Britain and West Germany.* Durham, NC: Duke University Press.

Koopmans, Ruud. 1993. "The Dynamics of Protest Waves: West Germany, 1965 to 1989." *American Sociological Review* 58: 637–58.

———. 1995. *Democracy from Below: New Social Movements and the Political System in West Germany.* Boulder, CO: Westview Press.

Kriesi, Hanspeter. 1980. *Entscheidungsstrukturen und Entscheidungsprozesse in der Schweizer Politik.* Frankfurt: Campus.

———. 1991. *The Political Opportunity Structure of New Social Movements: Its Impact on Their Development.* Working Paper 91-103. Berlin: WZB.

———. 1995. "The Political Opportunity Structure of New Social Movements: Its Impact on Their Mobilization." In *The Politics of Social Protest. Comparative Perspectives on States and Social Movements,* edited by J. Craig Jenkins and Bert Klandermans, 167–98. Minneapolis: University of Minnesota Press.

———. 1996. "The Organizational Structure of New Social Movements in a Political Context." In *Comparative Perspectives on Social Movements: Political Opportunities, Mobilizing Structures, and Cultural Framings,* edited by Doug McAdam, John D. McCarthy, and Mayer N. Zald, 152–84. Cambridge: Cambridge University Press.

Kriesi, Hanspeter, Ruud Koopmans, Jan Willem Duyvendak, and Marco G. Giugni. 1995. *New Social Movements in Western Europe.* Minneapolis: University of Minnesota Press.

Kumar, Krishnan. 1993. "Civil Society: An Inquiry into the Usefulness of an Historical Term." *British Journal of Sociology* 44: 375–95.

Lamont, W., and S. Oldfield. 1975. *Politics, Religion, and Literature in the Seventeenth Century.* London: J. M. Dent.

Lamounier, Bolivar. 1979. "Notes on the Study of Re-Democratization." Working paper 58. Washington, DC: Wilson Center, Latin American Program.

Lange, P., S. Tarrow, and C. Irvin. 1990. "Party Recruitment: Mobilization, Social Movements and the Italian Communist Party since the 1960s." *British Journal of Political Science* 22: 15–42.

Laraña, Enrique, Hank Johnston, and Joseph R. Gusfield, eds. 1994. *New Social Movements: From Ideology to Identity.* Philadelphia: Temple University Press.

Lefort, Claude. 1986. "Politics and Human Rights." In *The Political Forms of Modern Society: Bureaucracy, Democracy, Totalitarianism,* edited by John B. Thompson, 239–72. Cambridge: MIT Press.

Leiva, Fernando, and James Petras. 1987. "Chile: New Urban Movements and the Transition to Democracy." *Monthly Review* 39: 209–26.

Lembruch, Gerhard. 1993. "Consociational Democracy and Corporatism in Switzerland." *Publius: The Journal of Federalism* 23: 43–59.

Lichbach, Mark. 1996. *The Rebel's Dilemma.* Ann Arbor: University of Michigan Press.

Liddington, Jill. 1984. *The Life and Times of a Respectable Rebel: Selina Cooper, 1864–1946.* London: Virago Press.

Lijphart, Arend. 1984. *Democracies: Patterns of Majoritarian and Consensus Government in Twenty-One Countries.* New Haven: Yale University Press.

Linder, Wolf. 1987. *La décision politique en Suisse: Genèse et mise en oeuvre de la législation.* Lausanne, Switzerland: Réalités sociales.

———. 1994. *Swiss Democracy: Possible Solutions to Conflict in Multicultural Societies.* New York: St. Martin's Press.

Lindkvist, Kent. 1990. "Mobilization Peaks and Declines of the Swedish Peace Movement." In *Towards a Comparative Analysis of Peace Movements,* edited by Katsuya Kodama and Unto Vesa, 147–67. Brookfield, VT: Gower Publishing Co.

Lipsky, Michael. 1970. *Protest in City Politics: Rent Strikes, Housing and the Power of the Poor.* Chicago: Rand McNally.

Lovenduski, Joni, and Vicky Randall. 1993. *Contemporary Feminist Politics: Women and Power in Britain.* Oxford: Oxford University Press.

Luhmann, Niklas. 1982. *The Differentiation of Society.* New York: Columbia University Press.

Mainwaring, Scott. 1986. *The Catholic Church and Politics in Brazil, 1916–1985.* Stanford, CA: Stanford University Press.

Maravall, José. 1978. *Dictatorship and Political Dissent.* London: Tavistock.

———. 1982. *The Transition to Democracy in Spain.* New York: St. Martin's Press.

Marks, Gary. 1992. "Structural Policy and 1992." In *Europolitics: Institutions and Policy Making in the "New" European Community,* edited by Albert Sbragia, 191–224. Washington, DC: Brookings Institution.

———. 1993. "Structural Policy and Multilevel Governance in the European Community." In *The State of the European Community,* edited by A. Cafruny and G. Rosenthal, 391–410. New York: Lynne Rienner.

Marks, Gary, and Doug McAdam. 1996. "Social Movements and the Changing Structure of Political Opportunity in the European Union." *Journal of West European Politics* 19: 249–78.

Marks, Gary, and Richard Haesly. 1996. "Thinking through Territorial Identity in Europe with Reference to Some Evidence." Paper presented at the International Conference of Europeanists, March, Chicago.

Marsh, David, and R. Rhodes 1992. *Policy Networks in British Government.* Oxford: Oxford University Press.

Marshall, T. H. 1964. *Class, Citizenship and Social Development.* Garden City, NY: Doubleday.

Marx, Gary T. 1974. "Thoughts on a Neglected Category of Social Movement Participant: The Agent Provocateur and the Informant." *American Journal of Sociology* 80: 402–42.

———. 1979. "External Efforts to Damage or Facilitate Social Movements: Some Patterns, Explanations, Outcomes, and Complications." In *The Dynamics of Social Movements,* edited by Mayer N. Zald and John McCarthy, 94–125. Cambridge: Winthrop Publishers.

Marx, Karl. 1978. "The Eighteenth Brumaire of Louis Bonaparte." In *The Marx-Engels Reader,* edited by Robert C. Tucker, 594–627. New York: Norton.

Marx, G., and J. L. Wood. 1975. "Strands of Theory and Research in Collective Behavior." In *Annual Review of Sociology,* Vol. 1, edited by A. Inkeles, 363–428. Palo Alto, CA: Annual Reviews.

Masnata, François. 1963. *Le parti socialiste et la tradition démocratique en Suisse.* Paris: Armand Colin.

McAdam, Doug. 1982. *Political Process and the Development of Black Insurgency, 1930–1970.* Chicago: University of Chicago Press.

———. 1983. "Tactical Innovation and the Pace of Insurgency." *American Sociological Review* 48: 735–54.

———. 1996. "Conceptual Origins: Current Problems, Future Directions." In *Comparative Perspectives on Social Movements: Political Opportunities, Mobi-*

lizing Structures, and Cultural Framings, edited by Doug McAdam, John D. McCarthy, and Mayer N. Zald; 23–40. Cambridge: Cambridge University Press.

McAdam, Doug, and Dieter Rucht. 1993. "The Cross-National Diffusion of Ideas." *Annals of the American Academy of Political and Social Science* 528: 56–74.

McAdam, Doug, John D. McCarthy, and Mayer N. Zald, eds. 1996. *Comparative Perspectives on Social Movements: Political Opportunities, Mobilizing Structures, and Cultural Framings.* Cambridge: Cambridge University Press.

McAdam, Doug, Sidney Tarrow, and Charles Tilly. 1996. "To Map Contentious Politics." *Mobilization* 1: 7–34.

———. 1997. "Toward an Integrated Perspective on Social Movements and Revolutions." In *Comparative Politics: Rationality, Culture, and Structure,* edited by Mark I. Lichbach and Alan S. Zuckerman, 142–73. Cambridge: Cambridge University Press.

McCarthy, John D., and Clark McPhail. 1998. "The Institutionalization of Protest in the USA." In *The Social Movement Society,* edited by David Meyer and Sidney Tarrow, 83–110. Lanham, MD: Rowman & Littlefield.

McCarthy, John D., Clark McPhail, and John Crist. 1995. "The Emergence and Diffusion of Public Order Management Systems: Protest Cycles and Police Responses." Paper presented at the Conference on Cross-National Influences and Social Movement Research, 15–18 June, Mont-Pèlerin, Switzerland.

McCarthy, John D., and Mayer N. Zald. 1973. *The Trend of Social Movements in America: Professionalization and Resource Mobilization.* Morristown, NJ: General Learning Press.

McPhail, Clark, Davis Schweingruber, and John D. McCarthy. 1998. "The Policing of Demonstrations in the USA, 1963–1993." In *Policing Mass Demonstrations in Contemporary Democracies,* edited by Donatella della Porta and Herbert Reiter, 49–69. Minneapolis: University of Minnesota Press.

Medhurst, Kenneth. 1984. "Spain's Evolutionary Pathway from Dictatorship to Democracy." In *The New Mediterranean Democracies,* edited by Geoffrey Pridham, 30–49. London: Frank Cass.

Melucci, Alberto. 1981. "New Movements, Terrorism, and the Political System: Reflections on the Italian Case." *Socialist Review* 56: 97–136.

———. 1984. "An End to Social Movements?" *Social Science Information* 23: 819–35.

———. 1989. *Nomads of the Present: Social Movements and Individual Needs in Contemporary Society.* London: Hutchinson Radius.

———. 1996a. *Challenging Codes: Collective Action in the Information Age.* Cambridge and New York: Cambridge University Press.

———. 1996b. *The Playing Self: Person and Meaning in the Planetary Society.* Cambridge and New York: Cambridge University Press.

(El) Mercurio. 1990. Entrevista con Enrique Krauss, 14 January.

Meyer, David S., and Suzanne Staggenborg. 1996. "Movements, Countermovements, and the Structure of Political Opportunity." *American Journal of Sociology* 101: 1628–60.

Meyer, David S., and Sidney Tarrow. 1998. *The Social Movement Society*. Lanham, MD: Rowman & Littlefield.

Meyer, David S., and Nancy Whittier. 1994. "Social Movement Spillover." *Social Problems* 41: 277–98.

Meyer, John W., and Brian Rowan. 1977. "Institutionalized Organizations: Formal Structure as Myth and Ceremony." *American Journal of Sociology* 83: 340–63.

Meyer, John W., John Boli, and George M. Thomas. 1987. "Ontology and Rationalization in the Western Cultural Account." In *Institutional Structure: Constituting State, Society, and the Individual*, edited by George M. Thomas, John W. Meyer, Francisco O. Ramirez, and John Boli, 12–37. Newbury Park, CA: Sage.

Meyer, John, John Boli, George M. Thomas, and Francisco O. Ramirez. 1997. "World Society and the Nation State." *American Journal of Sociology* 103: 166–81.

Michels, Robert. 1962 (1911). *Political Parties: A Sociological Study of the Oligarchical Tendencies of Modern Democracy*. New York: Free Press.

Minkoff, Debra C. 1997. "The Sequencing of Social Movements." *American Sociological Review* 62: 779–99.

Monchablon, A. 1988. "L'UNEF en Mai 1968." Paper presented to the Colloque sur acteurs et terrains du mouvement social de 1968, November, Paris, CRSMSS.

Moore, Barrington, Jr. 1970. *Social Origins of Dictatorship and Democracy*. Boston: Beacon Press.

Morand, Charles Albert. 1991. "Les nouveaux instruments d'action et le droit." In *Les instruments d'action de l'Etat*, edited by Charles Albert Morand, 181–219. Bâle, Switzerland: Helbing et Lichtenhahn.

Morris, Aldon. 1984. *The Origins of the Civil Rights Movement*. New York: Free Press.

Morris, Aldon D., and Carol McClurg Mueller, eds. 1992. *Frontiers in Social Movement Theory*. New Haven and London: Yale University Press.

Moshiri, Farrokh. 1991. "Iran: Islamic Revolution against Westernization." In *Revolutions of the Late Twentieth Century*, edited by Jack A. Goldstone, Ted Robert Gurr, and Farrokh Moshiri, 116–35. Boulder, CO: Westview Press.

Muller, Edward N. 1985. "Income Inequality, Regime Repressiveness, and Political Violence." *American Sociological Review* 50: 47–61.

Muller, Edward, and Mitchell Seligson. 1987. "Inequality and Insurgency." *American Political Science Review* 81: 425–52.

Myrdal, Alva. 1982. *The Dynamics of European Nuclear Disarmament*. Chester Springs, PA: Dufour Editions.

Neidhart, Leonhard. 1970. *Plebiszit und pluralitäre Demokratie: Eine Analyse der Funktionen des schweizerischen Gesetzesreferendum*. Bern, Switzerland: Francke.

Noonan, Rita K. 1995. "Women against the State: Political Opportunities and Collective Action Frames in Chile's Transition to Democracy." *Sociological Forum* 10: 81–111.

North, Douglas C. 1990. *Institutions, Institutional Change, and Economic Performance*. New York: Cambridge University Press.

Oberschall, Anthony, and Hyojoung Kim. 1996. "Identity and Action." *Mobilization* 1: 63–86.

O'Donnell, Guillermo. 1986. "Introduction to the Latin American Cases." In *Transitions from Authoritarian Rule: Latin America,* edited by Guillermo O'Donnell, Philippe Schmitter, and Laurence Whitehead, 3–18. Baltimore, MD: Johns Hopkins University Press.

O'Donnell, Guillermo, and Philippe Schmitter. 1986. *Transitions from Authoritarian Rule: Tentative Conclusions.* Baltimore, MD: Johns Hopkins University Press.

———. 1988. *Transições do Regime Autoritário, Primeiras Conclusões.* Rio de Janeiro: Editora Vertice.

Offe, Claus, and Helmut Wiesenthal. 1980. "Two Logics of Collective Action—Theoretical Notes on Social Class and Organisational Form." In *Political Power and Social Theory,* edited by M. Zeitlin, 67–115. Greenwich, CT: JAI Press.

Olson, Mancur. 1967. *The Logic of Collective Action.* Cambridge: Harvard University Press.

Opello, Walter C., Jr. 1985. *Portugal's Political Development: A Comparative Approach.* Boulder, CO: Westview Press.

Opp, Karl-Dieter, and Wolfgang Roehl. 1990. "Repression, Micromobilization, and Political Protest." *Social Forces* 69: 521–47.

Orren, Karen. 1991. *Belated Feudalism: Labor, the Law, and Liberal Development in the United States.* New York: Cambridge University Press.

Oxhorn, Philip. 1995. *Organizing Civil Society: The Popular Sectors and the Struggle for Democracy in Chile.* University Park: Pennsylvania State University.

Palermo, Vicente. 1987. "Movimientos sociales y partidos politicos: Aspectos de la cuestion en la democracia emergente en la Argentina." In *Movimientos sociales e democracia emergente 2,* edited by Elizabeth Jelin, 132–75. Buenos Aires: Centro Editor de América Latina.

Papadopoulos, Yannis. 1995. *Complexité sociale et politiques publiques.* Paris: Montchrestien.

Passeron, J.-C. 1986. "1950–1980: L'université mise à la question: changement de décor ou changement de cap?" In *Histoire des universités en France,* edited by J. Verger, 367–420. Toulouse: Privat.

Passy, Florence. 1995. "Supranational Political Opportunities as a Channel of Globalization of Political Conflicts: The Case of the Conflict around the Rights of Indigenous Peoples." Paper presented at the Conference on Cross-National Influences and Social Movement Research, 15–18 June, Mont-Pélerin, Switzerland.

Pastrano, Ernesto, and Monica Threlfall. 1974. *Pan, techo y poder: El movimiento de pobladores en Chile 1970–1973.* Buenos Aires: Ediciones S.A.P.

Pateman, Carol. 1970. *Participation and Democratic Theory.* Cambridge: Cambridge University Press.

Pfeffer, Jeffrey, and Gerald R. Salancik. 1978. *The External Control of Organizations.* New York: Harper and Row.

Pickvance, C. F. 1992. "Social Movements and Local Politics in the Transition from State Socialism: A Preliminary Report on the Housing Movement in Moscow." Paper presented at the European Conference on Social Movements, Berlin.

Pimlott, Ben. 1977. *Labour and the Left in the 1930s.* London: Allen and Unwin.

Piven, Frances Fox, and Richard A. Cloward. 1971. *Regulating the Poor: The Functions of Public Welfare.* New York: Pantheon.

———. 1977. *Poor People's Movements. Why They Succeed, How They Fail.* New York: Pantheon.

———. 1979. *Poor People's Movements. Why They Succeed, How They Fail.* New York: Vintage.

Polletta, Francesca. 1996. "Book Review." *Contemporary Sociology* 25: 483–85.

Polsby, N. 1985. "Prospects for Pluralism." *Society* 22: 30–34.

Pore, Renate. 1981. *A Conflict of Interest: Women in German Social Democracy, 1919–1933.* Westport, CT: Greenwood Press.

Powell, Walter W., and Paul J. DiMaggio, eds. 1991. *The New Institutionalism in Organizational Analysis.* Chicago: University of Chicago Press.

Przeworski, Adam. 1986. "Some Problems in the Study of the Transition to Democracy." In *Transitions from Authoritarian Rule: Comparative Perspectives,* edited by Guillermo O'Donnell, Philippe Schmitter, and Laurence Whitehead, 47–63. Baltimore, MD: Johns Hopkins University Press.

———. 1991. *Democracy and the Market.* Cambridge: Cambridge University Press.

Quataert, Jean H. 1979. *Reluctant Feminists in German Social Democracy, 1885–1977.* Princeton, NJ: Princeton University Press.

Raschke, Joachim. 1985. *Soziale Bewegungen: Ein historich-systematischer Grundriss.* Frankfurt: Campus.

Richardson, R. C. 1973. "Puritanism and the Ecclesiastical Authorities in the Case of the Diocese of Chester." In *Politics, Religion, and the English Civil War,* edited by Brian Manning, 3–36. New York: St. Martin's Press.

Rochon, Thomas R. 1990. "The West European Peace Movement and the Theory of New Social Movements." In *Challenging the Political Order: New Social and Political Movements in Western Democracies,* edited by Russell J. Dalton and Manfred Kuechler, 105–21. Cambridge: Polity Press.

Rochon, Thomas R., and Daniel A. Mazmanian. 1993. "Social Movements and the Policy Process." *Annals of the American Academy of Political and Social Science* 528: 75–87.

Rodrigues, Leoncio Martins. 1990. "A Composição Social das Lideranças do PT." In *Partido e Sindicatos: Escritos de Sociologia Política.* São Paulo: Editora Atica.

Rohrschneider, Robert. 1993. "Impact of Social Movements in European Party Systems." *Annals of the American Academy of Political and Social Science* 528: 157–70.

Rokkan, Stein. 1975. "Dimensions of State Formation and Nation-Building: A Possible Paradigm for Research on Variations within Europe." In *The Formation of National States in Western Europe,* edited by Charles Tilly, 562–600. Princeton, NJ: Princeton University Press.

Rokkan, S., with the collaboration of A. Campbell, P. Torsvik, and H. Valen. 1970.

Citizens, Elections, Parties: Approaches to the Comparative Study of the Processes of Development. New York: David McKay.

Rose, R. 1980. *Do Parties Make a Difference?* Chatham, NJ: Chatham House.

Roth, Roland. 1997. *Demokratie von Unten: Neue soziale Bewegungen auf dem Weg zur politischen Institution.* Köln: Bund Verlag.

Rowan, Caroline. 1982. "Women in the Labour Party, 1906–1920." *Feminist Review* 12: 74–91.

Rucht, Dieter. 1990. "Campaigns, Skirmishes, and Battles: Anti-Nuclear Movements in the USA, France, and West Germany." *Industrial Crisis Quarterly* 4: 193–222.

———. 1992. "Studying the Effects of Social Movements: Conceptualization and Problems." Paper presented at the ECPR Joint Sessions, 30 March–4 April, Limerick, Ireland.

———. 1995. "Parties, Associations, and Movements as Systems of Political Interest Mediation." In *Political Parties in Democracy*, edited by J. Thesing and W. Hofmeister, 103–25. Sankt Augustin, Germany: Konrad-Adenauer-Stiftung.

———. 1996a. "The Impact of National Contexts on Social Movement Structures: A Cross-Movement and Cross-National Comparison." In *Comparative Perspectives on Social Movements: Opportunities, Mobilizing Structures, and Cultural Framings*, edited by Doug McAdam, John D. McCarthy, and Mayer N. Zald, 185–204. Cambridge and New York: Cambridge University Press.

———. 1996b. "The Structure and Culture of Political Protest in Germany since 1950." Paper presented at the Tenth International Conference of Europeanists, 14–16 March, Chicago.

Rüdig, Wolfgang. 1991. *The Green Wave: A Comparative Analysis of Ecological Parties.* Cambridge and New York: Cambridge University Press.

Rupp, L., and V. Taylor. 1987. *Survival in the Doldrums: The American Women's Rights Movement, 1945 to the 1960s.* New York: Oxford University Press.

Ryan, Charlotte. 1991. *Prime Time Activism.* Boston: South End Press.

Sader, Eder. 1988. *Quando Novos Personagens Entram em Cena.* Rio de Janeiro: Editora Paz e Terra.

Salmon, P. 1982. "France, the Loi d'Orientation and Its Aftermath." In *Universities, Politicians and Bureaucrats*, edited by H. Daalder and E. Shils, 63–101. Cambridge: Cambridge University Press.

Sandoval, Salvador A. M. 1994. *Labor Unrest and Social Change in Brazil since 1945.* Boulder, CO: Westview Press.

Schild, Andreas. n.d. *Politique étrangère et société civile en Suisse: Un essai sur la coopération au développement en Suisse.* Bern, Switzerland: Intercooperation.

Schirmer, Jennifer G. 1982. *The Limits of Reform: Women, Capital and Welfare.* Cambridge, MA: Schenkman Publishing Company.

Schmitter, Philippe C. 1977. "Modes of Interest Mediation and Models of Societal Change in Western Europe." *Comparative Political Studies* 10.

———. 1981. "Interest Intermediation and Regime Governability in Contemporary Western Europe and North America." In *Organizing Interests in Western Europe*, edited by Suzanne Berger, 285–327. Cambridge: Cambridge University Press.

Schnapp, A., and P. Vidal-Naquet. 1988. *Journal de la commune étudiante: Textes et documents, Novembre 1967–Juin 1968*. 2nd ed. Paris: Seuil.

Schneider, Cathy Lisa. 1992. "Radical Opposition Parties and Squatters' Movements in Pinochet's Chile." In *The Making of Social Movements in Latin America*, edited by Sonia Alvarez and Arturo Escobar, 260–75. Boulder, CO: Westview Press.

———. 1995. *Shantytown Protest in Pinochet's Chile*. Philadelphia: Temple University Press.

Schumaker, Paul D. 1975. "Policy Responsiveness to Protest-Group Demands." *Journal of Politics* 37: 488–521.

Scott, W. Richard. 1995. *Institutions and Organizations*. Thousand Oaks, CA: Sage.

Sewell, William, Jr. 1985. "Ideologies and Social Revolutions: Reflections on the French Case." *Journal of Modern History* 57: 57–85.

———. 1992. "A Theory of Structure: Duality, Agency, and Transformation." *American Journal of Sociology* 98: 1–29.

Shorter, Edward, and Charles Tilly. 1974. *Strikes in France, 1830–1968*. Cambridge: Cambridge University Press.

Sikkink, Kathryn. 1992. "Ideas and Economic Policy-Making: Paradigm Shift and the Economic Commission for Latin America." Paper presented at the annual meeting of the American Political Science Association, Chicago.

Skidmore, Thomas E. 1988. *The Politics of Military Rule in Brazil, 1964–85*. New York: Oxford University Press.

Skocpol, Theda. 1979. *States and Social Revolution: A Comparative Analysis of France, Russia and China*. Cambridge: Cambridge University Press.

Slater, David. 1985. "The Peruvian State and Regional Crises: The Development of Regional Movements, 1968–1980." In *New Social Movements and the State in Latin America*, edited by David Slater, 147–70. Amsterdam: CEDLA.

Smelser, Neil J. 1963. *Theory of Collective Behavior*. New York: Free Press.

Smith, Jackie, and Ronald Pagnucco. 1992. "Political Process and the 1989 Chinese Student Movement." *Studies in Conflict and Terrorism* 15: 169–84.

———. 1995. "Global Strategies of Social Protest: Transnational Social Movements Organizations." Paper presented at the Conference on Cross-National Influences and Social Movement Research, 15–18 June, Mont-Pèlerin, Switzerland.

Smith, Jackie, Charles Chatfield, and Ron Pagnucco, eds. 1997. *Solidarity beyond the State: The Dynamics of Transnational Social Movements*. Syracuse, NY: Syracuse University Press.

Smith, M. 1993. *Pressure, Power and Policy*. Hemel Hempstead, UK: Harvester Wheatsheaf.

Snow, David A., and Robert D. Benford. 1988. "Ideology, Frame Resonance, and Participant Mobilization." In *From Structure to Action: Comparing Social Movement Research across Cultures*, edited by Bert Klandermans, Hanspeter Kriesi, and Sidney Tarrow, 197–218. Greenwich, CT: JAI Press.

———. 1992. "Master Frames and Cycles of Protest." In *Frontiers in Social Movement Theory*, edited by Aldon Morris and Carol McClurg Mueller, 133–55. New Haven, CT: Yale University Press.

Snow, David A., E. Burke Rochford Jr., Steven K. Worden, and Robert D. Benford. 1986. "Frame Alignment Processes, Micromobilization, and Movement Participation." *American Sociological Review* 51: 464–81.

Soule, Sarah. 1995. "The Student Anti-Apartheid Movement in the United States: The Diffusion of Protest Tactics and Policy Reform." Ph.D. diss., Department of Sociology, Cornell University.

Staggenborg, Susan. 1988. "The Consequences of Professionalization and Formalization in the Pro-Choice Movement." *American Sociological Review* 53: 585–605.

Steinmo, Sven, Kathleen Thelen, and Frank Longstreth, eds. 1992. *Structuring Politics: Historical Institutionalism in Comparative Analysis.* New York: Cambridge University Press.

Stokes, Susan C. 1995. *Cultures in Conflict: Social Movements and the State in Peru.* Berkeley: California University Press.

Stone, Norman, 1983. *Europe Transformed, 1878–1919.* Cambridge: Harvard University Press.

Swidler, Ann. 1986. "Culture in Action: Symbols and Strategies." *American Sociological Review* 51: 273–86.

Tarrow, Sidney. 1988. "Social Movement and National Politics." *Annual Review of Sociology* 14: 421–40.

———. 1989a. *Democracy and Disorder: Protest and Politics in Italy, 1965–1975.* Oxford: Oxford University Press.

———. 1989b. "Struggle, Politics and Reform: Collective Action, Social Movements, and Cycles of Protest." Western Societies Papers 21. Ithaca, NY: Cornell University Press.

———. 1991. "Transitions to Democracy as Waves of Mobilization with Applications to Southern Europe." Paper presented at SSRC Subcommittee Conference on Democratization in Southern Europe, 4–7 July, Delphi.

———. 1992. "Mentalities, Political Cultures, and Collective Action Frames." In *Frontiers in Social Movement Theory,* edited by Aldon D. Morris and Carol Mueller, 174–202. New Haven, CT: Yale University Press, 1992.

———. 1994a. *Power in Movement: Social Movements, Collective Action, and Mass Publics in the Modern State.* New York: Cambridge University Press.

———. 1994b. "Social Movements and Democratic Development." Working paper 190. New York: Center for Studies of Social Change, New School for Social Research.

———. 1995. "Transitions to Democracy as Waves of Mobilization with Applications to Southern Europe." In *The Politics of Democratic Consolidation: Southern Europe in Comparative Perspective,* edited by Richard Gunther, P. Nikiforos Diamandouros, and Hans-Jürgen Puhle, 204–30. Baltimore, MD: The Johns Hopkins University Press.

———. 1996. "Social Movements in Contentious Politics: A Review Article." *American Political Science Review* 90: 874–83.

———. 1997. "Popular Contention in a Composite State: Ordinary People's Conflicts in the European Union." Unpublished paper.

———. 1998. *Power in Movement: Social Movements and Contentious Politics.* 2d ed. Cambridge: Cambridge University Press.

Taylor, A. J. P. 1958. *The Troublemakers: Dissent over Foreign Policy*. Blooming-ton: Indiana University Press.

Taylor, Verta. 1989. "Social Movement Continuity: The Women's Movement in Abeyance." *American Sociological Review* 54: 761–75.

te Brake, Wayne. 1997. *Making History: Ordinary People in European Politics, 1500–1700*. Berkeley: University of California Press.

Thomis, Malcolm I., and Peter Holt. 1977. *Threats of Revolution in Britain, 1789–1848*. London: Macmillan.

Tilly, Charles. 1978. *From Mobilization to Revolution*. Reading, MA: Addison-Wesley Publishing Co.

———. 1982. "Britain Creates the Social Movement." In *Social Conflict and the Political Order in Modern Britain*, edited by James Cronin and Jonathan Schneer. London: Croom Helm.

———. 1984. "Social Movements and National Politics." In *Statemaking and Social Movements*, edited by Charles Bright and Susan Harding, 297–317. Ann Arbor: University of Michigan Press.

———. 1986. *The Contentious French*. Cambridge: Harvard University Press.

———. 1993. *European Revolutions, 1492–1992*. Cambridge, MA: Blackwell.

———. 1994. "Social Movements as Historically Specific Clusters of Political Performances." *Berkeley Journal of Sociology* 38: 1–30.

———. 1995a. *Popular Contention in Great Britain, 1758–1834*. Cambridge: Harvard University Press.

———. 1995b. "Democracy Is a Lake." In *The Social Construction of Democracy*, edited by George Reid Andrews and Herrick Chapman, 365–87. New York: New York University Press.

———. 1995c. "Globalization Threatens Labor's Rights." *International Labor and Working-Class History* 47: 1–23.

———. 1998. *Durable Inequality*. Berkeley and Los Angeles: University of California Press.

———. Forthcoming. "From Interactions to Outcomes in Social Movements." In *How Movements Matter*, edited by Marco Giugni, Doug McAdam, and Charles Tilly. Minneapolis: University of Minnesota Press.

Tilly, Charles, Louise Tilly, and Richard Tilly. 1975. *The Rebellious Century, 1830–1930*. Cambridge: Harvard University Press.

Tingsten, Herbert. 1973. *The Swedish Social Democrats: Their Ideological Development*. Totowa, NJ: Bedminster Press.

Tocqueville, Alexis de. 1955. *The Old Regime and the French Revolution*. New York: Doubleday.

Touraine, Alain. 1977. *The Self-Production of Society*. Chicago: University of Chicago Press.

———. 1984. *Le retour de l'acteur*. Paris: Fayard.

———. 1995. *Critique of Modernity*. Translated by David Macey. Oxford and Cambridge: Blackwell.

Tuchman, Gaye. 1978. *Making the News*. New York: The Free Press.

Últimas Noticias. 1990. "Carabineros desalojó las tomas," 7 August.

Valenzuela, Arturo, and J. Samuel Valenzuela. 1986. "Party Opposition under the

Chilean Authoritarian Regime." In *Military Rule in Chile: Dictatorship and Opposition,* edited by J. Samuel Valenzuela and Arturo Valenzuela, 184–229. Baltimore, MD: Johns Hopkins University Press.

van der Linden, W. H. 1987. *The International Peace Movement, 1815–1874.* Amsterdam: Tilleul Publications.

Vernus, M. 1988. "La F. C. P. E. en Mai 1968." Paper presented to the Colloque sur acteurs et terrains du mouvement social de 1968, November, Paris, CRSMSS.

Volker, Frank. 1994. "Acuerdo y conflictos: Signos contradictorios de nuevas relaciones laborales en la transición chilena a la democracia?" *Estudios Sociologicos* 12, no. 36 (September–December): 581–602.

Waarden, Franz van. 1992. "Dimensions and Types of Policy Networks." *European Journal of Political Research* 21: 29–52.

Wahl, A. 1988, November. "Le mai des footballeurs." Paper presented to the Colloque sur acteurs et terrains du mouvement social de 1968, Paris, CRSMSS.

Walder, Andrew G. 1995. "Collective Protest and the Waning of the Communist State: Reflections on 1989 from the Perspective of Beijing." Paper presented at the conference on Structure, Identity and Power: The Past and Future of Collective Action; Conference in Honor of Charles Tilly, 2–4 June, Amsterdam.

Wälti, Sonia. 1993. "Neue Problemlösungsstrategien in der nuklearen Entsorgung." *Schweizerisches Jahrbuch für Politische Wissenschaft* 33: 205–24.

Walton, John. 1984. *Reluctant Rebels.* New York: Columbia University Press.

———. 1992. *Western Times and Water Wars.* Berkeley and Los Angeles: University of California Press.

Wank, Solomon. 1988. "The Austrian Peace Movement and the Hapsburg Ruling Elite, 1906–1914." In *Peace Movements and Political Cultures,* edited by Charles Chatfield and Peter van den Dungen, 40–64. Knoxville: University of Tennessee Press.

Wapner, Paul. 1995. *Environmental Activism and World Civil Politics.* Albany: State University of New York Press.

Webb, Catherine. 1927. *The Woman with the Basket: The History of the Women's Co-operative Guild, 1883–1926.* Manchester, UK: Cooperative Society Printing Works.

Weber, Max. 1978. *Economy and Society.* Edited by Guenther Roth and Claus Wittich. Berkeley: University of California Press.

Weede, Erich. 1987. "Some New Evidence on Correlates of Political Violence: Income Inequality, Regime Repressiveness, and Economic Development." *European Sociological Review* 3: 97–108.

Weidner, Helmut. 1993. "Der verhandelnde Staat: Minderung von Vollzugskonflikten durch Mediationsverfahren." *Schweizerisches Jahrbuch für Politische Wissenschaft* 33: 225–44.

Wellmer, Albrecht. 1984. "Terrorism and the Critique of Society." In *Observations on 'The Spiritual Situation of the Age,'* edited by Jürgen Habermas, 283–307. Translated by Andrew Buchwalter. Cambridge: MIT Press.

Wetstein, Matthew E. 1996. *Abortion Rates in the United States.* Albany: State University of New York Press.

Wheatcroft, Andrew. 1983. *The World Atlas of Revolution.* New York: Simon and Schuster.

White, Robert. 1989. "From Peaceful Protest to Guerrilla War: Micromobilization of the Provisional Irish Republican Army." *American Journal of Sociology* 94: 1277–1302.

Whittier, Nancy. 1995. "Turning It Over: Personnel Change in the Columbus, Ohio, Women's Movement, 1969–1984." In *Feminist Organizations: Harvest of the New Women's Movement,* edited by M. M. Ferree and P. Y. Martin, 128–34. Philadelphia: Temple University Press.

Wildavsky, Aaron. 1974. *The Politics of the Budgetary Process.* Boston: Little, Brown.

Willke, Helmut. 1991. "Trois types de structures juridiques: programmes conditionnels, programmes finalisés, programmes relationnels." In *L'Etat propulsif: Contribution à l'étude des instruments d'action de l'Etat,* edited by Charles Albert Morand, 65–94. Paris: Editions Publisuc.

———. 1992. *Ironie des Staates.* Frankfurt: Campus.

Winn, Peter. 1986. *Weavers of Revolution.* Oxford and New York: Oxford University Press.

Woolrych, Austin. 1968. "Puritanism, Politics, and Society." In *The English Revolution, 1600–1660,* edited by E. W. Ives, 87–100. New York: Harper and Row.

Wozniak, Lynn. 1990. "Economic Orthodoxy and Industrial Protest: Consolidating Spanish Democracy." Ph.D. diss., Cornell University.

Wright, Gordon. 1987. *France in Modern Times: From the Enlightenment to the Present.* New York: Norton.

Zald, Mayer N., and John D. McCarthy, eds. 1979. *The Dynamics of Social Movements.* Cambridge, MA: Winthrop Publishers.

———, eds. 1987. *Social Movements in an Organizational Society.* New Brunswick, NJ: Transaction Books.

Zucker, Lynne G. 1987. "Institutional Theories of Organization." *Annual Review of Sociology* 13: 443–64.

Index

271

Elligson, Stephen, 119
England: protest, revolution, and reform in early modern, 135–36; Puritan movement in, 133, 134, 135–36;
Revolution of 1640 and, 127, 135,
136. *See also* Great Britain
Enlightenment, 134
environmental movement, 66, 67–68; in
Brazil, 165, 229; in Ecuador, 229,
237–38; in Europe, 242; in France,
xxiii–xxiv, 90, 92, 98–100, 101–2,
104–5; "green" culture and, 221; in
Switzerland, xxiii–xxiv, 90, 92, 98–
100, 101–2, 104–5
Environmental Protection Agency
(EPA), 85
ethnic conflicts, contentious collective
action and, 143–44
Europe: Enlightenment in, 134; environmental movement in, 242, 243;
ghetto parties in, 115; incorporation
of social movements into political
parties in, xxii–xxiii, 3–30; monastic
movement in medieval, 134; multiple institutional levels in, 242, 243;
racial equality movement and, 127.
See also specific countries
European Union (EU), 240; lack of social movements in, 243–45; multiple
institutional levels in, 242, 243
experiential knowledge, social movements using, 58
exportation, of social movement form,
237–39

factionalization, protest waves and,
41–43
Faure, Edgar, 33, 35, 38, 39, 40, 41, 42,
43–44, 45, 46, 47
Fédération de l'Education Nationale
(FEN) (France), 43, 44
Fellowship of Reconciliation (FoR)
(Great Britain), 22
Féminisme Chrétien, The (France), 8
feminists. *See* women's movements
Finland: labor movements in, 16; wom-
en's movements in, 11, 14

Flast v. Cohen, 67
Flores, Hugo, 161
Fontanet, Joseph, 47
framing, 118, 130, 219
France: career open to talents movement in, 133; cooperation of environmental and solidarity
movements in, xxiii–xxiv, 90, 92,
93–95, 98–102; French Revolution
and, 110–11, 127, 238; labor movements in, 8, 9, 12, 13, 16; May 1968
protest wave and, xxiii, 31–56, 134;
peace movements in, 8, 9, 10, 20,
21–23; Popular Front in, 50; wom-
en's movements in, 8, 11, 14
Franco, Francisco, 197
Franco-Prussian War of 1870–1871, 12
French National Movement of Struggle
for the Environment, 99
French Revolution, 110–11, 127, 238
Friends of the Earth, 238
Fujimoro, 197
fundamentalists, collective action and,
221–22
future, of social movements, xxvi,
229–46

Gambetta, Léon, 12
Garretón, Manuel Antonio, 152
Gauche Proletarienne (France), 27
Gaullist party (France), 37, 38, 41, 43,
44, 47, 51
gay movement, 83. *See also* AIDS
George, David Lloyd, 10
Germany, 28; labor movements in, 12,
16, 23, 27; peace movements in, 9;
policing of protest in, 233; political
violence in, 233; protest activity in,
231, 232; student movements in, 48;
terrorism in, 134–35; women's
movements in, 11, 14, 19
ghetto parties, in Europe, 115
Giesel, Ernesto, 176
Giugni, Marco, 29
Gleichheit (Germany), 6
Goldstone, Jack, 111
Gorbachev, Mikhail, 142

About the Contributors

Elisabeth S. Clemens is associate professor of sociology at the University of Arizona. Her work addresses the role of voluntary organizations and social movements in processes of political change. She is the author of *The People's Lobby: Organizational Innovation and the Rise of Interest Group Politics in the United States, 1890–1925* (1997), as well as coeditor of *Private Action and the Public Good* (1998). Her current research addresses the relationship of organizational heterogeneity to institutional change, exploring the consequences of the growth and centralization of the U.S. federal government for the autonomy and diversity of both state governments and private associations.

William A. Gamson is a professor of sociology and codirects the Media Research and Action Project (MRAP) at Boston College. He is the author of *Talking Politics* (1992) and *The Strategy of Social Protest* (2nd edition, 1990) among other books and articles on political discourse, the mass media, and social movements. He is a past president of the American Sociological Association.

Marco G. Giugni is a researcher at the Department of Political Science, University of Geneva, Switzerland. He has authored or coauthored several books and articles on social movements. He is the author of *Entre stratégie et opportunité* (1995) and coauthor of *New Social Movements in Western Europe* (1995) and *Histoires de mobilisation politique en Suisse* (1997). He is currently working on a comparative research on migration policies in France and Switzerland.

Jack A. Goldstone is professor of sociology at the University of California, Davis. He is the author of *Revolution and Rebellion in the Early Modern World*, which was awarded the Distinguished Scholarly Publication Award of the American Sociological Association. He is also editor of the forthcoming *Encyclopedia of Political Revolutions,* and is finishing a book titled *Understanding Revolutions, Social Movements, and Social Change: A Theory of Structures, Cultures, and Processes.* Professor Goldstone has held fellowships from the American Council of Learned Societies, the Canadian Institute for Advanced Study, the Australian Research School of Social Sciences, and the Center for Advanced Study in the Behavioral Sciences.

Michael Hanagan has published books and articles on historical collective action and European social history. He is the coeditor of *Challenging Authority: The Historical Study of Collective Action* (1998) and of *Extending Citizenship, Reconfiguring States* (forthcoming). He is currently involved in a comparative study of the origins and development of the welfare state in Europe and the United States. He teaches comparative and social history at the New School for Social Research in New York City.

Patricia Hipsher is assistant professor of political science at Oklahoma State University. She has published several pieces concerning the role of social movements in democratizing Latin America, including an article in *Comparative Politics* and a chapter in Sidney Tarrow and David Meyer's book *The Social Movement Society* (1998). She is currently conducting research on the feminist movement in El Salvador and on the framing and collective identity processes of "heretical" social movement organizations.

Timo Lyyra is a Ph.D. candidate in sociology at the Graduate Faculty of the New School for Social Research, New York. His research focuses on collective action, mass media, politics, and the concept of the public sphere in complex societies. He has published articles on social movements and social change.

Doug McAdam is professor of sociology at the University of Arizona and author of two major monographs on the dynamics of social movements, *Political Process and the Development of Black Insurgency* (1982) and *Freedom Summer* (1988). The latter book was accorded the C. Wright Mills Award for 1991 and was also a finalist for the American Sociological Association's Best Book Award in the same year. He is currently at work, with Charles Tilly and Sidney Tarrow, on an ambitious theoretical book, tentatively titled *Dynamics of Contention.*

Alberto Melucci is professor of cultural sociology and on the faculty of the postgraduate school of clinical psychology at the University of Milan. He has taught extensively in Europe and the United States and has contributed to many international journals. He is the author of more than fifteen books on social movements, cultural change, and personal and collective identity, including *Nomads of the Present* (1989), *The Playing Self* (1996), and *Challenging Codes* (1996).

Florence Passy is assistant professor at the Department of Political Science at the University of Geneva. She is currently working on a comparative research on the impact of social movements on migration policies in France and Switzerland. Among her works, *Histoires de mobilisation politiques en Suisse* (coauthored, 1997) and *L'Action altruiste* (forthcoming).

Salvador A. M. Sandoval received his Ph.D. from the University of Michigan in political science. He has taught extensively in Mexico and Brazil and is currently professor of political psychology at the Graduate School of the Pontifical Catholic University of São Paulo, where he conducts research on social and labor movement topics. He is the author of *Labor Unrest and Social Change in Brazil since 1945* (1994). His present research interests include the psychosociological dynamics of social movement mobilization and demobilization and the factors affecting the current demobilization of the Brazilian labor movement under neoliberalism.

Sidney Tarrow is Maxwell M. Upson Professor of Government at Cornell, where he teaches social movements and West European politics. Tarrow is the author of *Democracy and Disorder: Protest and Politics in Italy, 1965–1975* (1989), *Power in Movement: Social Movements and Contentious Politics* (2d ed., 1998), and is coeditor (with David Meyer) of *The Movement Society* (1998). He is currently at work on a book, *Dynamics of Contention,* to be coauthored with Doug McAdam and Charles Tilly.

Charles Tilly studied at Oxford and served in the U.S. Navy before receiving a Ph.D. from Harvard in 1958. He has held long-term teaching appointments at Delaware, Harvard, Toronto, Michigan, the New School, and Columbia, where he is now Joseph L. Buttenwieser Professor of Social Science. His first book was *The Vendee* (1964), his most recent *Durable Inequality* (1998).